Giorgio Agambe[n]
Aziz + Cucher//[G]
Ballengée//Gre[g]
Bergson//Josep[h]
Boettger//Roger Caillois//Oron Catts//Mel Chin//
Emma Cocker//Steven Connor//Lynne Cooke//Critical
Art Ensemble//Walter De Maria//Jacques Derrida//
herman de vries//Mark Dion//Vilém Flusser//George
Gessert//Oliver Grau//Tim Griffin//Félix Guattari//
Hans Haacke//Henrik Håkansson//Peter Halley//
Donna Haraway//Helen & Newton Harrison//David
Harvey//Pierre Huyghe//Eduardo Kac//Bruno Latour//
Pamela M. Lee//Jean-François Lyotard//Tom
McDonough//Denise Markonish//Mary Mattingly//
Ana Mendieta//Laurent Mignonneau//Jacques
Monod//Robert Morris//Arne Naess//Thomas Nagel//
Trevor Paglen//Jane Prophet//Ingeborg Reichle//
Alexis Rockman//Nikolas Rose//Andrew Ross//Tomás
Saraceno//Mark Sheerin//Bonnie Sherk//Robert
Smithson//Christa Sommerer//Alan Sonfist//Stelarc//
Paul Tebbs//Rirkrit Tiravanija//Mierle Laderman
Ukeles//Vladimir Vernadsky//Victoria Vesna//Carl
Zimmer//Andrea Zittel//Ionat Zurr

Nature

Whitechapel Gallery
London
The MIT Press
Cambridge, Massachusetts

Edited by Jeffrey Kastner

NATURE

Documents of Contemporary Art

Co-published by Whitechapel Gallery
and The MIT Press

First published 2012
© 2012 Whitechapel Gallery Ventures Limited
All texts © the authors or the estates of the authors,
unless otherwise stated

Whitechapel Gallery is the imprint of Whitechapel
Gallery Ventures Limited

All rights reserved. No part of this publication
may be reproduced, stored in a retrieval system
or transmitted in any form or by any means,
electronic, mechanical, photocopying or otherwise,
without the written permission of the publisher

ISBN 978-0-85488-196-3 (Whitechapel Gallery)
ISBN 978-0-262-51766-9 (The MIT Press)

A catalogue record for this book is available from
the British Library

Library of Congress Cataloging-in-Publication Data

Nature / edited by Jeffrey Kastner.
   p.   cm. — (Whitechapel : Documents of
contemporary art)
Includes bibliographical references and index.
ISBN 978-0-262-51766-9 (pbk. : alk. paper)
1. Nature (Aesthetics) 2. Arts, Modern—Themes,
motives. I. Kastner, Jeffrey.
BH301.N3N39   2012
111'.85—dc23
                          2011034641

10 9 8 7 6 5 4 3

Series Editor: Iwona Blazwick
Commissioning Editor: Ian Farr
Project Editor: Sarah Auld
Design by SMITH
Justine Schuster, Sarah Newitt
Printed and bound in China

Cover, Justine Cooper, *Sulphur Butterflies (Phoebis
rurina)*, from the series *Saved by Science* (2005),
C-type print (detail). © Justine Cooper. Courtesy
of the artist and Jan Manton Gallery.

Whitechapel Gallery Ventures Limited
77-82 Whitechapel High Street
London E1 7QX
whitechapelgallery.org
To order (UK and Europe) call +44 (0)207 522 7888
or email MailOrder@whitechapelgallery.org
Distributed to the book trade (UK and Europe only)
by Central Books
www.centralbooks.com

The MIT Press
Cambridge, MA 02142
http://mitpress.mit.edu

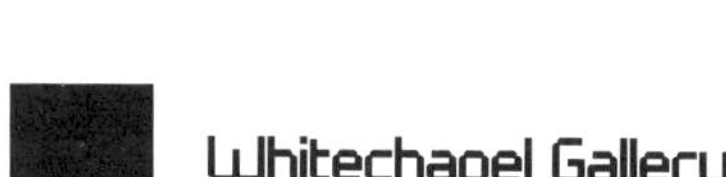
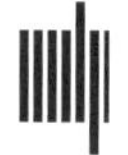

Documents of Contemporary Art

In recent decades artists have progressively expanded the boundaries of art as they have sought to engage with an increasingly pluralistic environment. Teaching, curating and understanding of art and visual culture are likewise no longer grounded in traditional aesthetics but centred on significant ideas, topics and themes ranging from the everyday to the uncanny, the psychoanalytical to the political.

The Documents of Contemporary Art series emerges from this context. Each volume focuses on a specific subject or body of writing that has been of key influence in contemporary art internationally. Edited and introduced by a scholar, artist, critic or curator, each of these source books provides access to a plurality of voices and perspectives defining a significant theme or tendency.

For over a century the Whitechapel Gallery has offered a public platform for art and ideas. In the same spirit, each guest editor represents a distinct yet diverse approach – rather than one institutional position or school of thought – and has conceived each volume to address not only a professional audience but all interested readers.

Series Editor: Iwona Blazwick; Commissioning Editor: Ian Farr; Project Editor: Sarah Auld; Editorial Advisory Board: Achim Borchardt-Hume, Roger Conover, Neil Cummings, Mark Francis, David Jenkins, Kirsty Ogg, Gilane Tawadros

FOR YEARS

I HAD THIS

STRATEGY AS

AN ARTIST

TO BECOME

ANIMAL

Marcus Coates, 2010

PUT THE BEST OBJECT YOU KNOW NEXT TO THE
GRAND CANYON, NIAGARA FALLS, REDWOODS

THE

BIG

THINGS

ALWAYS

WIN.

Walter De Maria, 'On the Importance of Natural Disasters', 1960

Jeffrey Kastner
Introduction//Art in the Age of the Anthropocene

At the beginning of her 1998 essay 'Nature by Design', the historian Lorraine Daston presents for consideration a trio of curious objects: an onyx cameo, probably Hellenistic in origin, depicting two figures in profile; a 'stone' in the form of what appear to be five interlocking rocks, once held in the seventeenth-century *Wunderkammer* of Paris's Bibliothèque de Sainte-Geneviève; and a small limestone panel painted with a biblical scene, a decoration on a cabinet of curiosities presented by the citizens of Augsburg, Germany, to the Swedish King Gustavus Adolphus in 1632.[1]

Daston is interested in these objects because, she writes, 'all at one time or another [were] viewed as straddling the boundary between art and nature'. The cameo, for instance, is mentioned in the *Book of Minerals*, one of the many studies produced by the legendary scholar of the Middle Ages, Albertus Magnus. The polymathic natural philosopher judged the object, despite seeming to our contemporary eyes indisputably a work of human facture, to have been 'made naturally and not artificially'.[2] The Parisian artefact, known as the 'Stone of Hammon', was described by the English philosopher John Locke in his *Travels* as being among the 'great many … natural & artificiall curiositys' he encountered among the collections at Sainte-Geneviève. Their curator, Claude du Molinet, called the object – in all likelihood a fossilized ammonite – 'a game of nature', noting that 'most of those who have seen it have believed it to be artificial, but the most able Sculptors in Paris have judged it natural'.[3] Meanwhile, writes Daston, the limestone panel, one of several hundred ornamenting the Augsburg cabinet – a nine-foot-tall oak and ebony structure that held nearly a thousand natural and manmade objects[4] – represents, with its 'deliberate juxtaposition and even fusion of art and nature … a game of forms played across that same boundary'.

Fast-forward a few hundred years to three contemporary scenes, each another (now quite deliberate) boundary-crossing game of form. The first takes place in a genetic research laboratory in Jouy-en-Josas, France, the birthplace of Alba, a rabbit 'commissioned' in 2000 from scientists at France's Institut National de la Récherche Agronomique by the artist Eduardo Kac. An albino, the animal had at Kac's request been implanted with a synthesized version of the naturally occurring protein that causes green fluorescence in the marine invertebrate *aequorea victoria*, commonly known as the crystal jellyfish. The project, an example of what Kac has referred to as 'transgenic art',[5] was to have continued with the adoption of the glow-in-the-dark bunny by the artist and his family, but the lab reneged on the agreement and the whereabouts and status of Alba are today unknown. The second venue is a gallery space in the capital city of Luxembourg, the site of a November 1995 performance called *Fractal Flesh* by Stelarc (Stelios Arkadiou). In this piece, the Cypriot-Australian artist attached networked sensors to various parts of his body and allowed himself to be physically 'remote-controlled' by users in Paris, Amsterdam, Hamburg, Helsinki, Vienna, Milwaukee and Toronto.[6] And our final location is New York's Museum of Modern Art and, somewhat improbably, a round beaker set in the galleries there, the vessel for the contribution of the Australian group SymbioticA to the museum's 2008 exhibition 'Design and the Elastic Mind'. An incubator of sorts, it contained a hunk of live mouse stem cells that the artists had coaxed into the shape of a small coat – an example of what SymbioticA's members Oron Catts and Ionat Zurr have characterized as 'victimless leather' – until, that is, MoMA curator Paola Antonelli was forced effectively to 'kill' the work by denying it nutrients after the cells began multiplying too quickly, clogging its glass den.

These two sets of examples may be separated by centuries, but they also share striking similarities in the kinds of questions they provoke about the distinct character of natural and artificial creation, and the uncanniness of gestures that seem to elude the strict definitions of either. In many ways, it is these kinds of questions – which are both ancient and utterly contemporary – that lie at the heart of this volume. Though the pre-modern moment of wonder and confusion conjured by Daston's anecdotes may at first strike us as a quaint illustration of a less discerning age, our present moment is in many ways just as inflected with astonishment and perplexity about such distinctions – which is precisely why our contemporary artists have devised so many practices designed to probe, shift, cross and even erase them. This anthology is not, strictly speaking, a historical project, but it is necessarily informed by historical perspectives, not least because the pedigree of its theme reaches so far back and across many different disciplinary borders. It stretches from philosophy to science to anthropology to poetics; from pantheistic ritual that treats nature simultaneously as subject and object, to the eclectic, undifferentiated agglomerations of made things and *lusus naturae*, or freaks of nature, that populated the European cabinets of curiosity which would give rise to the modern museum.[7] From the inscriptive, post-Minimalist gestures of early Land art to following generations' practices in nature – influenced by feminist, ecological and other anti-institutional political discourses – to contemporary transdisciplinary programmes that draw freely on scientific and technological modes of address and practical implementation, the spaces between (or of overlap among) different concepts of the natural and the artistic continue to offer productive sites for creative activity.

Culture has long been understood to be a fluid, artificial complex, the result of a range of interdependent forces – social, political, economic and more. For enormous stretches of human history, the contingency of civilization, and in particular of its cultural products, was read in contradistinction to the supposed integral essentialism of the natural world. From Socrates, Plato and Aristotle forward, art was understood, for ill (or good), to be merely mimetic; forever attempting, and failing, to replicate the wonders of nature. Yet thinkers (and makers) in subsequent periods continually sought to reconceive the relationship between humans and nature and the products of each.[8] Ultimately, whether constituted as muse or foil, as contestant or collaborator, nature continues to loom as the elusive, originary Other – a system we are fundamentally native to, but unavoidably separate from; one that produces us, even as we (physically, conceptually, discursively) produce it; a complex of spaces, structures and organisms inexhaustibly good to think (and work) with.

This volume is structured around three different sections – *Material Zones*, *Evolutionary Ideas* and *Cognition and Conscience* – designed to tease out both the various strands of discourse around the natural world and the ways in which the ideas and influences contained within them have been translated into operations and objects by contemporary artists. The temporal frame for these artefacts is exclusively the post-war period, although the textual material ranges more widely across the entire twentieth and twenty-first centuries, tracking as it does a construction of 'nature' that is defined not just as the physical world around us but also, and especially, the conditions of our physical, metaphorical, political and social interactions with it.

The first section, *Material Zones*, opens with an extract from Gaston Bachelard's 1942 essay 'Imagination and Matter', in which the philosopher sets out the most basic structures of his developing poetics of the material world. This introduces the primary concern here with the ways that spatial environments and the organisms that populate them (including humans) are understood as products of certain fundamental biological processes, but also as subjects that lend themselves, to greater and lesser degrees, to various systems of categorization, mapping, inscription, networking, and more. It is here that we find the well-known figures from the first generation of 'land artists', such as Robert Smithson and Walter De Maria, as well as artists who engaged with nature in ways that unsettle conventional wisdom about the character of earthworks: from the systems aesthetics of Hans Haacke to the ritual enactments of Ana Mendieta; from Hamish Fulton's rambles to Mierle Laderman Ukeles' brand of radical domesticity and social ecology. Meanwhile, scholar Suzaan Boettger's examination of the practices of a number of female land artists – including Nancy Holt, Alice Aycock, Mary Miss, Harriet Feigenbaum and Athena Tacha, among others whose work is often overlooked in canonical narratives of the late 1960s and early 1970s – asks important questions about the role of gender in this history.

Further considerations of the landscape itself – the site for these largely inscriptive activities, both physical and metaphorical – are also developed here via thinkers like Michel Serres, whose topological 'shapes of thought' are discussed by Steven Connor, and artists who reconceive the environment as site (such as Jane Prophet) and system (like Christa Sommerer & Laurent Mignonneau). Central to this section's concern with materiality are questions of mutability and hybridity, explored via a range of entities and organisms from the level of DNA (in George Gessert's brief history) to the entire body, both animal (in Kac, for example) and human (via artists such as Victoria Vesna, Aziz + Cucher, and Oron Catts & Ionat Zurr of SymbioticA). And in the excerpt from Jane Bennett's eloquently provocative book *Vibrant Matter*, larger-scale questions about what she calls 'vibrant materialism' are routed through figures ranging from Lucretius, Spinoza and Henri Bergson to Bruno Latour, in a project designed, she says, 'to awaken what [Bergson] described as "a latent belief in the spontaneity of nature"'.[9]

The organizing principle of *Evolutionary Ideas*, our next section, is the continuous tracking of developments in science and philosophy, and in particular the ways in which new ideas about what constitutes the natural world – and the natural state of human *being* – have been mobilized by artists. It begins with two early twentieth-century texts, the first by Bergson, who coined the term *élan vital* – a vital force or 'current of life' – in an attempt to map notions of consciousness and agency onto biological systems. Here he begins to consider the relationship between intellect and intuition and the role each plays in the production of knowledge.[10] In the second, the relatively little-known Russian geologist Vladimir Vernadsky outlines his concept of the 'biosphere' which, with its successor the 'noosphere' (or the sphere of human thought), has significantly influenced discourse around environmental philosophy of the later twentieth century.[11] Following on from these early, generative observations, different notions of what might be meant by the concept of ecology – with a variety of social, political and poetical inflections – are examined in excerpts from Gregory Bateson, Arne Naess and Félix Guattari. The thread then turns back towards the question of artistic production within this web of discourse. Peter Halley's essay proposes an overview of the dialectics of nature and culture in post-war American art, and in an important roundtable discussion, published in a 2005 special issue of *Artforum* devoted to land- and nature-based practices, the critics Claire Bishop, Lynne Cooke, Tim Griffin and Pamela M. Lee, and the artists Pierre Huyghe, Rirkrit Tiravanija and Andrea Zittel provide a kind of snapshot of thought and praxis at the beginning of the twenty-first century. Texts by the theorist Trevor Paglen and artists Tomás Saraceno and Helen & Newton Harrison consider, in different ways, questions around new ways of understanding the 'production of space', through elements of both geography and the built environment.

This impulse towards reconceiving the external world as a site for politico-artistic analysis and activity is also reflected in a turning inward, towards body-as-site. Texts by scholars and artists here consider the various ways in which the body has become the locus for processes of technologization – whether constituted in the form of the mechanical cyborg, the telepresented being, or the phantom avatar conjured from the realm of capital, as in the case of Annlee, the *manga* character at the heart of Pierre Huyghe and Philippe Parreno's distributed artwork *No Ghost Just a Shell*.

The closing section, *Cognition and Conscience*, ranges widely over what might usefully be understood as the terrain of perceptual and ethical implications that flow from our ever-growing attention to and knowledge of the natural world and the place we might occupy in relation to it. It begins with Roger Caillois' lyrical meditation on the 'natural fantastic', the eruption of the wondrous amidst 'the general commotion that tends to conceal the profound unity of nature'.[12] Though, as always for Caillois, it is the world of the mineral that holds the most intriguing potential for the staging of his dialectic of the animate and inanimate,[13] here he also gathers up the animal kingdom in his quest for what he calls his 'material mysticism', a quest in which, translator Claudine Frank notes, Caillois 'grasps for the cosmos'. 'In doing so', she continues, 'he both dehumanizes man's creation within the natural order, in the Taoist tradition, and humanizes nature by recasting it in his own terms, in the Western tradition.'[14] Complicated questions about the de/humanization of nature are explored in extracts from the philosophers Giorgio Agamben (*The Open: Man and Animal*), Jacques Derrida (*The Animal That Therefore I Am*), Thomas Nagel, in his famous thought experiment, the essay 'What is It Like to be a Bat?' and Bruno Latour, whose provocative essay 'Will Non-Humans Be Saved: An Argument in Ecotheology', concludes this section and the book.[15]

Questions of research, display and intervention are also vital parts of this spectrum, constituted in diverse ways: the historical biology of the pioneering Alan Sonfist; the transdisciplinary collaboration seen in the work of artists such as Mel Chin, Natalie Jeremijenko, Mary Mattingly and Brandon Ballengée; the interrogation of museological tropes (Mark Dion), or of zoological practices (Zhao Renhui's project *The Institute of Critical Zoologists*). It is perhaps not surprising that some of these modes of practice dovetail with a certain strain of the utopic. Yet in works such as *The Farm* – Bonnie Sherk's communal agricultural enterprise of the late 1970s – or Marcus Coates' shamanistic interventions in geopolitical strife, the sense of optimism about a new basis for our interactions with nature (and through it, with others) is underpinned by pragmatism or self-aware humour.[16] Which is not to say that research inevitably leads either the thinkers or the artists included here to positive conclusions. Important contrarian voices and astute assessments are also present, from Andrew Ross's socially engaged critique of the strategies of the environmental movement to the Critical Art Ensemble's cautionary analyses of the burgeoning techniques of genetic modification, and particularly their increasing enlistment in the service of dehumanizing capital-generation.

Nature has repeatedly been rejected and reclaimed by artists over the last half century. Art that is engaged with it – informed by philosophical and political trends, by scientific advances and by the evolution of theoretical frameworks within the field of visual culture – has been uniquely positioned to benefit from the dislocation of disciplinary specificities. As forms of technology have made our interventions into natural systems both increasingly refined and profound, and advances in biological and communication technology have altered the way we 'present' ourselves, so too have artistic re-presentations of nature (human and otherwise) evolved. These new modes of working, in some fundamental, structural sense, return the oppositional concepts of *culture* and *nature* to the dialectical balance hinted at in their etymological roots: the former once again understood not as separate from but actively engaged with the latter, and artists seen as potential *mediators between the two worlds – cultivators* of a natural world full to bursting with material. Just as forward-looking scientists increasingly acknowledge the wide and complex range of interdependencies between the world that made us and the world that we have made (we have, they tell us, emerged from the Holocene epoch into the Anthropocene, literally the age of the 'new human' – a term that recognizes the degree to which we are full actors in the natural systems of the planet), so too will the artistic avant-garde continue to develop new tools and strategies that unsettle conventional wisdom about our relationships with and within nature.

1   Lorraine Daston, 'Nature by Design', in *Picturing Science, Producing Art*, ed. Caroline A. Jones and Peter Galison (New York and London: Routledge, 1998) 233–53.

2   Daston, op. cit., 232. She goes on to point out that as late as the end of the seventeenth century, scholars continued to debate whether objects that to us are obviously works of the human hand – such as Etruscan vases or early implements – were in fact the results of natural processes. For more on this, see Frank Dawson Adams, *The Birth and Development of the Geological Sciences* (Baltimore: The Williams & Wilkins Company, 1938) 120–23; 255.

3   Daston, op. cit., 233. Also see Lorraine Daston and Katherine Park, *Wonders and the Order of Nature, 1150–1750* (New York: Zone Books, 1998) 287–90.

4   The cabinet has been held in the collection of the Museum Gustavianum at Sweden's Uppsala University since 1694. For a detailed examination of its design and contents, see the museum's

richly interactive website (http://konstskapet.gustavianum.uu.se/webb/index.html).

5   See Eduardo Kac, 'Transgenic Art', *Leonardo Electronic Almanac*, vol. 6, no. 11, December 1998; reprinted in *Ars Electronica '99: Life Science*, ed. Gerfried Stocker and Christine Schopf (Vienna and New York: Springer, 1999) 289–95.

6   For more on the artist's work, see *Stelarc: The Monograph*, ed. Marquard Smith (Cambridge, Massachusetts: The MIT Press, 2005).

7   There are a number of excellent treatments of this history; see especially Paula Findlen, *Possessing Nature: Museums, Collecting and Scientific Culture in Early Modern Italy* (Berkeley and Los Angeles: University of California Press, 1994) and the anthologies *Museum Origins: Readings in Early Museum History & Philosophy*, ed. Hugh H. Genoways and Mary Anne Andrei (Walnut Creek, California: Left Coast Press, 2008) and *Cultures of Natural History*, ed. Nicholas Jardine, James A. Secord and Emma Spary (Cambridge: Cambridge University Press, 1996).

8   The numerous pre-Enlightenment and Enlightenment figures – from Descartes and Spinoza to Leibniz and Kant, among others – who were engaged with these questions in degrees of complexity and nuance well beyond the scope of this project are especially important for our contemporary notions of the nature/culture divide. For pithier takes, see also Francis Bacon, *A Description of the Intellectual Globe* (c. 1612), trans. Robert Leslie Ellis, in *The Philosophical Works of Francis Bacon* (London: George Routledge and Sons, 1905) 678–9: 'I am the rather induced to set down the history of arts as a species of natural history, because it is the fashion to talk as if art were something different from nature, so that things artificial should be separated from things natural, as differing totally in kind; whence it comes that most writers of natural history think it enough to make a history of animals or plants or minerals, without mentioning the experiments of mechanical arts (which are far the most important for philosophy); and not only that, but another and more subtle error finds its way into men's minds; that of looking upon art merely as a kind of supplement to nature; which has power enough to finish what nature has begun or correct her when going aside, but no power to make radical changes, and shake her in the foundations; an opinion which has brought a great deal of despair into human concerns.' And, later, Voltaire in his entry for 'Nature', from his *Philosophical Dictionary* (1764), trans. anon (London: William Dugdale, 1843) 248: 'PHILOSOPHER: We are curious. I should be pleased to know how it is, that while so rough and coarse in your mountains, and deserts and seas, you are at the same time so ingenious and finished in your animals and vegetables? NATURE: My poor child, shall I tell you the real truth? I have had bestowed upon me a name that does not at all suit me: I am called nature, while I am all art. PHILOSOPHER: That word deranges all my ideas. What! is it possible that nature should be nothing but art? NATURE: It is undoubtedly the case …'

9   See also Bennett on 'political ecologies', where she opens up the Latourian notion of the 'actant' with help from Charles Darwin, John Dewey, Jacques Rancière, and some worms, to ask questions about the potential for the constitution of a 'non-human' public. Jane Bennett, *Vibrant Matter: A Political Ecology of Things* (Durham, North Carolina: Duke University Press, 2010) 94–109.

10   Also see Gilles Deleuze's important reconsiderations of Bergson, in both his essay 'Bergson, 1859–1941', included in Deleuze, *Desert Islands and Other Texts, 1953–1974*, trans. Christopher

Bush (New York: Semiotext(e), 2004) and in his later *Bergsonism*, trans. Hugh Tomlinson and Barbara Habberjam (New York: Zone Books, 1991). Meanwhile, see the excerpt from Jacques Monod, *Chance and Necessity*, trans. Austryn Wainhouse (New York: Alfred A. Knopf, 1971) in this volume for a vigorous critique of both the 'metaphysical' and 'scientistic' vitalist traditions.

11 For interesting interpretations and extensions of Vernadsky, see also Teilhard de Chardin's writing on nature, and those of the Gaia theorists, such as James Lovelock.

12 'The Natural Fantastic' (1971), in *The Edge of Surrealism: A Roger Caillois Reader* (Durham, North Carolina: Duke University Press, 2003) 356–7 (extract reprinted in this volume, 142–4).

13 For more on Caillois' rich involvement with the geological, see his *The Writing of Stones*, trans. Barbara Bray (Charlottesville: The University of Virginia Press, 1985).

14 Claudine Frank, introduction to 'The Natural Fantastic', in *The Edge of Surrealism*, op. cit., 348.

15 See, too, Donna J. Haraway, *When Species Meet* (Minneapolis: University of Minnesota Press, 2008), for an eclectic, often personal account of potential forms of human/non-human intersubjectivity. And for an intriguing early perspective on zoology that, according to Agamben, expresses 'the unreserved abandonment of every anthropocentric perspective in the life sciences and the radical dehumanization of the image of nature', see Jakob von Uexküll, 'A Stroll through the Worlds of Animals and Men: A Picture Book of Invisible Worlds' (1934), in *Instinctive Behaviour: The Development of a Modern Concept*, ed. and trans. Claire H. Shiller, (New York: International Universities Press, 1957) 5–80.

16 For a foundational moment of the pragmatic impulse in the realm of land-based artistic practice, and one routed through a wonderfully cranky sensibility, see Robert Morris, 'Notes on Art as/and Land Reclamation' (1979), *October*, vol. 12 (Spring 1980) 87–102 (extract reprinted in this volume, 170–73).

NO MATTER HOW ALIENATED WE MAY BECOME, WE PRODUCE PATTERNS THAT MIRROR THE NATURAL WORLD

Victoria Vesna, 'Mind and Body Shifting: From Networks to Nanosystems', 2002

MATERIAL ZONES

Gaston Bachelard
Imagination and Matter//1942

Let us help the hydra clear away the fog.
Stéphane Mallarmé, *Divagations*

The imagining powers of our mind develop around two very different axes.

Some get their impetus from novelty; they take pleasure in the picturesque, the varied and the unexpected. The imagination that they spark always describes a springtime. In nature these powers, far from us but already alive, bring forth flowers.

Others plumb the depths of being. They seek to find there both the primitive and the eternal. They prevail over season and history. In nature, within us and without, they produce seeds – seeds whose form is embedded in a substance, whose *form is internal.*

By speaking philosophically from the outset, we can distinguish two sorts of imagination: one that gives life to the formal cause and one that gives life to the material cause – or, more succinctly, a *formal imagination* and a *material imagination.* Thus abbreviated, these concepts seem to me indispensable for a complete philosophical study of poetic creation. Causes arising from the feelings and the heart must become formal causes if a work is to possess verbal variety, the ever-changing life of light. Yet besides the images of form, so often evoked by psychologists of the imagination, there are – as I will show – images of matter, images that stem *directly from matter.* The eye assigns them names, but only the hand truly knows them. A dynamic joy touches, moulds and refines them. When forms, mere perishable forms and vain images – perpetual change of surfaces – are put aside, these images of matter are dreamt substantially and intimately. They have weight; they constitute a heart.

Of course, there are works in which the two imagining powers cooperate. It is not even possible to separate them completely. Even the most fleeting, changing and purely formal reverie still has elements that are stable, dense, slow and fertile. Yet even so, every poetic work that penetrates deeply enough into the heart of being to find the constancy and lovely monotony of matter, that derives its strength from a substantial cause, must bloom and bedeck itself. It must embrace all the exuberance of formal beauty in order to attract the reader in the first place.

Because of this need to fascinate, the imagination ordinarily works where there is joy – or at least one kind of joy – produced either by forms and colours, variety and metamorphosis, or by what surfaces become. Imagination deserts depth, volume and the inner recesses of substance.

However, it is to the intimate imagination of these vegetating and material powers that I would like to pay most attention. Only an iconoclastic philosopher could undertake the long and difficult task of detaching all the suffixes from beauty, of searching behind the obvious images for the hidden ones, of seeking the very roots of this image-making power.

In the depths of matter there grows an obscure vegetation; black flowers bloom in matter's darkness. They already possess a velvety touch, a formula for perfume.

When I began meditating on the concept of the beauty of matter, I was immediately struck by the neglect of the *material cause* in aesthetic philosophy. In particular it seemed to me that the individualizing power of matter had been underestimated. Why does everyone always associate the notion of the individual with form? Is there not an individuality in depth that makes matter a totality, even in its smallest divisions? Meditated upon from the perspective of its depth, matter is the very principle that can dissociate itself from forms. It is not the simple absence of formal activity. It remains itself despite all distortion and division. Moreover, matter may be given value in two ways: by deepening or by elevating. Deepening makes it seem unfathomable, like a mystery. Elevation makes it appear to be an inexhaustible force, like a miracle. In both cases, meditation on matter cultivates an *open imagination*.

Only after studying forms and attributing each to its proper matter will it be possible to visualize a complete doctrine on human imagination. Then one can appreciate the fact that an image is a plant – which needs earth and sky, substance and form. Images discovered by men evolve slowly, painfully; hence Jacques Bousquet's profound remark: 'A new image costs humanity as much labour as a new characteristic costs a plant.' Many attempted images cannot survive because they are merely formal play, not truly adapted to the matter they should adorn.

Therefore I believe that a philosophic doctrine of the imagination must, above all, study the relationship between material and formal causality. […]

Gaston Bachelard, extract from introduction, *L'eau et les rêves* (Paris: José Corti, 1942); trans. Edith Farrell, *Water and Dreams: An Essay on the Imagination of Matter* (Dallas: Dallas Institute of Humanities and Culture, 1983) 1–3.

Walter De Maria
On the Importance of Natural Disasters//1960

I think natural disasters have been looked upon in the wrong way.

Newspapers always say they are bad, a shame.

I like natural disasters and I think that they may be the highest form of art possible to experience.

For one thing they are impersonal.

I don't think art can stand up to nature.

Put the best object you know next to the Grand Canyon, Niagara Falls, redwoods.

The big things always win.

Now just think of a flood, forest fire, tornado, earthquake, typhoon, sand storm.

Think of the breaking of the ice jams. Crunch.

If all of the people who go to museums could just feel an earthquake.

Not to mention the sky and the ocean.

But it is in the unpredictable disasters that the highest forms are realized.

They are rare and we should be thankful for them.

Walter De Maria, 'On the Importance of Natural Disasters' (May 1960), in *An Anthology of Chance Operations*, ed. Jackson Mac Low and La Monte Young (Bronx, New York: self-published by the editors, 1963; reprinted, New York: Heiner Friedrich, 1970).

Robert Smithson
In Conversation with Dennis Wheeler//1969–70

Dennis Wheeler The footprints around the second mirror displacement [in *Incidents of Mirror Travel in the Yucatan*, 1969] are strange … That's something that draws you out … The footprints are one of the few humanist comparatives which manage to penetrate the piece. They lend an increased actuality …

Robert Smithson To make that even clearer, you could trace it to the *Dog Tracks* [a location photograph for *Six Stops on a Section*, 1968] – that particular observation in terms of the tracking … the observations on the dog tracks leading to that kind of uncertainty, of the constellation of the mirrors, you know, as you move around it, this residue builds out …

Wheeler Especially when simply sky, or vacuous-appearing space, is caught up in the mirror, as if the mirror were actually a hole punched into the soft earth; then you get the sense that it's a hole but it's lined with something.

Smithson It's like a negative hole.

Wheeler … a negative hole, it's … the end of a column without the column, it's really a strange image. And revealing on the other side, or interior to itself, a deeper, or another, more mercurial, difficult and abstracting world than what we have managed to tame. The world for ourselves … 'That camera is a portable tomb. You must remember that.'[1] That's a strange statement. Can you explain something about that?

Smithson Well, because of the arrested moment, that perhaps is even spelled out in the thing from Santayana: 'Living beings dwell on their expectations rather than their senses.'[2]

Wheeler Right, the fleeting moment caught.

Smithson 'If they are ever to see what they see, they must first – in a manner – stop living; they must suspend the will.' Well, that's the arrestment of the moment, stopped. 'They must suspend the will, as Schopenhauer put it; they must photograph the idea that is flying past, veiled in its very swiftness.'[3] What you're really doing is fixing something out of duration. […]

Smithson I was talking with Steve Heizer[4] about the difference between two types of scientists, the one who has the controlled studio experiment, and then the field scientist, who is working in a sense with the uncontrollable aspect. And the conflict that arises from the perfect isolation as opposed to the chance disruption. The security that comes from working in a lab is very similar to the security that comes from working in a studio. So there's a parallel there. The studio and the lab become places where you can control your information. But at the same time, the information you're controlling is not that interesting. It tends to be rather unneccessary. The stability of that is constantly challenged by the instability of these extra forces, like the storm over the island …

Wheeler Or the storm of butterflies over the mirrors in the third displacement …

Smithson That stormy aspect, that kind of lightning in the head, you know.

Wheeler I keep seeing, there's the storm in the sky, which is this kind of low level … it's the basement of the sky, it tends to blend with the earth … and then the blending of the earth itself. And then the instance or occasion of the work between the two strengths, the forces, like the mirrors inserted in the earth reflecting the sky contained in the earth with the earth spilling over … and those mirrors are like a slash in between it, that act as a release.

Smithson Well, that's what I talk about in the beginning, with the sacrifice of matter as a kind of very primordial idea. Not a human sacrifice, but there's a disjunction. And that disjunction releases a certain kind of awareness. And this is what Georges Bataille, in his book *Death and Sensuality*, points out. The disjunction was what was so liberating to the primitives. But to us, the disjunction becomes almost disgusting; this revulsion enters into it …

Wheeler These are isolated energy occasions, and as such, they're definitely disjunctive … like there's a cleavage, or break, or fracturing in between those obvious realities like earth and heaven.

Smithson That it's caught.

Wheeler Yeah, that it opens up, like when I said 'punched a hole in the earth', I literally meant it opened up, or displays a possibility into an abstraction …

Smithson There's a kind of cutting in, the cantilevering in of the piece, of the geometric abstraction into the inchoate, or the rawness. Its just a surface, and the surface is unlocatable between those two things, so the way the thing is held in there is once again like a kind of slicing.

Wheeler It's as though they're spun off. It's like the gyrostasis made material in its energy. Like something moving out, as you said, in the cyclonic action, but capturing the shattering as if it was a frozen … and the shatterings were caught in the earth in the spin-off and inserted. And that's why they're so energized … it's like a karate chop. […]

And you're always moving towards the wasteland, that reduced landscape. Except the wasteland isn't like the kind of T.S. Eliot romantic …

Smithson … No, no, there's no lament for anything. It's inevitable. And there's no hatred of that aspect … We have almost a kind of rinky-dink idea of nature – Mickey Mouse … Like the people of my generation have grown up in the industrial blight, and it's not rustic woodside that we remember.

Wheeler That's like the Disneyland experience.

Smithson And they're trying to make the jump back to a kind of Romanticism … so you just have a picture-book sentimental, very trite romanticism of what the balance of nature is … Even in the supposedly stable universe of matter as it was viewed by nineteenth-century scientists, new problems constantly appear … The discovery by physicists that anti-matter particles have electric charges, opposite to those that compose our world and unable to exist in concert with known matter, raises the question of whether after all our corner of the universe is representative of the entire potentialities that may exist elsewhere. Elsewhere. That's how the Yucatan runs. 'Yucatan is elsewhere.'[5] So it's a kind of Anti-Yucatan. […]

1 [footnote 39 in source] Robert Smithson, 'Incidents of Mirror-Travel in the Yucatan', *Artforum* (September, 1969).

2 [40] George Santayana, *Scepticism and Animal Faith* (New York: Dover, 1955). Quoted in 'Incidents of Mirror-Travel in the Yucatan'.

3 Ibid.

4 [44] The artist Michael Heizer's brother, an environmentalist.

5 [45] 'Incidents of Mirror-Travel in the Yucatan'.

Robert Smithson and Dennis Wheeler, extract from 'Four Conversations between Dennis Wheeler and Robert Smithson (1969–1970)', in *Robert Smithson: The Collected Writings*, ed. Jack Flam (Berkeley and Los Angeles: University of California Press, 1996) 227–30.

Hans Haacke
Systems Aesthetics: Conversation with Jeanne Siegel//1971

Jeanne Siegel You have been called a naturalist because of your extensive interest in physical elements as well as grass, birds, ants and animals.

Hans Haacke I don't consider myself a naturalist, nor for that matter a conceptualist or a kineticist, an earth artist, elementalist, minimalist, a marriage broker for art and technology, or the proud carrier of any other button that has been offered over the years. I closed my little statement of 1965 with 'articulate something natural'.[1] That has an intended double meaning. It refers to 'nature', and it means something self-understood, ordinary, uncontrived, normal, something of an everyday quality. When people see the wind stuff or the things I have done with animals, they call me a 'naturalist'. Then they get confused or feel cheated when they discover, for example, my interest in using a computer to conduct a demographic survey. This is inconsistent only for those with a naïve understanding of nature – nature being the blue sky, the Rockies, Smokey the Bear. The difference between 'nature' and 'technology' is only that the latter is man-made. The functioning of either one can be described by the same conceptual models, and they both obviously follow the same rules of operation. It also seems that the way social organizations behave is not much different. The world does not break up into neat university departments. It is one supersystem with myriad subsystems, each one more or less affected by all the others.

If you take a grand view, you can divide the world into three or four categories – the physical, biological, social and behavioural – each of them having interrelations with the others at one point or another. There is no hierarchy. All of them are important for the upkeep of the total system. It could be that there are times when one of these categories interests you more than another. So, for example, I now spend more thought on things in the social field, but simultaneously I'm preparing a large water-cycle for the Guggenheim show[2] that uses the peculiarities of the building. […]

Siegel What is your definition of a system that is also a work of art?

Haacke A system is most generally defined as a grouping of elements subject to a common plan and purpose. These elements or components interact so as to arrive at a joint goal. To separate the elements would be to destroy the system. The term was originally used in the natural sciences for understanding the behaviour of physically interdependent processes. It explained phenomena of directional change, recycling and equilibrium. I believe the term system should be reserved for sculptures in which a transfer of energy, material or information occurs, and which do not depend on perceptual interpretation.

I use the word 'systems' exclusively for things that are not systems in terms of perception, but are physical, biological or social entities which, I believe, are more real than perceptual titillation.

Siegel Do you originate systems? Do you demonstrate existing systems?

Haacke Both, but not for didactic reasons. Let me give you an example. Take the cycle of water trickling out of holes in a hose, which I laid out around the periphery of the roof of my studio building. The water was following the uneven surface of the roof, down to a central pool from which it was pumped back into the hose. This is a system which I originated. On the other hand, the invitation to come to the same roof on a given day and view the weather was a demonstration of the meteorological system. This was later complemented by that day's weather chart and the weather statistics of the month. [...]

Haacke A very important difference between the work of minimal sculptors and mine is that they were interested in inertness, whereas I was concerned with change. From the beginning the concept of change has been the ideological basis of my work. All the way down there's absolutely nothing static – nothing that does not change, or instigate real change. Most minimal work disregards change. Things claim to be inert, static, immovably beyond time. But the status quo is an illusion, a dangerous illusion politically.

Siegel How did your attitude about change manifest itself in these works?

Haacke Well, first, by the use of water I got rid of the static illusion and introduced real motion. (At first one only stumbles over the more obvious.) Then I saw the rain boxes condensing[3] and I was very intrigued by it – there was this fantastic cycle of evaporation, condensation, then the droplets falling. That is a process evolving all by itself. This was the first time I had something that was literally responding to its environment. And the response was so subtle that one had to come back after a while to notice it – it had a history. One could decipher the history of the process from the condensation patterns on the inside of the container's walls. It was like a living organism reacting in a flexible manner to its environment. It would be more appropriate however, to liken it to our weather system. [...]

Siegel How did you make the transition from physical systems to biological ones?

Haacke The condensation, as much as the formation of ice [in *Ice Stick*, 1966], figuratively speaking, is related to growth. It was a natural step, then, to introduce actual growth, namely, biological growth. The grass pieces[4] went through a life cycle: they were seeded a few days before the exhibition; the seedlings came out of the ground at the time of the opening of the exhibition, they grew during the show, and at the end of the exhibition they were about to die.

Siegel Growth is obviously a manifestation of change. Are there conditions other than change upon which a work can depend?

Haacke Interference is an existing situation which thereby affects it – this is something that intrigues me. I've brought water into a rather dry forest, a sort of irrigation system, which then changed the existing vegetation.

Siegel Is there any difference in communication between social systems and physical or biological ones?

Haacke For physical or biological processes to take their course, there is no need for the presence of viewers – unless, as with some participatory works, their physical energy is required (they then become an indispensable part of the system's physical environment). However, there is no need for anybody to get mentally involved. These systems function on their own, since their operation does not take place in the viewer's mind (naturally this does not prevent a mental or emotional response). [...]

1   [First published as an untitled statement in Peter Selz, *Directions in Kinetic Sculpture* (Berkeley: University of California Press, 1966) 37.]
2   [Haacke's planned 1971 solo exhibition at the Guggenheim Museum, cancelled by trustees due to their objections to *Shapolsky et al. Manhattan Real Estate Holdings, a Real-Time Social System*.]
3   [as in *Condensation Cube*, 1963–65.]
4   [such as *Grass Grows*, 1969.]

Hans Haacke and Jeanne Siegel, extracts from interview in *Arts Magazine*, vol. 45, no. 7 (May 1971); reprinted in Jeanne Siegel, ed., *Artwords: Discourse on the 60s and 70s* (Ann Arbor: UMI Research Press, 1985) 211–12; 212–13; 214–15.

Suzaan Boettger
Looking at, and Overlooking, Women Working
in Land Art in the 1970s//2008

[…] In the decade between the tumultuous 1960s and the flush 1980s, Cecile Abish, Alice Adams, Alice Aycock, Agnes Denes, Harriet Feigenbaum, Suzanne Harris, Nancy Holt, Mary Miss, Patsy Norvell, Jody Pinto, Patricia Johanson and Athena Tacha, among others, most based in New York City, began to be recognized as a distinctive contingent within the new genre of Land art. In a 1978 article, 'Six Women at Work in the Landscape', critic April Kingsley asserted, 'Women seem to be making most of the really innovative moves in this art form at the moment.'

Did you know that? Probably not. Think of the most famous sculpture made by a woman in the 1970s, and scrolling through your mental file system will probably pop up Judy Chicago's *The Dinner Party* (1974–79), which became the zenith – or nadir, depending on personal/political preference – of the goddess-worship central to the decade's feminist art movement. The historical view of the early to mid 1970s sculptural zeitgeist, as being female-coded or conceptual/disembodied, seems to have swept women sculptors who used architectural and landscape procedures to focus on phenomenological issues into a kind of Bermuda Triangle of historical invisibility. Last summer, to address that lacuna, the SculptureCenter, Long Island City, presented 'Decoys, Complexes and Triggers: Feminism and Land Art in the 1970s', guest-curated by Catherine Morris [4 May – 28 July 2008]. […]

The women sculptors who worked outdoors in the 1970s became active after great notice was given to the earthen excavations, mounds, piles and markings of Michael Heizer, Richard Long, Dennis Oppenheim and Robert Smithson, the first generation earthworkers who began delving into distant dirt around 1967. In contrast to those artists' customary practice of using earth unreinforced by extraneous supports, the next generation of Land artists working in the earth brought wood, metal and concrete. As Kingsley put it: 'Alien materials are brought to the site and something is built with them that is more or less meant to endure through time.'

Works by Aycock, Holt, Miss and Stuart, the four artists mentioned by Kingsley who also participated in 'Feminism/Land Art', generally confirm that definition. Holt is the archetypal Land artist in terms of the expansive scale of her projects exploring perceptions of space and astronomy. She brought concrete pipes of varying diameters to a Hamptons beach for *Views through a Sand Dune* (1972); to Artpark in Lewiston, New York, where they sunk into the earth and filled with water for *Hydra's Head* (1974); and to the Nevada desert for the solstice-aligned *Sun Tunnels* (1976). *Sun Tunnels* and *Stone Enclosure: Rock Rings* (1977–78) at

Bellingham, Washington, may be the only still-extant 1970s outdoor works documented in the show.

Stuart transferred a more fragile medium, paper, to the outdoors in *Niagara Gorge Path Relocated*, made at Artpark in 1975. After impressing local rocks and earth into muslin-backed rag paper and polishing the surface, she joined the panels to form a 420-inch-long ribbon that unfurled as it rolled down a terraced hillside where Niagara Falls was located at the time of the last glacier, about 12,000 years ago, an earthen remembrance of a former flow. By contrast, her *Stone Alignments/Solstice Cairns* (1979), which used only rocks from a plateau at the Columbia River Gorge in Oregon to create an astronomically aligned X within a circle with cairns on the perimeter, was an earthwork. Likewise, Denes' *Rice/Tree/Burial* at Artpark and dramatic *Wheatfield – A Confrontation* (1982) at the Battery Park City landfill brought non-indigenous seeds to the sites as a kind of transgressive agriculture. These were very much about positive generative forces through the growth of edible plants in unlikely places.

Aycock's precise plan for *Project for Elevation with Obstructed Sight Lines* (1972) exemplifies the importance of participatory discovery of the environment in both earthworks and Land art. As she wrote on her drawing, 'only as the observer completed the ascent of a given slope does the next slope become apparent.' Her 14-foot-high pine *Stairs (These Stairs Can Be Climbed)* (1974/2008), reconstructed inside SculptureCenter, demonstrated Aycock's practice of putting the viewer/participant in uncomfortable spaces: when one climbed the stairs the ceiling height prevented ascent to the top. Conforming to the show's themes, Aycock should also have been represented by photographs of her signature early *Land Art: Low Building with Dirt Roof* (1973), with its dank earthen hole to crawl around in, and *Circular Building with Narrow Ledges for Walking* (1976), a scary descent to another pit. Her work is compelling in its experiential perversity, but one had no sense of that from the broad blond staircase at the SculptureCenter.

In comparison, Miss's inventive designs focusing attention on unmediated spaces and exploring contrasts of enclosed and unobstructed space were well represented in photographs, including *Untitled (Battery Park)* (1973), a series of panels installed 50 feet apart on rough landfill, with disks cut out to suggest a setting sun, and *Perimeters/Pavilions/Decoys* (1978), a mini-city of excavated rooms and projecting towers with ladders, on the grounds of the Nassau County Museum in Roslyn, New York. Miss's plywood and steel mesh Screened Court (1979) demonstrated her characteristic preference for contrasting industrial weave and solidity in abstract forms, as well as a sensibility that thwarted the viewer's ability to penetrate to the centre, akin to the frustrations perpetrated by Aycock in works such as *Wooden Post Surrounded by Fire Pits* (1976).

Aycock's and Miss's early works were very architectural in structure, a fact that Lucy Lippard brought to attention in her 1979 article 'Complexes: Architectural Sculpture in Nature', probably the source of curator Morris's use of 'Complexes' in her exhibition title. Of the seven women Lippard discusses, three were included in the show: Aycock, Harris and Holt. Documentation of Harris's *Locus One Up*, built in 1976 on the sand and rock landfill of the future Battery Park City, would have been more appropriate to the Land art theme than the boxy interior-scale works chosen by Morris. As Lippard described it, 'One entered a temporary shelter, an underground passageway that led to a doubled experience: absolute enclosure (in a solid white cube nearly filling the circular well) and open expanse (the sky seen when one looked up instead of ahead).' [...]

The other women discussed by Lippard were like sisters missing from the reunion staged by Morris. Lippard describes Harriet Feigenbaum's works at Artyard, Brooklyn, and Art on the Beach in Lower Manhattan; Feigenbaum would go on to remediate a strip-mined site in Pennsylvania (1983). Lippard also describes Jody Pinto's *Triple Well Enclosure* (1976), with ladders for descent into what might be a burial chamber or libation pit, and Audrey Hemenway's trellised and planted *Garden Web* (1977–78), which was featured in the feminist journal *Heresies*, in an article on 'Environmental Sculpture' that also illustrated and discussed Patricia Johanson's design for *Leaf Garden* (1974). Johanson started making site-specific sculptures in nature out of wood or cement in 1968; her subsequent architect's licence gave her comprehensive control as artist/designer of complex environmental remediation projects.

Others making relevant work who were omitted by Morris include Athena Tacha, who in the 1970s created 'chiselled mountains stippled with pines and boulders' and expansive, thinly terraced hillsides in public art projects for casual public seating. Another is Patsy Norvell whose *Lifeline* (1977) 'consists of a series of fences of different heights and materials which define paths, creating both boundaries and openings. These different spaces and passageways re-create symbolically the passage of life – time/space that is occasionally easy and flowing and other times cramped and unclear.' And Cecile Abish's shallow excavations and low heaps, as in *4 into 3* (1974), illustrated in Kingsley's article, and *Shifting Concern* (1975), display the qualities of environmental embeddedness and expansive scale characteristic of Land art. [...]

We can be sure that the women making Land art, as vanguard artists in a cutting-edge milieu, were aligned in various ways, intellectually, socially, with feminism. But the works in the show, and Land art by women in general, do not display an explicit relation to gender and sexuality in their subject matter. Holt and Stuart encouraged a connection between viewers and the cosmos through solstice alignments; Aycock's dark crawl spaces may be constricted wombs, but her mazes or forests of poles that we can't enter evoke emotional aloofness.

Denes planted crops to feed the world and later trees to sustain it, and Feigenbaum, Pinto and especially Johanson designed environments to sustain and recycle natural resources for the public good while providing visually stimulating recreational areas. But spatially and materially, a number of women sculptors' oeuvres are not distinctly feminine: the large scale of the works, the rough, industrially associated materials, the architectural forms and the constructive procedures are aspects traditionally associated with masculinity.

Consider the gender androgyny implied in Kingsley's analogy between the development of Land art and American territorialism. Writing of 1960s earthworkers as 'pioneers' who 'scouted' the new genre, she wrote, 'Just as women shouldered half of the backbreaking workload of civilizing the wilderness in those early days of our country, so do they now share equally with male artists in this new wave of creative intellectual domination over nature.' So, on the one hand, the large number of women who worked in Land art in the 1970s evokes an archaic identification with the dyad of women and nature. But on the other hand, their creation of abstract and architectural forms on land, followed by their development into designers of large-scale, constructed public environments, suggests an antipathy to earth mother codification in favour of alignment with (male) culture's manipulation of nature as Other. Despite this being a decade after the publication of Rachel Carson's *Silent Spring*, few of these ambitious male and female artists (Alan Sonfist was the exception) directly connected their works or themes to political environmentalism. The women's position – working in nature but making increasingly complex architectural structures – suggests a gender fusion ahead of the fluidity of subsequent decades, which allowed women artists to predominate in current reparative environmental projects. [...]

Suzaan Boettger, extracts from 'Looking at, and Overlooking, Women Working in Land Art in the 1970s' (2008), *WEAD Magazine*, no. 1 (2009), Women Environmental Artists Directory (http:weadartists.org)

Ana Mendieta
In Conversation with Linda Montano//1988

Linda Montano In your work, you embody the earth, become it, leave your impression on it. Can you remember an instance from your past that may have encouraged you to leave images of yourself on the earth?

Ana Mendieta I came from a tropical country, Cuba, and I have pictures of myself, seven months old, crawling around on the sandy beach. We had a house there, and I would be outside from 7.30 a.m. to 2.00 in the afternoon – out in the water and the sand. I learned about my body from doing that. Now I continue to use my body to communicate with the world, so that things that I have learned are things that I have experienced and internalized. I'm five feet tall, so I even measure things with my body. I started doing imprints to place myself and my body in the world. That way I can do something, step away from it, and see myself there afterwards. [...]

Montano Was anyone in your family a healer? [...]

Mendieta No, my family was against anything like that. It was considered to be low class and an activity of the uneducated. However, I became interested in these things after I had been working for a while and I found that my work shares a lot of healing imagery. [...] I did an interesting piece that crosses the line between art and life. The Santeros use a tree that in Spanish is called *sela* and in English is called a cotton silkwood tree. It has very long roots that stick out. In Miami there is a tree like that, which the Santeros have claimed, and the people do things to that tree when a healer tells them that they have to make a sacrifice. When I was there I decided to do a piece on the tree. I was in the Cuban section and collected human hair from the different beauty shops, so I knew that it was Cuban hair. Then I made an image of a figure on the tree. A root was sticking out, so the figure appeared to be either a male or female being screwed. There were also three knots on it that happened to look like female genitalia, so I surrounded them with hair that I glued on. It's amazing how Elmer's glue withstands weather, because I did it in 1981 and it's still there. The last time I saw the tree, people had added coconuts, chicken wings, all kinds of offerings. For a while they put the figure of Santa Barbara underneath it, cut an opening in what would be the face, and stuck a shell in the mouth. They have really activated the image and claimed it as their own. [...]

Ana Mendieta and Linda Montano, extracts from interview, *Sulfur*, no. 22 (Spring 1988) 69.

Michael Auping
A Nomad among Builders//1987

There is something venerable about the nomad, moving across the surface of the planet with no need to take possession of it. For such peoples, architecture has a unique meaning. It is often impermanent, collapsible and mobile, not a monument to colonization or a system of controlling a place. In this sense architecture is not a 'thing' but a temporary state of being. Hamish Fulton attempts to make an art that parallels this state. In working with nature as subject, Fulton's approach is not one of displacement and construction but a nomadic odyssey that embraces a spiritual sense of place.

Since 1969 Fulton's art has stemmed from walks he has taken in the landscape. He represents these walks through the combined media of words and photographs, his reaction to the character of the landscape determining the length of the walk and the number of photographs made during the journey. He tends to distil his experience of a walk into precise images, often representing a journey with a single photograph placed behind glass in a large, dark wood frame. Each of the photographs is set in a mat upon which is printed a text giving factual information about the walk and brief details of the experience culled from an ongoing diary. These are essentially country walks, but they take place on what seems a McLuhanesque scale. Fulton has walked literally thousands of miles in Nepal, India, Bolivia, Canada, Peru, Iceland, England, Scotland, America, Mexico, Australia, France and Italy.

Fulton's art was initially inspired by his interest in the [Native] American Indian. In a recent letter, he stated specifically that it was his admiration for two books he read on the subject in 1962 – *Black Elk Speaks* by J.G. Neihardt and *Wooden Leg* by T.B. Marquis – that led to a 1969 trip to the United States. Fulton's interest in the American Indian remains a guiding force in his art, and one of his ambitions is to produce an extended series on the American Indian and 'their landscape'.[1]

Fulton is not, however, a twentieth-century version of the Victorian voyager who transported easels and sketchbooks to the far corners of the world in search of the exotic native, unpoisoned by civilization. [...]

What Fulton envies in American Indian culture, or that of the Australian Aboriginal, is the lack of a monumental architecture mediating between these people and their natural environment. For such cultures, the land is not to be captured but followed judiciously if not spiritually. Fulton recently sent me the following quotation of Narritjin Maymura, an Australian Aboriginal, in response to a question about the inspirational sources for his art:

We belong to the ground
It is our power and we must stay
Close to it or maybe
We will get lost[2]

For Fulton, this philosophy is expressed most poignantly in the simple act of walking. He sees walking as the central aspect of his art. 'No walk, no work'[3] has been one of his maxims. In Fulton's art, walking is presented as one man's most basic dialogues with nature, a dialogue not coincidentally central to the nomadic peoples who have helped inspire his art. Fulton does not approach nature as 'landscape', in the traditional sense of a still image, but as a physical experience. The texts that accompany his photographs relay the time, the distance, and in a number of cases, the condition of a walk. Time is compared to distance, which is measured in relation to terrain and weather. The interpretation of nature, the reasons he chooses to photograph particular images, is a direct result of his physical involvement with it. As he moves, each footstep is a form of measurement that mediates between his body and the landscape. When Fulton takes his photographs, he is not separated from the 'scenery' as it were; he is walking through it, incorporated into it. Thus the different types of terrain become a crucial element of chance in the work, determining the length of the walk, the direction and the number of photographs taken. Fulton has commented, 'My work is about nature and it seems proper to allow nature to determine events en route.'[4] [...]

While Michael Heizer and Robert Smithson chose to rearrange the landscape, Fulton prefers that the landscape impose itself on him. Avoiding alteration of place, the photographs document his attraction for 'unspoiled' landscape and the fact that 'he was there'. Fulton agrees with the idea that the only things you should take out of the landscape are photographs and the only things you should leave are footprints. [...]

1   Undated letter to the author, received May 1984.

2   Ibid.

3   Conversation with the artist, October 1981.

4   Peter Turner, in 'An Interview with Hamish Fulton', *Landscape Theory* (New York: Lustrum Press, 1980) 81.

Michael Auping, extracts from 'A Nomad Among Builders', *Places*, vol. 3, no. 4 (Fall 1987) 4–7.

Jean-François Lyotard
Scapeland//1988

[...] Landscapes could be classified in terms of how easily they can be nibbled, BITTEN. It would take a bite of tungsten steel to savour the frozen flesh of the lakes of Minnesota in the bitter cold or the Rimouski shore in winter. Given that we don't have that bite, that different judgement, we draw back. But as we do so, we still evoke that impracticable ordeal.

The walls will never be really cast down. Hence the MELANCHOLIA of all landscapes. We owe them a debt. They immediately demand the deflagration of the mind and they obtain it immediately. Without it, they would be places, not landscapes. And yet the mind never burns enough.

It is a question of MATTER. Matter is that element in the datum which has no destiny. Forms domesticate it, make it consumable. Especially visual perspectives and modes and scales of sound. Forms of sensibility which have come under the control of the understanding without difficulty. Things are less clear when it comes to their lower sisters who smell, drink in and touch. For a beautiful visual landscape, walking without any goal, strolling and the desire to wander simply authorize a transfer of material powers to scents, to the tactile quality of the ground, of walls, of plants. Your foot savours the *morbidezza* of the mossy heathland and the undergrowth which flank and contradict the sharp stones of the path. In New York, the cars hurtle down Forty-third Street towards SoHo, crossing the ruts that criss-cross the street in every direction, their back ends bobbing up and down like badly moored rubber boats. They make the ground ring with the hollow sound of a percussion instrument; their tyres make the noise of suckers being pulled off the road. So many untameable states of matter.

It used to be said that landscapes – *pagus*, those borderlands where matter offers itself up in a raw state before being tamed – were wild because they were, in Northern Europe, always forests. *FORIS*, outside. Beyond the pale, beyond the cultivated land, beyond the realm of form. Estrangement procures an inner feeling of being outside thanks to an intimist exoticism. In cities, in minds. States of mind are states of spiritual matter. Suspended between two mental intrigues. See Rimbaud. Beside himself.

Whether or not you 'like' a landscape is unimportant. It does not ask you for your opinion. If it is there, your opinion counts as nothing. A landscape leaves the mind DESOLATE. It makes lymph (the soul) flow, not blood. You do not associate. No more synthesis. It doesn't follow on. Leave it for later. You pray to heaven, to provide for you in your wretchedness. The wretchedness of a soul rubbed raw by the tide race of matter.

A lonely traveller, a lonely walker. It is not only that conversation, even conversations with yourself, and the intrigue of desires and understanding have to be silenced. As in a temple, a *TEMPLUM*, a neutralized space-time where it is certain that something – but what? – might perhaps happen. (What I mean is that this 'templation' is the price that has to be paid so that even the cacophony of the Place de la République can become a landscape at 5.30 p.m. on a winter's day, when it is choked with thousands of jammed vehicles.) Not only solitude, but the disconcertment of the powers and therefore the defences, of the mind. Not alone with oneself, but behind oneself. The self is left behind, sloughed off, definitely too conventional, too sure of itself and over-arrogant in the way it puts things into scale. It is tempting to speak, yet again, of what Cézanne calls 'little sensations'. Inner desolation.

There are a thousand ways of obtaining this surrender. Feasting or fasting, tobacco, grass, *farniente*, overwork. But it always requires something that is TOO … (if only too little). In order to have a feel for landscape you have to lose your feeling of place. A place is natural, a crossroads for the kingdoms and for *homo sapiens*. The mineral, vegetable and animal kingdoms are ordered by knowledge and knowledge takes to them quite spontaneously. They are made, selected for one another. But a landscape is an excess of presence. My *savoir-vivre* is not enough. A glimpse of the inhuman and/or of an unclean non-world [*l'immonde*] […]

[…] It is not estrangement which procures landscape. It is the other way around. And the estrangement that landscape procures does not result from the transfer of a sensorial organization into another sensorium, such as the transfer of the fragrance of scents into the flagrance of colours or into the light of timbres. This estrangement is absolute; it is the implosion of forms themselves, and forms are mind. A landscape is a mark, and it (but not the mark it makes and leaves) should be thought of, not as an inscription, but as the erasure of a support. If anything remains, it is an absence which stands as a sign of a horrifying presence in which mind FAILS and misses its aim. Fails, not because it was looking for itself and did not find itself, but (we are forced to fall back on comparisons) in the sense that one can say that one missed one's footing and fell, or that one's legs gave way, as one sits on a bench, watching a window which is lit up but empty. […]

Jean-François Lyotard, extracts from *L'Inhumain: Causeries sur le temps* (Paris: Éditions Galilée, 1988); trans. David Macey, 'The Inhuman: Reflections on Time', in The Lyotard Reader' (Oxford: Blackwell, 1989) 214–15; 217.

David Harvey
Between Space and Time//1990

[…] I often ask beginner geography students to consider where their last meal came from. Tracing back all the items used in the production of that meal reveals a relation of dependence upon a whole world of social labour conducted in many different places under very different social relations and conditions of production. That dependency expands even further when we consider the materials and goods used in the production of the goods we directly consume. Yet we can in practice consume our meal without the slightest knowledge of the intricate geography of production and the myriad social relationships embedded in the system that puts it upon our table.

This was the condition that Karl Marx picked up on in developing one of his most telling concepts – the fetishism of commodities.[1] He sought to capture by that term the way in which markets conceal social (and, we should add, geographical) information and relations. We cannot tell from looking at the commodity whether it has been produced by happy labourers working in a cooperative in Italy, grossly exploited labourers working under conditions of apartheid in South Africa, or wage labourers protected by adequate labour legislation and wage agreements in Sweden. The grapes that sit upon the supermarket shelves are mute; we cannot see the fingerprints of exploitation upon them or tell immediately what part of the world they are from. We can, by further enquiry, lift the veil on this geographical and social ignorance and make ourselves aware of these issues (as we do when we engage in a consumer boycott of non-union or [apartheid-era] South African grapes). But in so doing we find we have to go behind and beyond what the market itself reveals in order to understand how society is working. This was precisely Marx's own agenda. We have to get behind the veil, the fetishism of the market and the commodity, in order to tell the full story of social reproduction.

The geographical ignorance that arises out of the fetishism of commodities is in itself cause for concern. The spatial range of our own individual experience of procuring commodities in the marketplace bears no relationship to the spatial range over which the commodities themselves are produced. The two space horizons are quite distinct, and decisions that seem reasonable from the former standpoint are not necessarily appropriate from the latter. To which set of experiences should we appeal in understanding the historical geography of space and time? Strictly speaking, my answer will be both because both are equally material. But it is here that I insist we should deploy the Marxian concept of fetishism with its full force. We will arrive at a fetishistic interpretation of the world (including the objective social definitions of space and time) if we take the realm of individual experience (shopping in the supermarket, travelling to work and picking up money at the bank) as all there is. These latter activities are real and material, but their organization is such as to conceal the other definitions of space and time set up in accordance with the requirements of commodity production and capital circulation through price-fixing markets.

A pure concern for the material base of our own daily reproduction ought to dictate a working knowledge of the geography of commodity production and of the definitions of space and time embedded in the practices of commodity production and capital circulation. But in practice most people do without. This also raises important moral issues. If for example, we consider it right and proper to show moral concern for those who help put dinner on the table, then this implies an extension of moral responsibility throughout the whole intricate geography and sociality of intersecting markets. We cannot reasonably go to church on Sunday, donate copiously to a fund to help the poor in the parish, and then walk obliviously into the market to buy grapes grown under conditions of apartheid. We cannot reasonably argue for high environmental quality in the neighbourhood while still insisting on living at a level which necessarily implies polluting the air somewhere else (this is, after all, the heart of the ecologists' argument). Our problem is indeed precisely that in which Marx sought to instruct us. We have to penetrate the veil of fetishisms with which we are necessarily surrounded by virtue of the system of commodity production and exchange and discover what lies behind it. In particular, we need to know how space and time get defined by these material processes which give us our daily bread.

1   [footnote 2 in source] Karl Marx, *Capital. Volume 1* (1867) (New York: International Publishers, 1967) 71–83.

David Harvey, extract from 'Between Space and Time: Reflections on the Geographical Imagination', in *Annals of the Association of American Geographers*, vol. 80, no. 3 (September 1990).

Mierle Laderman Ukeles
Flow City (1983–91)//1995

[...] When the department of sanitation began redesigning the waste disposal system for the city of New York in the early 1980s, they invited me to sit in on the meetings. During my *Touch Sanitation* work, I had fallen in love with one of the locations they now wanted to redevelop. It was at the base of 59th Street, on the Hudson River. In 1983 I proposed to the department a permanent public environment that would become an organic part of an operating garbage facility. I designed *Flow City* with the design engineers from Greeley Hanson.

The site is one of the most beautiful on the Hudson River, midway between the George Washington Bridge and the Statue of Liberty. It is a marine transfer station that handles a waste flow equivalent to that of a city the size of San Francisco. Garbage trucks transfer their payloads into barges that wait in the finger of the Hudson River that flows through the station. The barges are then switched out in a beautiful nautical manoeuvre and taken by tug boat to the Fresh Kills Landfill on Staten Island.

Flow City is a radical penetration of art into the workplace. The penetration begins with the *Passage Ramp* that leads to the *Glass Bridge*. From the bridge, visitors will observe the operation of the station. The end of the bridge is called *Media Flow Wall*. [...]

When we first proposed *Flow City*, the Department of Ports and Terminals said, 'You can't do that, because it's never been done before.' The sanitation department replied, 'Yes we can. It is time to lift the veil on the subject, and this is the way to do it.'

Passage Ramp will be a 248 foot-long procession made of ten to twelve recyclable materials, including 20 feet of crushed glass and 20 feet of shredded rubber. I want visitors to feel the extreme diversity in different materials, because if you can appreciate this, then you can't watch them all getting dumped together in the barge without thinking, 'How stupid.' I want visitors to see the materials in a kind of hovering state of flux: thrown out, not yet back. I want the visitors to pass through a state of potentiality.

I have designed the recycling panels in the shape of a running spiral, a form that can be found in every culture and is universally seen as a symbol of regeneration and continuity – the essence of recycling. This work is about a paradigm shift in how we relate to materials in the world. We need to grow beyond the self-destructive cycle of acquiring materials, owning them, using them, and then leaving them as if they don't exist any more.

At the top of the ramp visitors will enter the *Glass Bridge* that is 40 feet long and 18 feet wide. On one side of the bridge is the formal city with the icons of New York: the Empire State Building and the World Trade Center. On the other side is the city in flux. The trucks, in fourteen dumping bays, lift their hoppers and dump their payloads into the waiting barges. As the barges are loaded, the visitors will see them passing beneath their very feet, under the *Glass Bridge*. They will be able to watch all of the things they worked so hard to buy go to waste. I call it the 'Violent Theatre of Dumping.'

At the end of the bridge is the *Media Flow Wall*, a 10 by 18 foot crushed glass wall with 24 monitors set into it. The video wall will be programmed with live cameras, located on and off site, and prepared disc and tape sources. It is an electronic permeable membrane that will enable visitors to pass 'through' this physical point in order to get a broader understanding of how this kind of place links up with the systems of the planet. The wall will transmit three kinds of flow-imagery: river, landfill and recycling.

Six live cameras, 350 feet away from the facility, will focus continually on the mighty Hudson River. The fact that the garbage is collected and transferred in this particular place prompts a great sense of loss, because the facility bars access to our primal source: the river. This river makes the city live. It will flow back in real time across the *Media Flow Wall*, as cameras focus down-river, up-river, midway, close-up on the face of the water, and even beneath the surface, where thirty species of fish presently live in midtown Manhattan.

The wall will also document the accumulation of our garbage at the Fresh Kills Landfill that will eventually be the highest point on the eastern sea coast, rising almost 500 feet.

The third source of imagery is the great social revolution of our time: recycling, in which each of us becomes a sanitation worker, a participating partner in the care of the environment.

I also plan to have an intercom system set up to create a flow of communication between visitors and any available sanitation worker. As citizens, we consume the services of those who work in these places, we produce the product that is serviced in these places; we own these places. These are public facilities. We have every reason to be here.

There are many reasons why there are veils between ourselves and our waste. Hopefully, in a short while, we can lift these veils and see who we are, where we come from and what we can do. [...]

Mierle Laderman Ukeles, extracts from 'Mierle Laderman Ukeles' in Baile Oakes, ed., *Sculpting with the Environment* (New York: Van Nostrand Reinhold, 1995) 184–9.

Steven Connor
Topologies: Michel Serres and the Shapes of Thought//2002

[…] One of the most important of Michel Serres' applications of topological thought is to thinking about history. In place of the line of history, Serres proposes a series of different figurings of time, based on dynamic volumes, or topologies. Time is seen as a river, forking, branching, slewing, slowing, rolling back on itself. It can be a flame, leaping out and resiling. It can even be a crumpled handkerchief, in which apparently widely separated points may be drawn together into adjacency.[1] All of these structures involve apprehending time as what David Bohm called an 'implicate order', as a complex volume that folds over on itself, and in the process does not merely transform in time, but itself gathers up and releases time, as though time were like the intricately folded structure of a protein.[2]

'Physics and history are founded in the same time', writes Serres in his *Rome*, a book in which Serres confronts and attempts to outflank imperial, foundational and progressive time.[3] This leads him to a remarkable, extended reflection on a further metaphor for time and history, the kneading of dough. Kneading is seen as a woman's art, conflating it with the complex imbrications of the developing foetus – indeed, embryology should be thought of as a kind of topology, Serres observes in *Atlas*.[4] Serres is not the only contemporary philosopher to have been concerned with the action and implication of the fold. In one of his rare acknowledgements of the work of a contemporary, Serres approves Deleuze's generalization of the metaphor of the fold in his study of Leibniz (1993): 'This is what the classical or baroque age discovered, along with Leibniz and his calculus: the infinitesimal germ of form, the topological atom of the fold, beside the algebraic or ensemblist atom of the element; from this moment and this philosophy on, everything is folding, as Gilles Deleuze has rightly said of it.'[5] Perhaps both Serres and Deleuze have behind them, as well as Leibniz, a memory of the remarkable evocation of kneading in Bachelard's *La Terre et les rêves de la volonté* (1948). In his chapter on the soft matter of the earth, Bachelard sees the workings of oils, creams and doughs as derivatives from what he calls an ideal of primary 'paste', 'the perfect synthesis of stiffness and softness, a marvellous equilibrium of yielding and resisting forces'.[6] Bachelard's discussion of this primary paste occurs as the first in a series of discussions of dreams of terrene matter, as these are played out between the alternatives of the hard (rock, crystal, diamond, iron) and the soft (clay, putty, oil). It is the ideal of such a paste which allows Bachelard to posit the existence of a new kind of *cogito*, or sense of self. In between the neutral *cogito* of mere self-knowing and the more active kind of self-recognition which arises in the 'phenomenology of the against', the sense of straining or striving against things (and perhaps before both of these allotropes of the *cogito*), there is 'a cogito of kneading' (*un cogito pétrisseur*).[7] The action of kneading is a process that turns slack mud, mire or waste into a dough or paste that is taut with potential, whether as nutriment or cement. Mixing in is vital to this process, in particular the addition of oil, butter or other fatty substances to powder or flour. The aim of kneading is to blend together the joined and the disjoined, breadth and depth, the virtue of oil's smooth spread and the density of pulverized substance. In kneading, one repeatedly folds the outer skin of the substance inwards, until it is as it were crammed with surface tension, full of its outside. The result, for Bachelard, is no mere mixture, but a tonic mass, full of tensile potential: the strudel dough that can be drawn out almost indefinitely. The action of kneading makes the material alive because it invests it with energy. One seems literally to put work into the substance one kneads, inducing kinetic potential into the previously dead substance. When one kneads dough or clay, it is as if one were winding a spring. A lump of worked dough is a negentropic niche in things. Time has been folded into it along with work and air, and so, having undergone a transition from an in-itself to a for-itself, it has a future. Dough is quickened mass: not amorphous, but incipient of shape, not slack but charged. Erotic life may begin with the caress, but without the action of kneading, moulding your partner into new life, eros cannot be long protracted. The body is quickened as the soil is quickened, by turning it over, by folding it into itself, with the addition of air. When air is folded into pastry, time is folded in too: the time of growth, of the swelling of the soufflé, the breathed-in dish. In one sense, the skin is the antagonist of a kneaded world, for the skin is what holds individual lives separate and aloof; it is integument which guarantees the integrity of shape and signifies the suspension of decomposition that is all life. But skin, which Serres always represents topologically, also holds the dream of the kneaded body, the dough-body, the *cogito pétrisseur*.

Although Serres uses the automorphic self-touching of the skin as a way of reflecting on what Deleuze calls the 'inclension of the soul'[8] he is interested in much more than the curvature of the *cogito*.[9] The discussion of baker's dough in *Rome* is an image of the complex overlayering of time in history, an image not of time moving on and dissipating, but of endlessly regathering itself: 'The system grows old without letting time escape; it garners age – the new emblems are caught up and subsumed by old ones; the baker moulds memory … Time enters into the dough, a prisoner of its folds, a shadow of its folding over.'[10] Serres imagines trying to map or model the involutions of the dough as it is moulded, perhaps by making a mark and plotting its changes of position in three or more dimensions through successive stretchings and foldings. To those who can think of progress only as the extension or unrolling of a straight line, the trajectory of this point relative to other points in the dough would very quickly become undetermined, irrational, as seemingly random as the flight of a fly. This apparent unassimilability to the spatial intelligence occurs because

we simple blind people, simplistic, short-sighted, have not imagined implication, inclusion, fold; we have never known what a tissue is, never noticed or listened to women, never known what a mélange might be, and never understood, or even imagined, time.[11]

In the folding and refolding dough of history, what matters is not the spreading out of points of time in a temporal continuum, but the contractions and attenuations that ceaselessly disperse neighbouring points and bring far distant points into proximity with one another. The totality of these foldings would assume the fractal or fluctuating forms of natural structures, rather than the straight lines of the geometrical imagination:

The route from local time to global time, from the instant to time, from the present to history, is unforeseeable; it is not integrable by reason, as analysis has shaped it. It seems to go crazily, no matter where, and drunkenly, no matter how. If the baker knew how to write, she would lazily follow the fly's flight, the capricious foldings of proteins, the coastline of Brittany or of Île d'Ouessant, the fluctuating fringe of a mass of clouds.[12]

The image of history not as an inert or given shape, exposed and disposed to the investigating eye, but a dynamism, folding over automorphically on itself, makes the dough, as it had been for Bachelard, an image of the activity of thought or knowledge, as well as of the nature of its object. Serres describes this kind of knowledge as the opposite of analysis, or the separating of things one from another (for topological transformation disallows cutting). It is, or would be 'a knowledge that multiplies gestures in a short time, in a limited space, so that it renders information more and more dense, until it forms a rarer place that sometimes becomes a dark solid'.[13] It is an image of time gathering into history, but also the image of the way in which time is thought, in time. It is as though history gains its shape from the ways in which it reads itself or gathers itself up, as we say, reflexively, as well as the ways in which its time happens to fall out. History is the shape that time can take and the shape that historical reflexion (doubling back, doubling over) will make of it. The kneaded dough is only one in a huge ensemble of images for fluctuation that Serres has allowed to propagate across and between his works, which includes skins, textiles, bags, tapestries, kimonos, rivers, coastlines, clouds, vortices, mountain ranges and flames. But it is also a kind of meta-metaphor, which figures the topological generation of metaphor itself. Indeed, it may even be an image for the relations between Serres' different works, in which it is similarly extremely hard to mark out any clear and determinate progress from origins to ends, so full is that work of anticipations, dawdlings, accelerations, rewindings, recapitulations. The more Serres writes, the more he finds himself crossing the path of his own sylleptic footsteps. [...]

The ethical claims for synthesis, a holistic grasping of the complete shape of things, which seem increasingly to complete and justify Serres' rapprochements of science and the humanities, fact and value, may in fact be the coarsest and least compelling aspects of his thought. The very power to integrate complex phenomena which the idea of topology offers may be its weakness, in a world in which the acceptance and management of discontinuity may be a better hope than the effort to see and entertain every possibility.

Serres' topological mode of thinking offers great possibilities of transformation and renewal for thinking and writing in the humanities and science, as well as offering a model for how they might begin to include each other. His work makes it clear how crudely mechanical or frankly magical (the same thing perhaps) our conceptions of the nature and workings of social life and time can be. Characteristically he has done this not through critique but the invention of new shapes of thought. Nick Bingham, for example, has argued that we may be able to rouse ourselves from dulling contemporary fantasies of the 'technological sublime' through Serres' idea of the binding mobility of the quasi-object, which holds together complex societies as the movement of the ball may be said to focus and bind together the movements and purpose of two opposed teams.[14] Serres' work offers to contemporary thought the same kind of reinvigoration that the work of Bergson did a century ago, except that where Bergson attempted to make a clean break between the fixative illusions of spatial thinking, in favour of thought in motion, Serres offers ways of thinking time spatially and morphologically. For the historian of ideas, forms and feelings in particular, Serres' versatile development of Bachelard's insight into the material imagination – the imagining of the material world, and the materiality of the imagination – offers a thesaurus of shapes of thought and thoughts of shape that promise enrichment to historical thought. Bachelard's explication of the poetics of matter and space could only take shape in a reserved space of dream and reverie, set aside from the forms of scientific knowledge that formed the subject of his earlier historical analyses. Serres' topologies of space and time disclose and project new and more inclusive, less sequestered forms in which to hold together science and culture, and to incubate new forms of historical poetics. His greatest contribution is surely his inventive cultivation of the spatial and topological imagination, the ways in which we project how and where we live, as embodied beings who are nevertheless incapable of not being beside themselves, not living beyond the here-and-now of their bodies, not being taken up in the flamboyant dramatics of topology. Serres has always spurned schools and disciplines, and it may be that we can do most with his work by effecting a partial break with it, by declining to accept as definitive the ethical and political shape within which he encloses it. [...]

1   Michel Serres and Bruno Latour, *Conversations on Science, Culture and Time*, trans. Roxanne Lapidus (Ann Arbor: University of Michigan Press, 1995) 60–61.

2   David Bohm, *Wholeness and the Implicate Order* (London: Routledge and Kegan Paul, 1980).

3   Michel Serres, *Rome: The Book of Foundations*, trans. Felicia McCarren (Stanford: Stanford University Press, 1983) 267.

4   Michel Serres, *Atlas* (Paris: Éditions Julliard, 1994) 47–8.

5   Ibid., 49.

6   Gaston Bachelard, *La Terre et les rêveries de la volonté* (Paris: José Corti, 1948) 78.

7   Ibid., 79.

8   Gilles Deleuze, *The Fold: Leibniz and the Baroque*, trans. Tom Conley (London: Athlone Press, 1993) 3.

9   Michel Serres, *Les Cinq Sens* (Paris: Hachette, 1998) 20.

10   Michel Serres, *Rome: The Book of Foundations*, op.cit., 81.

11   Ibid., 82.

12   Ibid., 82.

13   Ibid., 78.

14   Nick Bingham, 'Unthinkable Complexity? Cyberspace Otherwise', in *Virtual Geographies: Bodies, Space and Relations*, ed. Mike Crang and Jon May (London and New York: Routledge, 1999).

Steven Connor, extracts from 'Topologies: Michel Serres and the Shapes of Thought', paper for 'Literature and Science' conference, Ascoli, Piceno, Italy (May 2002); *Anglistik*, no. 15 (2004).

Emma Cocker
Heather and Ivan Morison: *Earthwalker//2006*

The image conjured by slide-projected travelogues relayed to others in the comfort of a domestic space is now synonymous with the banal clichés of middle-class tourism: photographic residues of holiday experiences served up to an often bored audience of friends and family. This cultural tradition also attests to the glitch in photography's promise: the image only infrequently captures the experience of the moment, more often stripping the event of meaningful content. Arguably the photographic memento of travel is only ever a pale echo of experiential encounter with a place, its documentary value serving merely as an *aide-mémoire* for those who participated in the actual journey. Here any transferable meaning is rendered void by the experiential chasm between what has authentically been seen or felt and its translation into a narrative or anecdote to be offered up to others.

The slide projection of travel images in a domestic context perhaps also draws on a tradition in which the gesture is seen as one of exclusivity: tales of exotic places serve to assert a cultural (often economic) separation, or shared sense of hierarchy, between the presenting host and invited guests. The slide show operates as a signal affirming the privileged status of a few individuals' experiences above the more pedestrian realities of others. With the democratization and standardization of travel, however, this now seems less about discovery, more about the compulsion of aimless repetition, the following of tried and tested paths. Perhaps, then, travel's photographic residue creates a dual dissatisfaction: it not only fails to capture the experiential moment but also invariably reiterates images that have already been collectively processed and approved by innumerable guidebooks and tourist boards.

The Morisons frequently make use of slide projection to relay or reiterate fragments from their expeditions. Their journeys are not determined by tourism's familiar routes but often follow highly personal and idiosyncratic itineraries or instructions from more unexpected sources. In *Chinese Arboretum*, for example, they follow the guidance of tree fanatics as they search for rare species; in more recent work the route of migrating storks presents a path for them to trace. Though their [2006] exhibition of work from the *Earthwalker* series is presented in the 'domestic' space of the Danielle Arnaud gallery, its slide projections might be seen as an attempt to subvert or sabotage conventions of popular travel and its reportage which rob the gesture of wandering of its critical or transformative function.

Earthwalker is a collection of fragments and traces in which photographic evidence from previous expeditions and projects appears to collide with an altogether more illusionary register. Echoing the preoccupations of the Victorian explorer or collector, the Morison's records reflect a natural world where the boundaries between the fictitious and factual are blurred and where strange hybrids and fantasy formations are the products of both imaginary and economic desires. The slides are presented as a disjointed, dislocated sequence that fails to communicate any stable idea of narrative trajectory or place, but seems instead to create spaces or gaps through which to reflect upon certain recurrent themes and preoccupations. References to collection and storage, taxonomy and organization, genetic modification and chimera play out over an eerily futuristic soundtrack, whose insistent electronic pulse seeps beyond the gallery space and functions both to underscore and disrupt the coherence of the work.

Rather than presenting a substitute for the performative experience of their travels, the documentary image in Heather and Ivan Morison's work offers both extraordinary (and at times equally prosaic) clues through which an audience must draw their individual conclusions, on account of the absent narrative. The slides present only partial references, separated or disrupted in projection by pauses and blank spaces, and in which stirs the promise of both possibility and unease. For Rosalind Krauss, the spacing of the photographic image itself is a form of syntax, indicating a 'break in the simultaneous experience of the real, a rupture that issues into sequence … a rupture in the continuous fabric of reality'.[1] And for Michel de Certeau the practice of walking is analogous to the 'speech act' and can also be understood to create a kind of 'spacing' or syntax in relation to how things are encountered. Walking and travel are described as a form of 'enunciation' that carries the possibility of breathing life, introducing a temporal beat or narrative, into the abstract spatial grid or dead text of the map. Both the photograph and the pedestrian act can thus be used as a means of disrupting the way in which things are habitually seen, presenting a more contingent and revelatory notion of space. Both work towards producing a form of anti-guide through which to encounter the everyday, where the normative methods of viewing or experiencing the world are bypassed in favour of more abstract, imaginative possibilities. Viewed in this light practices such as that of Heather and Ivan Morison can be argued to reclaim both a critical and a poetic function for travel and wandering, beyond the formulaic patterns of popular tourism: they reassert a mythic and transformative dimension of the traveller's tale, in which fantasy and superstition, science fiction and futuristic visions might operate alongside more familiar accounts of the world.

1   Rosalind Krauss, 'The Photographic Conditions of Surrealism', *October* (Winter 1981) 31.

Emma Cocker, 'Heather and Ivan Morison: *Earthwalker*', *Artists' Newsletter* (December 2006).

Jane Prophet
On *TechnoSphere//1996*

TechnoSphere is an online project that enables users to design artificial life forms and send them into a 3D virtual world where they interact with life forms designed by other users of the website. The 3D world has a fractally generated terrain in which trees self-seed at certain heights to make forests, and there are desert and mountainous regions in which the cyberbeasts artificially live. The current (June 1996) version is a prototype written between March and September 1995. [*TechnoSphere* is no longer online but documented at www.janeprophet. com/technoweb.html]

TechnoSphere has been produced by a team of people and is made up of four components: I am responsible for managing the project and for the website design, which has CGI commands written by Tony Taylor-Moran. The artificial life engine has been designed and written by Julian Saunderson from the Centre for Electronic Arts at Middlesex University; the rendering engine has been written by Gordon Selley from London College of Printing and Distributive Trades; and the email engine has been written by Selley and Saunderson. Andrew Kind, a computer graphics animator, models the component parts for the creatures.

On 1 September 1995 we opened *TechnoSphere*. Users who come to the website can choose whether to design a carnivore or a herbivore. They then build these artificial life forms by selecting from a limited range of body parts displayed on the website. Each body part carries with it certain behavioural characteristics; for example, different bodies store different amounts of food, and each head varies as to the rate at which it can eat, and how effective it is when used to defend itself or attack another creature. Once users have built their cyberbeast, they name it and tag it with their email address. Clicking on the 'submit' button saves the data description of that creature, and a CGI programme allocates it a unique identification number that is immediately displayed in the user's web browser window. It is necessary to give each creature an ID number as many creatures are either unnamed or similarly named ('Herbie' and 'Binkie' are especially popular).

Once placed in *TechnosSphere*, the creatures become part of the artificial life programme that controls their behaviour and traces their position in the 3D virtual landscape. The artificial life programme, *Creature Comforts*, written by Julian Saunderson, defines each beast's behaviour and monitors its interactions with other creatures. For example, a creature can splice digital DNA with another if they are similar, but only if both creatures are more than 50 per cent full of food; otherwise cybersex is out of the question and the search for food takes priority. There is one sex in *TechnoSphere*, and the creature that initiates reproduction takes care of the offspring. At key moments in its existence, an artificial life form will email its maker to inform him or her of important changes in its digital evolution. This is a bit like the Christmas cards that people receive on behalf of animals they have sponsored in sanctuaries, but in the case of the artificial life forms the postcard is prompted by a significant development such as death or reproduction. These events activate the email engine, which sends the email to the address that tags the beast. Where relevant these email messages also include the email address of whoever designed the other creature involved in the interaction, so it is possible for the Australian designer of Cyber Serpent (creature ID 2306) to email the German who designed Herbie (ID 19087), the beast with whom Cyber Serpent reproduced.

Users can also see 2D postcard images of their artificial life form. When a user requests a postcard image of a life form, *Creature Comforts* uses the ID number to trace its position in the 3D terrain, and this information is passed to the renderer, which in turn renders the appropriate scene. Animations of creatures interacting are produced in a similar manner: We tag a creature with a virtual camera and follow its movements, rendering the landscape and all the creatures by referring to data from *Creature Comforts* at each frame.

When we first opened the project we created a stock of 30,000 randomly designed creatures that can be identified by their negative ID numbers. These all coexist in a 16 kilometre-square area of fractal terrain. Since then users have added a further 30,000 randomly designed creatures that can be identified by their negative ID numbers. In early 1996, the population peaked at 90,000 as many of the surviving stock creatures, plus those designed by users in the first few weeks, reached sexual maturity and reproduced. Population then declined as creatures died from old age or starvation or as a result of predatory action by carnivores. The dying process also triggers email messages to users and it has an impact on the 3D environment. For example, when a creature dies it causes the grass to grow longer on the polygons of land where it falls. Grazing herbivores have to move on when they have depleted the grass in a particular location, and we have noticed interesting herding behaviour evolving from the simple rules that define the creatures' behaviour: herbivores tend to move in swathes back and forth across the terrain, forced onwards by the depletion of food. [...]

Artificial Life in *TechnoSphere*

Central to artificial life programmes is the assertion that life depends on a certain level of complexity. This might seem obvious to us now, as we live in an age where chaos theory has been popularized, but it was a radical proposition when first expounded in the 1950s. This dependence on complexity was a key step away from the reductionist approach to discovering the principles of evolution of biological organisms that was common in the physical sciences, and an interest in these areas underpins the *TechnoSphere* project and can be seen in Gordon Selley's applied research into fractal mathematics and the problems of using computers to model complex natural structures such as trees and fog.

A movement away from reductionist theories and towards ideas of synthesis again fits in with larger cultural shifts in the West that have seen us discard meta-narratives as viable interpretations of the world and move towards a postmodernist synthesis or eclecticism. Importantly, these complex systems can emerge from a relatively simple set of rules. The design of the artificial life engine in *TechnoSphere* was very difficult as we all struggled to decide the activities and parameters to focus on in our attempt to reduce the behaviour of the creatures to a simple set of rules. Our intention was not to create a groundbreaking artificial life environment, but rather to produce a project that made certain aspects of artificial life accessible to a wide audience. We hoped that complex and unpredictable behaviour would emerge from these rules, but as *TechnoSphere* was our first foray into artificial life we were concerned that we might end up with a digital ecology that either drifted into stasis or was prone to wild fluctuations in population. Stasis is partly avoided by the influx of new creatures designed by users visiting the website. The number of these creatures varies from week to week; sometimes only a few hundred are made each week, while at other times users add nearly a thousand a day. We have recently added an extra element to the project in the form of a digital whirlwind that travels through the terrain, destroying every creature in its path. The whirlwind's route is unpredictable as it is defined by a random fractal walk.

After some initial calibrating, the simple rules that define the behaviour of artificial life forms in *TechnoSphere* have resulted in some surprising moments, such as what we call 'vending machine valley'. At one point, carnivores formed a huge semicircular group at the mouth of a sealed valley flanked on three devices to attract the viewer's gaze. Trapped in the fractal corral, herds of herbivores grazed until the lack of grass drove them inevitably out of the valley and into the virtual jaws of the waiting carnivores (which had not ventured into the corral but merely waited outside).

The self-organizing artificial life systems that we have used in *TechnoSphere* depend on a 'bottom-up' approach, with behaviour emerging as artificial creatures interact, rather than on us imposing 'top-down' control on behaviour. This idea of bottom-up evolution has been applied to the whole project and carried through to the design process. By taking the calculated risk of developing the project online, starting with a simple version on the Internet, we can engage in bottom-up development in conjunction with the thousands of users who access the website and send us email about the project.

TechnoSphere is the result of each team member sharing an interest in the potential of the Internet for developing graphical, networked, interactive spaces, which can be seen as part of a larger cultural development. Interconnectivity has become one of the paradigms of the late twentieth century, as our interpretation of the world has been dramatically affected by new scientific discoveries, such as chaos theory, which has provided us with a model that recognizes the importance and power of interaction. There seems to be a paradox at the heart of *TechnoSphere* stemming both from its metaphors of artificial landscape and from our metaphoric use of terms like 'creature' to describe the artificial life forms and their underlying code. Also, there is a larger cultural unease with computer simulations of nature that is subtle but persistent. Rather than a paradox, it seems to us that *TechnoSphere* embodies a kind of gestalt effect: a merging of the metaphoric or allegorical and the mimetic. As you look at it, the 3D terrain seems recognizable, and there is a pleasure in that recognition, but then suddenly the mimesis is interrupted by a flat facet or an improbable life form and we are reminded of the digital source of the image.

Jane Prophet, extracts from 'Sublime Ecologies and Artistic Endeavours: Artificial Life and Interactivity in the Online Project *TechnoSphere*', *Leonardo*, vol. 29, no. 5 (1996) 339–40; 343–4.

Victoria Vesna
Mind and Body Shifting: From Networks to Nanosystems//2002

[…] My investigation into social networks online began with a piece that I started in 1996 and had pretty much completed by 1999, although the work is still online and actively growing. [www.bodiesinc.ucla.edu]

Its title, *Bodies© INCorporated*, plays on the juxtaposition of 'bodies' with the copyright symbol and the way that 'INCorporated' draws on the Latin root *corpus* while also alluding to a corporation: bodies are incorporated into the Internet and their information is copyrighted. The project's logo is a bronze head with a copyright sign on its third eye, signifying the inherent contradiction between efforts to control information flow and New Age ideals of interconnectedness.[1]

On entering the main site, participants are invited to create their own bodies and become 'members'. They have a choice of twelve textures with attached meanings, which are a combination of alchemical properties and marketing strategies. The body parts are female, male and infantile, left and right leg and arms, torso and head. The bodies themselves are wire-like frames based on 3-dimensional scans used for medical imaging. There are also twelve sounds to be attached to the body that can be viewed as an image. Although this work was completed in 1999 new bodies are generated almost every day. With this project came my fascination with the idea of a work that continues to change and grow without the artist's supervision. I now plan projects that have an open-ended architecture and no definitive end.

During the active phase that lasted from 1996–99, much of the project was developed in response to the audience demands. The best example of this is *Necropolis*, which was constructed in response to one member who threatened to sue unless his virtual body was deleted. It draws on the many different methods of death documented in crime archives on the Internet; participants have to choose a method, write an obituary and construct a grave.

The last, intriguing demand was for establishing a 'community'. I started researching online communities and wondered about the meaning of this. I realized that because of my own busy schedule, it was really difficult even for me to find time to spend in these online spaces. All my colleagues and friends were equally busy and not able to participate, no matter how fascinated by the concept. This led me to think about time, or lack of, due to technology that was designed to save us time. I was also interested in exploring other ways to visualize the online body and started exploring ideas of networks beyond the Internet. At this time I became fascinated with the tensegrity structures that were used by Kenneth Snelson in sculpture, Buckminster Fuller in architecture and explored in relation to the human body by Donald Ingber.[2]

I wondered if these same systems could be used to design information spaces, and in my search on the Web discovered a programmer, Gerald de Jong, who was doing exactly that. When invited to do a site-specific piece for an old mine in Germany, I decided to explore some of these ideas together with Gerald. We started working remotely and met only when the show was opening, which was an entirely new way of collaborating for me. The piece that resulted was 'Datamining Bodies'. This work was site-specific and the first to explore ways to represent the human body online as an energetic geometry and living database persona.[3]

nOtime (Building a Community of People with No Time)

Still thinking of networks, online communities and our relationship to time and technology, I continued to develop a concept that would actively engage the audience in a different time mode, depending on whether they occupied the physical or information spaces. Although I firmly believe that there is no separation between the virtual and the physical, I also recognize that these spaces create a very different experience of time, and ultimately believe that there is no time. There is only constant change. The constructed time we live in is not working very well for us at this point, as is seen by the number of stressed-out individuals that don't exclude you and me. We have moved too far away from any biological/ analogue measurements of change, to nanoseconds, and are overwhelmed with information, processed much faster than we were ever built to absorb.

As our bodies are reduced to large data-sets, we are entering into an entirely different age and need to start rebelling against industrial/product(ive) time. Whether digital technologies can help us solve some of those mysteries is an open question. The project that explored these issues was called *n0time (Building a Community of People with No Time)*. The physical installation was a collaboration with Gerald once again, along with David Beaudry and sculptor Tim Quinn. Once again, I found that the physical piece worked but I was not quite satisfied with the online aspect. Eventually it was reduced to a screensaver that would evolve while people were away from their desk. The information body would evolve in seconds, minutes, hours, months or years and in 1,000 increments would explode from too much information. This is then sent to the entire *n0time* community. Having no time is transformed to n(space) zero time. [...]

Exploring issues of time in relation to human networks and our bodies as elaborate networks has naturally shifted my attention to the molecular level. Working with tensegrity made me think more in terms of emerging patterns in nature – no matter how alienated we may become, we produce patterns that mirror the natural world. My work focuses on making these far-reaching connections between the social structures we unconsciously build and the ones that are inherently the building blocks of nature. Making the invisible traces of our connectivity and mirroring of nature visible is my long-term goal. [...]

1   http://bodiesinc.u~la.edu

2   Donald Ingber, 'Architecture of Life', *Scientific American* (January 1998).

3   http://notime.arts.ucla.edulmining

Victoria Vesna, extracts from 'Mind and Body Shifting: From Networks to Nanosystems', paper for *Artmedia VIII: 'L'Ésthétique de la Communication'* (Paris, 30 November 2002).

Jane Bennett
Vibrant Matter: A Political Ecology of Things//2010

Vibrant Matter has a philosophical project and, related to it, a political one. The philosophical project is to think slowly an idea that runs fast through modern heads: the idea of matter as passive stuff, as raw, brute or inert. This habit of parsing the world into dull matter (it, things) and vibrant life (us, beings) is a 'partition of the sensible', to use Jacques Rancière's phrase.[1] The quarantines of matter and life encourage us to ignore the vitality *of* matter and the lively powers *of* material formations, such as the way omega-3 fatty acids can alter human moods or the way our trash is not 'away' in landfills but generating lively streams of chemicals and volatile winds of methane as we speak.[2] I will turn the figures of 'life' and 'matter' around and around, worrying them until they start to seem strange, in something like the way a common word when repeated can become a foreign, nonsense sound. In the space created by this estrangement, *a vital materiality* can start to take shape.

Or, rather, it can take shape again, for a version of this idea already found expression in childhood experiences of a world populated by animate things rather than passive objects. I will try to reinvoke this sense, to awaken what Henri Bergson described as 'ardent belief in the spontaneity of nature'.[3] The idea of vibrant matter also has a long (and if not latent, at least not dominant) philosophical history in the West. I will reinvoke this history too, drawing in particular on the concepts and claims of Baruch Spinoza, Friedrich Nietzsche, Henry David Thoreau, Charles Darwin, Theodor Adorno, Gilles Deleuze and the early twentieth-century vitalisms of Bergson and Hans Driesch. […]

A guiding question: How would political responses to public problems change were we to take seriously the vitality of (nonhuman) bodies? By 'vitality' I mean the capacity of things – edibles, commodities, storms, metals – not only to impede or block the will and designs of humans but also to act as quasi agents or forces with trajectories, propensities or tendencies of their own. My aspiration is to articulate a vibrant materiality that runs alongside and inside humans to see how analyses of political events might change if we gave the force of things more due. How, for example, would patterns of consumption change if we faced not litter, rubbish, trash or 'the recycling', but an accumulating pile of lively and potentially dangerous matter? What difference would it make to public health if eating was understood as an encounter between various and variegated bodies, some of them mine, most of them not, and none of which always gets the upper hand? What issues would surround stem cell research in the absence of the assumption that the only source of vitality in matter is a soul or spirit? What difference would it make to the course of energy policy were electricity to be figured not simply as a resource, commodity or instrumentality but also and more radically as an 'actant'?

The term is Bruno Latour's: an actant is a source of action that can be either human or nonhuman; it is that which has efficacy, can *do* things, has sufficient coherence to make a difference, produce effects, alter the course of events. It is 'any entity that modifies another entity in a trial', something whose 'competence is deduced from [its] performance' rather than posited in advance of the action.[4] Some actants are better described as protoactants, for these performances or energies are too small or too fast to be 'things'.[5] I admire Latour's attempt to develop a vocabulary that addresses multiple modes and degrees of effectivity, to begin to describe a more *distributive* agency. Latour strategically elides what is commonly taken as distinctive or even unique about humans and so will I. At least for a while and up to a point. I lavish attention on specific 'things', noting the distinctive capacities or efficacious powers of particular material configurations. To attempt, as I do, to present human and nonhuman actants on a less vertical plane than is common is to bracket the question of the human and to elide the rich and diverse literature on subjectivity and its genesis, its conditions of possibility and its boundaries. The philosophical project of naming where subjectivity begins and ends is too often bound up with fantasies of a human uniqueness in the eyes of God, of escape from materiality, or of mastery of nature; and even where it is not, it remains an aporetic or quixotic endeavour. [...]

Why advocate the vitality of matter? Because my hunch is that the image of dead or thoroughly instrumentalized matter feeds human hubris and our earth-destroying fantasies of conquest and consumption. It does so by preventing us from detecting (seeing, hearing, smelling, tasting, feeling) a fuller range of the nonhuman powers circulating around and within human bodies. These material powers which can aid or destroy, enrich or disable, ennoble or degrade us, in any case call for our attentiveness, or even 'respect' (provided that the term be stretched beyond its Kantian sense). The figure of an intrinsically intimate matter may be one of the impediments to the emergence of more ecological and more materially sustainable modes of production and consumption. My claims here are motivated by a self-interested or conative concern for *human* survival and happiness: I want to promote greener forms of human culture and more attentive encounters between people-materialities and thing-materialities. [...]

In the 'Treatise on Nomadology', Deleuze and Félix Guattari experiment with the idea of a 'material vitalism', according to which vitality is immanent in matter-energy.[6] That project has helped inspire mine. Like Deleuze and Guattari, I draw selectively from Epicurean, Spinozist, Nietzschean and vitalist traditions, as well as from an assortment of contemporary writers in science and literature. I need all the help I can get, for this project calls for the pursuit of several tasks simultaneously: (1) to paint a positive ontology of vibrant matter, which stretches received concepts of agency, action and freedom sometimes to the breaking point; (2) to dissipate the onto-theological binaries of life/matter, human/animal, will/determination and organic/inorganic using arguments and other rhetorical means to induce in human bodies an aesthetic-affective openness to material vitality; and (3) to sketch a style of political analysis that can better account for the contributions of nonhuman actants.

I try to bear witness to the vital materialities that flow through and around us. Though the movements and effectivity of stem cells, electricity, food, trash and metals are crucial to political life (and human life per se), almost as soon as they appear in public (often at first by disrupting human projects or expectations), these activities and powers are represented as human mood, action, meaning, agenda or ideology. This quick substitution sustains the fantasy that 'we' really are in charge of all those 'its' – its that, according to the tradition of (non-mechanistic, non-teleological) materialism I draw on, reveal themselves to be potentially forceful agents.

Spinoza stands as a touchstone, even though he himself was not quite a materialist. I invoke his idea of conative bodies that strive to enhance their power of activity by forming alliances with other bodies and I share his faith that everything is made of the same substance. Spinoza rejected the idea that man 'disturbs rather than follows Nature's order' and promises instead to 'consider human actions and appetites just as if it were an investigation – into lines, planes or bodies'.[7] Lucretius, too, expressed a kind of monism in his *De Rerum Natura*: everything, he says, is made of the same quirky stuff, the same building blocks, if you will. Lucretius calls them *primordia*; today we might call them atoms, quarks, particle streams or matter-energy. This same-stuff claim, this insinuation that deep down, everything is connected and irreducible to a simple substrate, resonates with an *ecological sensibility*, and that too is important to me. But in contrast to some versions of deep ecology, my monism posits neither a smooth harmony of parts nor a diversity unified by a common spirit. The formula here, writes Deleuze, is 'ontologically one, formally diverse'.[8] This is, as Michel Serres says in *The Birth of Physics*, a turbulent, immanent field in which various and variable materialities collide, congeal, morph, evolve and disintegrate.[9] Though I find Epicureanism to be too simple in its imagery of individual atoms falling and swerving in the void, I share its conviction that there remains a natural *tendency* to the way things are – and that human decency and decent politics are fostered if we tune in to the strange logic of turbulence.

1   Jacques Rancière, 'Ten Theses on Politics', trans. Rachel Bowlby and Davide Panagia, *Theory &* *Event*, vol. 5, no. 3 (2001). Thesis 7: 'The Partition of the sensible is the cutting-up of the world … a partition between what is visible and what is not, of what can be heard from the inaudible.'

2   Rancière claims that 'politics in general is about the configuration of the sensible', meaning that politics consists in the contestation over just what *is* 'the given'. It is 'about the visibilities of the places and abilities of the body in those places'. (Rancière. 'Comment and Responses', *Theory &* *Event*, vol. 6, no. 3 [2003]). I agree that politics is the arranging and rearranging of the landscape that humans can sense or perceive, but I, unlike Rancière, am also interested in the 'abilities' of non-human bodies – of artefacts, metals, berries, electricity, stem cells, worms …

3   Henri Bergson, *Creative Evolution* (1907) (London: Macmillan, 1911) 45.

4   Bruno Latour, *Politics of Nature* (1999) (Cambridge, Massachusetts: Harvard University Press, 2004) 237.

5   On this point Latour says that the phrase *name of action* is more appropriate than *actant*, for 'only later does one deduce from these performances a competence'. (Latour, *Pandora's Hope* [Harvard, 1999] 303; 308).

6   Deleuze and Guattari, *A Thousand Plateaux* (1980) (Minneapolis: University of Minnesota, 2003) 351–423.

7   Spinoza, preface to *Ethics* (1677) (Princeton: Princeton University Press, 1985) 102–3.

8   Deleuze, *Expressionism in Philosophy: Spinoza* (1968) (New York: Zone Books, 1990) 67.

9   Serres, *Birth of Physics* (1977) (Manchester: Clinamen Press, 2000).

Jane Bennett, extract from preface, *Vibrant Matter: A Political Ecology of Things* (Durham, North Carolina: Duke University Press, 2010) vii–xi.

Vilém Flusser
Curie's Children//1988

Why is it that dogs aren't yet blue with red spots, and that horses don't yet radiate phosphorescent colours over the nocturnal shadows of the land? Why hasn't the breeding of animals, still principally an economic concern, moved into the field of aesthetics? It's as if nothing in the relationship between humanity and the biological environment had changed since the life-style revolutions of the Neolithic age. Yet at the same time that the farms of North America and Western Europe are today producing more food than we can consume, we also, not coincidentally, have learnt techniques that ultimately make conceivable the creation of plant and animal species according to our own programmes. Not only do we have mountains of butter and ham, rivers of milk and wine, but we can now make artificial living beings, living artworks. If we chose, these developments could be brought together and farming could be transferred from peasants, a class almost defunct anyway, to artists, who breed like rabbits and don't get enough to eat.

If you could make a film of the European landscape that covered the millennia of history, compressed into a convenient half-hour for the comfort of the public, it would show the following story: first, a cold steppe, populated by large ruminant animals migrating northwards in spring and southwards in autumn and followed by the beasts of prey, including humans, that hunted them. Then, an ever denser forest, inhabited by no-longer-nomadic peoples living and working in clearings kept open by the use of stone tools and fire. Then, a basically familiar scene of fields of edible grains, and pastures of edible animals, with occasional forests surviving as sources of newsprint. And if you could project your movie camera into the immediate future, you would see a continent-sized Disneyland full of people working very short weeks because of automation, and trying desperately to amuse themselves so as not to die of boredom. The question is: Who will be the Disney of the future? He or she might, I suggest, be a molecular biologist.

All the organisms of the Earth are coloured. We all secrete dyes in our skins and these dyes have important functions, supporting not only the individual (protective colouration) but also the species (sexual signals). We are now beginning to understand the chemical and physiological processes of these secretions and to be able to formulate the laws that govern them. Molecular biologists may soon be handling skin colour more or less as painters handle oils and acrylics. Then the internal dyes of animal and vegetable biology may acquire a crucial new use: they may help the human species to survive its boredom by filling the future-as-Disneyland with multicoloured fauna and flora.

Please don't think this fanciful conceit. Instead, take scuba gear and a torch, and jump into a tropical ocean. Down deep you'll see fields and forests of plant-like creatures whose red, blue and yellow tentacles sway with the currents, gigantic rainbow-coloured snails trailing through the scenery and swarms of silvery, gold and violet fish overflying it. This is what our familiar *terra firma* may someday look like. It has almost become feasible to transfer the genetic information that programmes deep-sea colouring into the inhabitants of the earth's surface. You might say that this painting of the future is a kind of land art, but of a much more complex type than the one we know. Instead of wrapping rocks in fabric or shoving them around with bulldozers, we may be able to compute and compose a complex living game.

There is a kind of potato that is pollinated by a single species of butterfly, which itself feeds exclusively on that potato. The butterfly may be said to be the potato's sexual apparatus, and the potato the butterfly's digestive system, the two forming a single organism. In this particular symbiosis, the butterfly's wing is exactly the same blue as the potato flower. The wing colour results from the reflection of sunlight by minuscule mirrors, that of the flower from the transformation of chlorophyll, but nevertheless they match, the consequence of a complex evolutionary chain of feedbacks and adjustments. The Disney of the future should be able to programme such effects at will. He or she may perhaps compose an enormous colour symphony, evolving spontaneously through endless variations (mutations), in which the colour of every living organism will complement the colours of every other organism and be mirrored by them. A gigantic living work of art, of a wealth and beauty as yet unimaginable, is definitely possible.

Today's environmentalists and ecologists, who stubbornly continue to call themselves 'green', will object that a landscape transformed into a Disneyland, a work of art, will no longer be 'natural'. But consider: when they planted fields, they accelerated the artifice. The future's Disneyland will simply continue it. And anyway, why can't art inform nature? When we ask why dogs can't be blue with red spots, we're really asking about art's role in the immediate future, which is menaced not only by explosions both nuclear and demographic, but equally by the explosions of boredom.

Vilém Flusser, 'Curie's Children', *Artforum* (October 1988) 9 [one of five texts under this title written for consecutive issues of *Artforum*].

George Gessert
A Brief History of Art Involving DNA//1996

Plants and Animals as Components of Art

Some pets and sporting animals are aesthetic creations, and performing animals used in theatre play roles in art. However, the first animals analogous to ornamental plants, that is, creatures kept solely for their aesthetic qualities, were probably birds like peacocks, or menagerie animals. Such creatures existed in ancient Eurasia and in Mexico. Fanciers' animals bred only for aesthetic effects did not arise until after the Renaissance.

The idea that landscape gardens are fine art appeared in the eighteenth century, most famously in Kant's *Critique of Judgement*. Two obvious implications of this idea are that plants can be components of art, and that works of art can consist largely or entirely of living things. However, Kant stopped short of recognizing *individual* plants as fine art. To do so would have been radical, even heretical. Kant maintained that nature was one thing and art quite another. This view was deeply rooted in Western culture. We find it, for example, in the book of *Genesis*, in which God creates humans separately from 'the beasts', and in his own image, while animals and plants exist only in their own, earthbound images. The message is clear: an unbridgeable chasm separates us from the rest of life.

Humankind's absolutely privileged place in the universe became a key Christian tenet, reinforced by borrowings from Greek philosophy. Until the late nineteenth century most aesthetic theory echoed church doctrine by arguing that art arose from the human mind or spirit and was therefore outside of nature.

Land Art and Ecological Art

Plants and animals appeared in many artworks in the late 1960s. Many earthworks were so gigantic that they provided habitats for small organisms, although no Land artist explored the implications. A few artists deliberately used living things as components of their work. For example, Alan Sonfist's *Time Landscape*, conceived in 1969 and first planted in 1978, recreates natural landscapes from New York City's past. On several sites he reintroduced plants that had grown in the area prior to European settlement. As long as Sonfist's reconstructions survive, the plants and animals that comprise them will undergo selective pressures from the city and from larger environmental forces such as weather, as well as from interaction among organisms that make up the work itself. Still, Sonfist did not emphasize the genetic aspects of this work.

Helen and Newton Harrison's life chain proposals – most not realized except on paper – encompass biological systems that would be preserved, or in some cases created through art. *Trümmerflora: On the Topography of Terrors* (1988) is typical of their approach. This work was to consist of rubble from two large piles that already existed on a site in Berlin near the Gropius-Bau, at the bureaucratic centre for the death camps of the Third Reich. Along with the rubble were *trümmerflora*, or plants that spring up in disturbed places. The rubble was to be dispersed over sites used by the Gestapo to plan the concentration camps. *Trümmerflora* would from then on inhabit those sites, and compose a living memorial to those who had suffered in the camps. The Harrisons designed this work to maintain an already existing biological process with genetic elements that would be destroyed unless sanctioned by art.

Some of the Harrisons' proposals span watersheds and bio-regions. *Sacramento Meditations* (1976–77) evaluated and proposed changes for the watersheds of California's two largest rivers, the Sacramento and the San Joachim. *Meditation on the Condition of the Great Lakes of North America* (1978) proposed a new nation to coincide with the watershed of the Great Lakes. *Tibet is the High Ground* (1990 to the present) presents a plan for the reforestation of Tibet. All of these projects favour genetic diversity.

The Harrisons told me that they consider genetics central to their work. However, the genetic component is implicit, not explicit, even in *The Lagoon Cycle* (begun in 1972), which involved breeding crabs. *The Lagoon Cycle* emerged from a search for edible organisms that could survive exhibition in art galleries. From a biological perspective, galleries are extremely inhospitable environments where few non-human organisms can survive for long. The search led the Harrisons to Sri Lanka, where they studied the crab *Scylla serrata*, an important food source in some parts of Southern Asia. After returning to the United States, the Harrisons raised these crabs in a studio and discovered how to breed them, something that had never been done before in captivity.

1980 to the Present

[Since 1980] many artists have produced projects to purify water, restore degraded sites, build community gardens, establish urban forests and create habitats for wildlife. Works such as *7,000 Oaks* (1982) by Joseph Beuys, *Leonhardt Lagoon* (1981–86) by Patricia Johanson, Dominique Mazeaud's *The Great Cleansing of the Rio Grande River* (1987 to the present) and *Revival Field* (1990 to the present) by Mel Chin, have genetic dimensions somewhat similar to those of Sonfist's projects or the Harrisons'. Genetics is implicit in such work but is not the focus.

Some contemporary artists incorporate imagery of DNA or other genetic elements into their work. Approaches vary. Suzanne Anker, for example, explores resemblances between chromosomes and hieroglyphics. Kevin Clarke paints what he calls portraits in which base sequences serve as key aspects of individual identity. Kevin Moore uses images of DNA as symbols of fate. In the *G-Nome Project* (1992) Andrew Leicester borrowed imagery from an impressively wide range of sources to explore the historical, ethical and social implications of genetic engineering. And many artists use genetic imagery for social criticism.

Alexis Rockman paints plants and animals in a style that draws on diverse sources including Dutch flower painting, nineteenth-century landscape painting, science fiction movies and natural history dioramas. Nature in Rockman's work is a Hobbesian spectacle in which ants devour butterflies, flowers drip sinister nectars and human creations proliferate amid faeces, traps and evolutionary cul-de-sacs. An atmosphere of luxurious decay pervades not only the subject matter, but colour and use of materials. Rockman favours sickly greens, lurid reds and golds and deep shadows. His glazes are so heavy that some canvases glisten like hams. Rockman's most blackly humorous works synthesize genetic engineering and pornography. In *The Trough* (1992) a pig mounts a duck; *Barnyard Scene* (1991) shows a raccoon sodomizing a rooster; and in *Jungle Fever* (1991) a preying mantis mates with a chipmunk.

In the 'Biosphere' paintings horror overwhelms humour. *Biosphere: Laboratory* shows a laboratory orbiting Saturn. The laboratory contains two-headed cows, a goat-cow-pig hybrid and a dog with a puppy grafted onto its neck. The scene recalls H.G. Wells' *The Island of Dr Moreau*. Both Wells and Rockman explore secret worlds, where under the rule of science, pathologies play themselves out. The most striking difference between Rockman's vision and Wells' is that while Dr Moreau had to leave civilization in order to pursue his experiments, Rockman's space station does not depart far from official practice. True, the station is modelled after the rebel station in the movie *Silent Running* (1972), but *Biosphere: Laboratory* is not about rebellion. Space stations express dominant forces of contemporary civilization and Rockman takes imagery directly from government-sponsored research. The grafted dogs, for instance are based on actual experiments carried out in Moscow. Rockman's rather nineteenth-century style and the similarity of his warnings to those that Wells issued more than a hundred years ago, suggest that fantasies about biology may have changed much less in the last century than we like to think.

Vilém Flusser, writing in *Artforum* in 1988, predicted that biotechnics would become an instrument of artists who someday might create wheat with the power of sight, photosynthetic horses and 'an enormous colour symphony ... in which the colour of every living organism will complement the colours of every other organism'. Flusser also wrote that the new artists would lay the 'foundations of mental processes that have never before existed'.[1]

The previous year Peter Gerwin Hoffmann had exhibited *Mikroben bei Kandinsky* in Graz. This work consisted of cultures of bacteria scraped from the surface of a Kandinsky painting. In the catalogue to the exhibition, Hoffmann wrote that 'gene technology has put ... an end [to] the polarity nature-art. The living organisms ... that surround us ... can only be understood and interpreted as works of art.'[2]

By the mid 1980s several artists began working with living things on the genetic level. In *Microvenus* (1984–5) Joe Davis configured a strand of DNA like the Germanic rune for life, inserted into the *E. Coli* bacterium. *Microvenus* is invisible under ordinary circumstances, so in the context of art it functions as a conceptual work.

Some contemporary artists breed larger organisms, or use genetically altered micro-organisms to create patterns visible to the unaided eye. David Kremers' *Somite* series, begun in 1992, consists of genetically-altered bacteria on agar-covered acrylic plates. There the bacteria interacted with dyes to produce complex stains. Kremers then sealed out moisture to arrest growth, and the works became stable but remained alive. My own work has been with irises, *streptocarpi* and other plants, which I hybridize and exhibit, along with documentation of the selection process. Eduardo Kac's development of genetically engineered animals such as the fluorescent rabbit Alba brings up an important ethical issue: what are our responsibilities to the creatures that we help create? Some artists who work with plants or micro-organisms ask this question, but it is especially relevant in Kac's projects and for any artist who would work with sentient creatures.

There are major obstacles to presenting plants and animals as art, but today these obstacles are less philosophical than ethical and architectural. Any exhibition that engages genetics and selection may awaken anxieties about eugenics, and those anxieties need to be addressed. Architectural obstacles can be quite difficult to overcome. Full exploration of genetic art will require new kinds of museums, spaces that welcome rather than exclude diverse forms of life and provide them with suitable habitats. We can imagine traditional gallery spaces combined with gardens, zoos and wilderness areas. Still, enough artists have exhibited living things in existing spaces to have made the presence of non-human organisms in galleries a fairly common occurrence today. As for genetic engineering, no one needs to prove that it can be a tool for artists. What remains to be proven is whether this tool can produce art that is more than conceptually interesting.

The most important question is: what kind of consciousness does art involving DNA serve? To what extent does it aestheticize the biological revolution, speed commodification of life and encourage the transformation of living things into consumer culture trivia? What kinds of genetic art can help remind people that plants and animals were not made for our sake, and that they create their own kinds of value? In the community of life, can we play some role other than self idolater?

I hope that acceptance of ornamental plants, fanciers' animals and various other organisms as art will encourage greater awareness in selection, which in turn will produce more wonderful organisms and perhaps even exalted ones. But above all I hope that art involving DNA will bring us closer to other living beings, who after all are our kin. Only as respectful kin are we likely to develop a true art of evolution.

1   Vilém Flusser, 'Curie's Children', see *Artforum*, vol. XXVI, no. 7 (March 1988) 15; vol. XXVI, no. 10 (Summer 1988) 18; and vol. XXVI, no. 2 (October 1988) 9.

2   Peter Gerwin Hoffmann, *Animal Art*, ed. Richard Kriesche (Graz: Steirischer Herst, 1987) n.p.

George Gessert, extracts from 'A Brief History of Art Involving DNA', *Art Papers* (September/October 1996); reprinted in *Ars Electronica 99: Life Science* (Vienna and New York: Springer Verlag, 1999) 228; 229; 232–5 [revised by the author for this publication, 2011].

Christa Sommerer & Laurent Mignonneau
Interactive Plant Growing (1993)//1999

[…] One of our first interactive computer installations to use a natural interface instead of then-common devices such as joysticks, mouse, trackers or other technical interfaces was *Interactive Plant Growing* (1993).[1] In this piece, living plants function as the interface between the human visitor and the artwork.[2]

This work involves interaction between five real plants and five or more human viewers who can, by moving their hands towards the plants, initiate and control three-dimensional real-time growth of artificial plants. By engaging in interaction with the real plants, the viewers become part of the installation: they influence how human-plant communication is translated into virtual growth on the computer display. The voltage difference between the viewer's body and the real plants is interpreted as electrical signals that determine how the virtual 3D plants will develop. By touching or merely approaching the real plants in the installations, the viewer engages in a dialogue with the virtual plants. He or she can stop, start, continue, deform and rotate the growth of the virtual plants, as well as develop new forms of plants in unexpected combinations. As the growing processes are programmed to be very flexible and are not predetermined, the result on the screen is always new and different, depending on the viewer-plant interaction.

Interactive Plant Growing was our first interactive installation that made visitors essential to the development of the piece: without their interaction, the piece could not exist, and images disappeared as soon as the visitors left. It was also unique in the sense that the subtle personality and interaction differences of the visitors could be interpreted in the form of complex scenery that solely depends on each viewer's identity. [...]

1   Sommerer and Mignonneau, 'Interactive Plant Growing', in Karl Gerbel and Peter Weibel, eds, *Electronica 93: Genetic Art Artificial Life* (Vienna: PVS Verleger, 1993) 408–14.

2   This work was called 'epoch making' by Toshiharu Itoh, for its use not only of an uncommon interface but the concept of interaction with a living being, the transformation and interpretation of this dialogue in virtual space. Itoh, 'Approach to Life – The World of Christa & Laurent', in *Christa Sommerer and Laurent Mignonneau* (Tokyo: ICC–NIT InterCommunication, 1994).

Christa Sommerer & Laurent Mignonneau, extract from 'Art as a Living System: Interactive Computer Artworks', *Leonardo*, vol. 32, no. 3 (June 1999) 165.

Eduardo Kac
Art That Looks You in the Eye//2007

[...] Society controls individuals cognitively (through ideology) and physically (through their bodies) in what Foucault aptly termed 'biopower' or 'biopolitics'.[1] We have now entered a social realm in which the minutest elements found inside the body (e.g. genes) can be externalized (through gene sequencing and amplification), and what is created outside (e.g. a synthetic chromosome) can be internalized (transgenics). In this new realm, certain features that belong to an individual can be transferred to another of the same kind (as in the cloning of the sheep Dolly) or to another of a completely different kind (as in the case of the rabbit Alba). Another characteristic of the reality produced by contemporary biotechnology is the reactivation of a certain genetic legacy long after its original owner has died, as dramatized by the cloning of endangered or extinct animals through frozen cells stored for over two decades in a literal gene bank. Likewise, human fertilization and pregnancy with frozen sperm of a deceased father has brought new legal and ethical issues to light.

Recent developments in human reproductive technology and successful cases of gene therapy have enabled human beings either to be born with new genetic configurations (e.g. children born via cytoplasmic transfer that have genetic material from 'three parents') or to have new genetic material added to their bodies without altering the germ line cells. Yet-to-be-developed human reproductive techniques will bring humans into the world through novel methods. These include oocyte fusion (fusion of two eggs from different females), haploidization (transformation of the nucleus of a male or female somatic cell into haploid (i.e., a cell that contains a single chromosome set) to make it function like a regular reproductive cell) and human cloning. However, once the novelty wears off and social curiosity recedes, provided they are safe, these techniques will become normal and routinely employed, like traditional *in vitro* fertilization (IVF). [...]

Clearly, it is impossible – and unacceptable – to circumscribe the questions raised by biotechnology within the realm of scientific research or industrial production, precisely because they take place in society at large. They affect the health of the individual but they also impact social relations. They dissolve species barriers and play a direct role in evolution. They create new life and unprecedented legal problems. They manufacture new products and redefine markets. Just as they influence notions of personal identity, they also change cultural patterns. On the one hand, critics, essayists, historians and philosophers suggest that our understanding of the phenomenon that once was aseptically divided between 'nature' and 'culture' is no longer sustainable on the pillars of this reductive dichotomy. On the other, artists openly defy premature obituaries of formal experimentation and innovation by literally working with living media – biomedia – and inventing ideas and forms impossible to produce until recently.

In art, to work with biomedia is to manipulate life, and any kind of life manipulation is part of the global network known as evolution. Mutation, selection and competition are evolutionary processes made more familiar through Darwin's writings and their popularization, but alone they cannot account for the complex ecology of species origination and development. Writing at the threshold of the twentieth century, the Russian political theorist Peter Kropotkin understood mutual aid to be 'a feature of the greatest importance for the maintenance of life, the preservation of each species, and its further evolution.'[2] Echoing this sentiment, scientist Lynn Margulis has demonstrated that symbiosis and cooperation are evolutionary factors as important (if not more important) than mutation and selection.[3] It is ideology that explains why individuals would privilege certain processes over others in their account of evolution. While Darwin was influenced by the emerging capitalism as developed by Scottish economists, Kropotkin embraced anarcho-communism. Darwin earned an income from his stock investments and, by his own account, in his formulation of the theory of natural selection, was directly influenced by Thomas Malthus (1766–1834), the conservative political economist who advocated regulating birth control of the lower class. As Richard Lewontin has so poignantly pointed out, what Darwin did 'was take early nineteenth-century political economy and expand it to include all of natural economy'.[4] Extending the analogy between evolution and market economy, one could say that today the most influential evolutionary forces operating at a global scale are Wall Street and FedEx. While the first decides what lives and reproduces, as well as what new life forms should be created, the second delivers them worldwide overnight. Undoubtedly, contemporary corporate business plans, institutional research agendas and individual initiatives of various kinds are collectively reshaping the Earth's evolutionary history. [...]

1   Michel Foucault, 'The Birth of Biopolitics', in *Michel Foucault: Ethics/The Essential Works, Volume 1*, ed. Paul Rabinow (London: Penguin, 1997) 73–9 [...].

2   Peter Kropotkin, *Mutual Aid: A Factor of Evolution* (1903) (Montreal: Black Rose, 1989) xxxvii.

3   Lynn Margulis, *Symbiotic Planet: A New Look at Evolution* (New York: Basic Books, 1998).

4   Richard C. Lewontin, *Biology as Ideology: The Doctrine of DNA* (New York: Harper, 1993) 10.

Eduardo Kac, extract from 'Art That Looks You in the Eye: Hybrids, Clones, Mutants, Synthetics and Transgenics', in idem., ed., *Signs of Life: Bio Art and Beyond* (Cambridge, Massachusetts: The MIT Press, 2007) 1–4.

Aziz + Cucher
In Conversation with Thyrza Nichols Goodeve//1999

Thyrza Nichols Goodeve In terms of the current work's relationship to the body, I think of Deleuze's notion of 'the body without organs' that was so influential in the late 1980s and early 1990s, because your *Chimeras* (1998) are really organs without the body, aren't they?

Anthony Aziz Yes, they are all the organs that didn't find a body! (*laughter*)

Goodeve I've never really understood what the body without organs meant but looking at these I certainly know what organs without a body are. Which is actually quite pertinent to the world we live in now, where there is a possibility of building whole organs from stem cells and so on. Yet these organ-like body-beings that appear in the *Chimera* series are what prompt the association with surrealism. I use Donna Haraway's term 'cyborg surrealism' to describe such work.

Aziz That could be a way to describe how we approached the sculptures in *Plasmorphica* (1997), the body of work that precedes this one. They were produced via the modernist method of assemblage – taking different materials and combining them to make a new form and then covering them with plastic skin.

Goodeve Which erases the sense of the different parts. By covering them with a plastic skin you erase the joints, so to speak, erase the premise that modernist assemblage is based on: the combining of disparate materials or genres in such a way as to shock. In *Plasmorphica* you were beginning to explore this notion of the creation of new beings. Kind of Frankenstein's monster without the sutures.

Aziz Yes, the sculptures in *Plasmorphica* are made up of electronic and consumer products that are combined in completely absurd ways. But something I'd like to stress is that it's important to us that these hybrid creatures come out of the material that is literally around us. The original sculptures were made from things that were all purchased at Radio Shack or on Canal Street or at Office Depot. In other words these are the forms that we live with, transformed through the assemblage process and now rephotographed and transformed yet further.

Sammy Cucher This is why the name chimera seems so apt to describe them because, as assemblage, they are a particular type of contemporary hybrid being based on the idea of these appliances as prosthesis.

Goodeve The monster is a broader term often used for the notion of the hybrid, but also associated with medical anomalies and often used as a figure in theory of the 1980s and early 1990s, a more 'gothic' period. I like shifting from the term 'monster' to 'chimera', as you have, in order to denote the texture of the transformations we are talking about. Such a difference in name signals a turn away from abjection. Also 'chimera' refers specifically to the fabula of myth. I think of the way Donna Haraway in her theory, or Matthew Barney in his art, use myth to go where we haven't yet been, but are certainly going in terms of biotechnology and new notions of what it is to be 'human'. And as I look at these images from the *Chimera* series they change into so many different things. I see torsos and amputated limbs as well as strange whole creatures, surrealistic objects, and so on.

Cucher Someone said to us recently that the *Chimeras* remind them of pieces in some strange game, such as chess, turned into fetishes. And we are happy with that interpretation because figures in a game of chess all carry a symbolic, almost animistic meaning. And we're interested in discovering a poetics, and some kind of depth, for this new biotechnological world we're entering into.

Aziz And I realize now that we are not dealing with hybridity only as a metaphor but also as an artistic process. In other words it's very important to see all of this work as a practice that conflates sculpture, photography and digital processes.

Goodeve What about the *Interiors* (1999–2001)?

Aziz The *Interiors* are our newest work. They represent a point of departure into work that is more lyrical and poetic, as well as maintaining the sense of objects that are deeply psychologically charged. Yet we see a connection with our *Dystopia* series (1994–95).

Goodeve In what sense?

Aziz In the sense that the viewer is presented with an enclosure of skin. But in this case, the viewer occupies metaphorically the space of the photograph. The *Dystopia* series were external portraits of subjects that had 'turned inwards'.

Goodeve I always felt they were subjects in the process of imploding. In other words, they were so muffled that the organ connecting them to the world had basically degenerated.

Cucher Perhaps. But these interiors take such a notion of 'turning inwards' into a phenomenological experience of the world. As a result, there occurs both a sense of disorientation and identification with the feeling one has of being inside one's body. Celeste Olalquiaga, in 'Megalopolis'[1] uses the term 'psychaesthenia' borrowed from Roger Caillois' 1935 essay, 'Mimicry and Legendary Psychaesthenia'. In her book she describes a subject incapable of demarcating the boundaries of its own body: a subject lost in the immensity that surrounds it.

Aziz What's interesting to us is the way Olalquiaga uses Caillois' discussion of psychaesthenia as a metaphor for contemporary or postmodern experience in general. Fredric Jameson describes a similar effect in his analysis of postmodern architecture, where the interplay between reflective and transparent surfaces creates a disorienting experience, such that the subject can no longer distinguish the exterior environment from the interior. In Caillois' example, taken from the insect world, the psychaesthenic organism abandons its own physical identity, taking on the markings of the environment outside of itself as a form of camouflage. Our interiors are perhaps a form of inverse psychaesthenia, where the external environment disappears utterly into the subject's consciousness.

Goodeve The subject's consciousness or the subject's perception?

Aziz Isn't consciousness developed through perception?

Goodeve What you are describing has roots in Romanticism, but of a kind that is induced by the nature of the new technology of digital and virtual realities rather than the psychological or emotional state of the viewer.

Aziz Perhaps that's what we are interested in – it's certainly what happens with our experience of cyberspace, where the whole informational universe is contained by the digital network and internalized by the user. Also one can look at a growing trend in architecture that uses computer technology to interface buildings with the body.

Cucher At MIT and other places people are talking about sentient rooms that are designed to become almost like a prosthetic human environment. Our interiors take the psychaesthenic utopia envisioned by so many techno and virtual reality gurus to its logical circuitous conclusion, fulfilling the dream of a regressive, womb-like space where there is no longer a separation between subject and environment; where all interaction is one steady stream of sensorial data.

Aziz But I really want to stress that with the *Interiors* we are in no way illustrating any of these cyborg theories. We are much more interested in looking for a visual poetics that generates a psychological response in the viewer. Of course, it may reflect our moment, but we would like to believe that these images have a staying power that goes beyond our time. We are indeed trying to approach that space of myth that you referred to earlier. [...]

1   Celeste Olalquiaga, *Megalopolis: Contemporary Cultural Sensibilities* (Minneapolis: University of Minnesota Press, 1992).

Aziz + Cucher and Thyrza Nichols Goodeve, extracts from 'These Are the Forms We Live With: A Conversation with Thyrza Nichols Goodeve' (1999) (www.azizcucher.net)

Oron Catts & Ionat Zurr
The Extended Body//2006

[…] A rough estimate would put the biomass of living cells and tissues, which are disassociated from the original bodies that once hosted them, in the millions of tons. In addition, there are tons of fragments of bodies (cells, tissues, organs) that are maintained in suspended animation in cryogenic conditions. All of this biomass requires an intensive technological intervention to prevent transformation to a non-living state. This type of being (or semi-being/semi-living) does not fall under current biological or even cultural classifications. The notion of the Extended Body can be seen as a way to define this category of life, maintaining the need for classification, while at the same time attempting to destabilize some of the rooted perceptions of classification of living beings. […]

In our *Victimless Utopia* series, we have explored the creation/construction of victimless meat in a project titled *Disembodied Cuisine* (2003). We ate, together with some brave volunteers, tiny semi-living frog steaks that were grown for more than two months in bioreactors, and used not only expensive resources but also animal-derived ingredients in the nutrient media. We referred to them ironically as extreme nouvelle cuisine, in the sense that they were luxury goods (and not necessarily tasteful ones). Still, the irony sometimes seems to be lost too easily, and now the discourse about a victimless society is being used by a university spin-off company that attempts to secure funding for tissue-engineered meat, as a possibility for eating meat without killing the animal.

We followed this project with *Victimless Leather – A Prototype of Stitchless Jacket Grown in a Technoscientific 'Body'* (2004), presenting a miniature leather-like jacket grown out of immortalized cell lines (a mix of human and mouse cells) that cultured and formed a living layer of tissue supported by a biodegradable polymer matrix, in a form of miniature stitchless coat. We were contacted by a company requesting more technical information for potential commercialization of such an idea.

The *DIY De-Victimizers* (2006) explores the hypocrisies involved in our relationship with other living and partially living systems, by taking the paradoxes and ironies involved in the production of a victimless utopia to somewhat extreme levels of absurdity. […]

The *DIY De-Victimizer Kit Mark One* (*DVK m1*) was set up to allay some of the guilt people feel when they consume parts of dead animals (as food, for aesthetic reasons or any other purpose) or cause the accidental death of a living being (by a car, a lawnmower, or any other piece of technology). The kit can maintain and in some cases even proliferate and extend the life of parts of the deceased bodies, at least until the guilt recedes. The *DIY DVK* utilizes off-the-shelf items to construct a basic tissue culture facility; a few specialized nutrients are needed – some of which contain animal-derived material – but the latter is so far removed from the end user that for most people remorsefulness is usually not an issue.

We made use of the *DIY DVK* for a performative installation in which we experimented with bringing back to life (literally) parts of meats. We attempted to reverse the 'destructive' effects of human technology by 're-lifing' its victims, and invited the audience to take an active role in the experiment by assisting us in caring for the fragments of life and making different ethical decisions with regard to these fragments' eventual fate.

Since this project had its debut in Barcelona, we felt compelled to reassess human relations to animals in the context of the Spanish bullfighting ritual. In drawing an analogy between participating in a bullfight ritual and eating McBurger, one may argue that in the bullfighting ritual, the killing of the animal for aesthetic/recreational reasons is more respectful, as it is exposed and even celebrated. However, the fate of the non-human animal is predestined. As a homage to the fighter bull, we relifted its tissue and grew it over a miniature replica of a tourist-shop figurine in the shape of a bull. We contrasted the tissue from the bull with that from a burger and tried to obtain viable cells for re-lifing. We also asked the audience to choose which one they would like to 'kill', that is, bring back to its cultural accepted position of dead meat.

As humans' ability to preserve ecological conditions for their survival is questionable, so is the Extended Body that is dependent on human care for its survival. The Extended Body is an extension of our own (or other living) body that takes the definition and perceptions of what a body is in different and alternative directions. The Extended Body is growing in size, presence, complexity and versatility, and can be a point of departure for addressing our limitations in the understanding of ourselves as an integral part of the ever transforming ecology.

Oron Catts & Ionat Zurr, extracts from 'Towards a New Class of Being: The Extended Body', *Intelligent Agent*, vol. 6, no. 2 (2006) (www.intelligentagent.com)

Up in the sky there will be this cloud, a habitable platform that floats in the air, changing form and merging with other platforms just as clouds////

///
///
///
///
///
///
///
///
///
///
///
///
///
///
///
///
///
///
///
//do.

Tomás Saraceno, in conversation with Stefano Boeri and Hans Ulrich Obrist, 2005

EVOLUTIONARY IDEAS

Henri Bergson
Creative Evolution//1907

[…] [Most philosophers] are at one in affirming the unity of nature, and in representing this unity under an abstract and geometrical form. Between the organized and the unorganized they do not see and they will not see the cleft. Some start from the inorganic and by compounding it with itself claim to form the living; others place life first, and proceed towards matter by a skilfully managed decrescendo; but for both there are only differences of degree in nature – degrees of complexity in the first hypothesis, of intensity in the second. Once this principle is admitted, intelligence becomes as vast as reality; for it is unquestionable that whatever is geometrical in things is entirely accessible to human intelligence, and if the continuity between geometry and the rest is perfect, all the rest must indeed be equally intelligible, equally intelligent. Such is the postulate of most systems. Anyone can easily be convinced of this by comparing doctrines that seem to have no common point, no common measure […].

At the root of these speculations, then, there are the two convictions correlative and complementary, that nature is one and that the function of intellect is to embrace it in its entirety. The faculty of knowing being supposed coextensive with the whole of experience, there can no longer be any question of engendering it. It is already given, and we merely have to use it, as we use our sight to take in the horizon. It is true that opinions differ as to the value of the result. For some, it is reality itself that the intellect embraces; for others, it is only a phantom. But, phantom or reality, what intelligence grasps is thought to be all that can be attained.

Hence the exaggerated confidence of philosophy in the powers of the individual mind. Whether it is dogmatic or critical, whether it admits the relativity of our knowledge or claims to be established within the absolute, a philosophy is generally the work of a philosopher, a single and unitary vision of the whole. It is to be taken or left.

More modest, and also alone capable of being completed and perfected, is the philosophy we advocate. Human intelligence, as we represent it, is not at all what Plato taught in the allegory of the cave. Its function is not to look at passing shadows nor yet to turn itself round and contemplate the glaring sun. It has something else to do. Harnessed, like yoked oxen, to a heavy task, we feel the play of our muscles and joints, the weight of the plough and the resistance of the soil. To act and to know that we are acting, to come into touch with reality and even to live it, but only in the measure in which it concerns the work that is being accomplished and the furrow that is being ploughed, such is the function of human intelligence. Yet a beneficent fluid bathes us, whence we draw the very force to labour and to live. From this ocean of life, in which we are immersed, we are continually drawing something, and we feel that our being, or at least the intellect that guides it, has been formed therein by a kind of local concentration. Philosophy can only be an effort to dissolve again into the Whole. Intelligence, reabsorbed into its principle, may thus live back again its own genesis. But the enterprise cannot be achieved in one stroke; it is necessarily collective and progressive. It consists in an interchange of impressions which, correcting and adding to each other, will end by expanding the humanity in us and making us even transcend it. [...]

Henri Bergson, extract from *L'Évolution créatrice* (Paris: Alcan, 1907); trans. Arthur Mitchell, *Creative Evolution* (New York: Henry Holt & Co., 1911) 200–201.

Vladimir Vernadsky
The Biosphere//1926

[...] Life presents an indivisible and indissoluble whole, in which all parts are interconnected, both among themselves and with the inert medium of the biosphere. In the future, this picture will no doubt rest upon a precise and quantitative basis. At the moment, we are only able to follow certain general outlines, but the foundations of this approach seem solid.

The principal fact is that the biosphere has existed throughout all geological periods, from the most ancient indications of the Archean. In its essential traits, the biosphere has always been constituted in the same way. One and the same chemical apparatus, created and kept active by living matter, has been functioning continuously in the biosphere throughout geologic times, driven by the uninterrupted current of radiant solar energy. This apparatus is composed of definite vital concentrations which occupy the same places in the terrestrial envelopes of the biosphere, while constantly being transformed. These vital films and concentrations form definite secondary subdivisions of the terrestrial envelopes. They maintain a generally concentric character, though never covering the whole planet in an uninterrupted layer. They are the planet's active chemical regions and contain the diverse, stable, dynamic equilibrium systems of the terrestrial chemical elements.

These are the regions where the radiant energy of the sun is transformed into free, terrestrial chemical energy. These regions depend, on the one hand, upon the energy they receive from the sun; and on the other, upon the properties of living matter, the accumulator and transformer of energy. The transformation occurs in different degrees for different elements, and the properties and the distribution of the elements themselves play an important role.

All the living concentrations are closely related to one another, and cannot exist independently. The link between the living films and concentrations, and their unchanging character throughout time, is an eternal characteristic of the mechanism of the Earth's crust.

As no geological period has existed independently of continental areas, so no period has existed when there was only land. [...] The land and the ocean have coexisted since the most remote geological times. This coexistence is basically linked with the geochemical history of the biosphere, and is a fundamental characteristic of its mechanism. From this point of view, discussions on the marine origin of continental life seem vain and fantastic. Subaerial life must be just as ancient as marine life, within the limits of geological times; its forms evolve and change, but the change always takes place on the Earth's surface and not in the ocean. If it were otherwise, a sudden revolutionary change would have had to occur in the mechanism of the biosphere, and the study of geochemical processes would have revealed this. But from Archean times until the present day, the mechanism of the planet and its biosphere has remained unchanged in its essential characteristics.

Recent discoveries in palaeobotany seem to be changing current opinions in the ways indicated above. The earliest plants, of basal Palaeozoic age, have an unexpected complexity which indicates a drawn-out history of subaerial evolution. Life remains unalterable in its essential traits throughout all geological times, and changes only in form. All the vital films (plankton, bottom [film of the hydrosphere] and soil) and all the vital concentrations (littoral, sargassic and fresh water) have always existed. Their mutual relationships, and the quantities of matter connected with them, have changed from time to time; but these modifications could not have been large, because the energy input from the sun has been constant, or nearly so, throughout geological time, and because the distribution of this energy in the vital films and concentrations can only have been determined by living matter – the fundamental part, and the only variable part, of the thermodynamic field of the biosphere. [...]

Vladimir Ivanovich Vernadsky, extract from *Biosfera* (Leningrad, 1926); trans. D.B. Langmuir, *The Biosphere* (New York: Copernicus/Springer Verlag, 1998) 148–9.

Jacques Monod
Chance and Necessity//1970

[…] Among vitalist theories a wide variety of tendencies may be discerned. Here we shall be content with distinguishing between what I shall refer to as 'metaphysical vitalism' and 'scientistic vitalism'.

There has probably been no more illustrious proponent of a metaphysical vitalism than Henri Bergson. Thanks to an engaging style and a metaphorical dialectic bare of logic but not of poetry, his philosophy achieved immense success. It seems to have fallen into almost complete discredit today, but in my youth no one stood a chance of passing his baccalaureate examination unless he had read *Creative Evolution*. This philosophy, as some will recall, rests entirely upon a certain idea of life conceived as an *élan*, a 'current', absolutely distinct from inanimate matter but contending with it, 'traversing' it so as to force it into organized form. Contrary to almost all other vitalisms and animisms, that of Bergson predicates no ultimate goal: it refuses to put life's essential spontaneity in bondage to any kind of predetermination. Evolution, identified with the *élan vital* itself, can therefore have neither final nor efficient causes. Man is the supreme stage at which evolution has arrived, without having sought or foreseen it. He is rather the sign and proof of the total freedom of the creative *élan*.

This conception is bound up with another, considered by Bergson fundamental: rational intelligence is an instrument of knowledge specially designed for mastering inert matter but utterly incapable of apprehending life's phenomena. Only instinct, consubstantial with the *élan vital*, can give a direct global insight into them. Every analytical and rational statement about life is therefore meaningless, or rather irrelevant. The high development of rational intelligence in *Homo sapiens* has brought on a grave and regrettable impoverishment of his powers of intuition, a lost treasure we today must strive to recover.

I shall not try to discuss this philosophy (which indeed does not lend itself to discussion). A captive of logic and poor in global intuitions, I feel myself disqualified. Be that as it may, I do not regard Bergson's attitude as insignificant; quite the contrary. Conscious or unconscious rebellion against the rational, respect given to the id at the expense of the ego are hallmarks of our times, and so too is creative spontaneity. Had Bergson employed a less limpid language, a more 'profound' style, he would be re-read today.

The 'scientific' vitalists have been more numerous, and they include some very distinguished scholars. But while fifty years ago the vitalists were recruited from among biologists (of whom the most renowned, Hans Driesch, gave up embryology for philosophy), those of our day come mainly from the physical sciences, like Walter Elsässer and Michael Polanyi.

It is understandable, certainly, that physicists should be still more impressed than biologists by the strangeness of living things. Summarized in a few words, for example, here is Elsässer's position:

The strange properties, invariance and teleonomy [apparent goal-directedness of structures/organisms], are doubtless not at fundamental odds with physics; but the physical forces and chemical interactions brought to light by the study of non-living systems do not fully account for them. Hence it must be realized that over and above physical principles and adding themselves thereto, others are operative in living matter, but not in non-living systems where, consequently, these electively vital principles could not be discovered. It is these principles – or, to borrow from Elsässer's terminology, these 'biotonic laws' – that must be elucidated.

Such hypotheses, it seems, were not dismissed by the great Nils Bohr himself. But he did not claim to have proof that they were necessary. Are they? That, finally, is the nub of it. That is what Elsässer and Polanyi assert. The least one can say is that the arguments of these physicists are oddly lacking in strictness and solidity. These arguments concern respectively each of the strange properties. As regards invariance, its mechanism is sufficiently well known today for us to be able to state that no non-physical principle is required for its interpretation.

This leaves us with teleonomy or, more exactly, with the morphogenetic mechanisms which put teleonomic structures together. It is perfectly true that embryonic development is in appearance one of the most miraculous phenomena in the whole of biology. It is also true that these phenomena, admirably described by embryologists, continue in large part (for technical reasons) to elude genetic and biochemical analysis, obviously the sole avenue to an understanding of them. The attitude of the vitalists who feel that physical laws are – or in any case will prove themselves – insufficient to explain embryogenesis draws its justification, therefore, not from precise knowledge or from definite observations, but from our present·day ignorance alone. On the other hand, our understanding of the molecular control mechanisms that regulate cellular growth and activity has progressed considerably and ought soon to contribute to the interpretation of organic development. [...] In order to survive as a point of view, vitalism requires that in biology there should remain, if not actual paradoxes, at least certain 'mysteries'. Developments in molecular biology over the past two decades have singularly narrowed the domain of the mysterious, leaving wide open to vitalist speculation little other than the field of subjectivity: that of consciousness itself. One runs no great risk in predicting that in this area as well, for the time being still 'off limits', such speculation will prove just as sterile as in all the others where it has hitherto been practiced.

Animist conceptions are in many respects a great deal more interesting than vitalist ideas. Reaching back to mankind's infancy, perhaps to before the appearance of *Homo sapiens*, they are still deep rooted in the soul of modern man. Our ancestors, we must presume, perceived the strangeness of their condition only very dimly. They did not have the reasons we have today for feeling themselves strangers in the universe upon which they opened their eyes. What did they see first? Animals, plants; beings whose nature they could at once divine as similar to their own. Plants grow, seek sunlight, die; animals stalk their prey, attack their enemies, feed and protect their young; males fight for the possession of a female. About plants and animals, as about man himself, there was nothing hard to explain. These beings all have an aim, a purpose: to live and to go on living in their progeny, even at the price of death. Its purpose explains the being, and the being makes sense only through the purpose animating it.

But around them our ancestors also saw other objects, far more mysterious: rocks, rivers, mountains, the thunderstorm, the rain, the stars in the sky. If these objects exist it must also be for a purpose; to nourish it they had also to have a spirit or soul. Thus was the world's strangeness resolved for those early human beings: in reality there exist no inanimate objects. For such a thing would be incomprehensible. In the river's depths, on the mountaintop, more subtle spirits pursue vaster and more impenetrable designs than the transparent ones animating men and beasts. Thus were our forebears wont to see in nature's forms and events the action of forces either benign or hostile, but never indifferent – never totally alien.

Animist belief, as I am visualizing it here, consists essentially in a projection into inanimate nature of man's awareness of the intensely teleonomic functioning of his own central nervous system. It is, in other words, the hypothesis that natural phenomena can and must be explained in the same manner, by the same 'laws', as subjective human activity, conscious and purposive. Primitive animism formulated this hypothesis with complete candour, frankness and precision, populating nature with gracious or awesome myths and myth-figures which have for centuries nourished art and poetry.

One would be wrong to smile, even out of the fondness and deference the childlike inspire. Do we imagine that modern culture has really forsaken the subjective interpretation of nature? Animism established a covenant between nature and man, a profound alliance outside of which seems to stretch only terrifying solitude. Must we break this tie because the postulate of objectivity requires it? Ever since the seventeenth century the history of ideas attests to the profuse efforts put forth by the greatest minds to avert that break, to forge the old bond anew.

Think of such mighty efforts as those of Leibniz, or of the colossal and ponderous monument Hegel raised. But idealism has not by any means been the only refuge for a cosmic animism. At the very core of certain ideologies said and claiming to be founded upon science, the animist projection, in a more or less disguised form, turns up again.

The biological philosophy of Teilhard de Chardin would not merit attention but for the startling success it has encountered even in scientific circles. A success which tells of the eagerness; of the need to revive the covenant. Teilhard revives it and does so nakedly. His philosophy, like Bergson's, is based entirely upon an initial evolutionist postulate. But unlike Bergson, he has the evolutive force operating throughout the entire universe, from elementary panicles to galaxies: there is no 'inert' matter and therefore no essential distinction between 'matter' and 'life'. His wish to present this concept as 'scientific' leads Teilhard to base it upon a new definition of energy. This is somehow distributed between two vectors, one of which would be (I presume) 'ordinary' energy, whereas the other would correspond to the upward evolutionary surge. The biosphere and man are the latest products of this ascent along the spiritual vector of energy. This evolution is to continue until all energy has become concentrated along the spiritual vector: that will be the attaining of 'point omega'.

Although Teilhard's logic is hazy and his style laborious, some of those who do not entirely accept his ideology yet allow it a certain poetic grandeur. For my part I am most of all struck by the intellectual spinelessness of this philosophy. In it I see more than anything else a systematic truckling, a willingness to conciliate at any price, to come to any compromise. Perhaps, after all, Teilhard was not for nothing a member of that order which, three centuries earlier, Pascal assailed for its theological laxness.

The idea of re-establishing the old animist covenant with nature, or of founding a new one through a universal theory according to which the evolution of the biosphere culminating in man would be part of the smooth onward flow of cosmic evolution itself – this idea did not of course originate with Teilhard. It is in fact the central theme of nineteenth-century scientistic progressism. One finds it at the very heart of Herbert Spencer's positivism and of the dialectical materialism of Marx and Engels as well. The unknown and *unknowable* force which, according to Spencer, operates throughout the universe creating variety, coherence, specialization and order, plays what amounts to exactly the same role in Teilhard's 'ascending' energy: human history is the extension of biological evolution, itself a component part of cosmic evolution. Thanks to this single principle, man at last finds his eminent and necessary place in the universe along with certainty of the progress which is forever pledged to him.

Spencer's differentiating force, like Teilhard's ascending energy, is a plain instance of animist projection. To give meaning to nature, so that man need not be separated from it by a fathomless gulf, and for it again to become decipherable and intelligible, *a purpose had to be restored to it*. Should no spirit be available to harbour this purpose, then one inserts into nature an evolutive, an ascending 'force', which in effect amounts to abandoning the postulate of objectivity. [...]

Jacques Monod, extract from *Le hasard et la nécessité. Essai sur la philosophie naturelle de la biologie moderne* (Paris: Éditions du Seuil, 1970); trans. Austryn Wainhouse, *Chance and Necessity* (New York: Alfred A. Knopf, 1971) 25–33.

Gregory Bateson
Steps to an Ecology of Mind//1972

[...] In the Second World War it was discovered what sort of complexity entails mind. And since that discovery, we know that wherever in the universe we encounter that sort of complexity, we are dealing with mental phenomena. It's as materialistic as that.

Let me try to describe for you that order of complexity, which is in some degree a technical matter. Alfred Russel Wallace sent a famous essay to Charles Darwin from Indonesia. In it he announced his discovery of natural selection, which coincided with Darwin's. Part of his description of the struggle for existence is interesting:

The action of this principle [the struggle for existence] is exactly like that of the steam engine, which checks and corrects any irregularities almost before they become evident; and in like manner no unbalanced deficiency in the animal kingdom can ever reach any conspicuous magnitude, because it would make itself felt at the very first step, by rendering existence difficult and extinction almost sure to follow.

The steam engine with a governor is simply a circular train of causal events, with a link in that chain such that the more of something, the less of the next thing in the circuit. The *wider* the balls of the governor diverge, the *less* the fuel supply. If causal chains with that general characteristic are provided with energy, the result will be (if you are lucky and things balance out) a self-corrective system.

Wallace, in fact, proposed the first cybernetic model.

Nowadays cybernetics deals with much more complex systems of this general kind; and we know that when we talk about the processes of civilization, or evaluate human behaviour, human organization, or any biological system, we are concerned with self-corrective systems. These systems are always *conservative* of something. As in the engine with a governor, the fuel supply is changed to conserve – to keep constant – the speed of the flywheel, so always in such systems changes occur to conserve the truth of some descriptive statement, some component of the status quo. Wallace saw the matter correctly, and natural selection acts primarily to keep constant that complex variable which we call 'survival'.

R.D. Laing noted that the obvious can be very difficult for people to see. That is because people are self-corrective systems. They are self-corrective against disturbance, and if the obvious is not of a kind that they can easily assimilate without internal disturbance, their self-corrective mechanisms work to sidetrack it, to hide it, even to the extent of shutting the eyes if necessary, or shutting off various parts of the process of perception. Disturbing information can be framed like a pearl so that it doesn't make a nuisance of itself; and this will be done according to the understanding of the system itself of what would be a nuisance. This too – the premise regarding what would cause disturbance – is something which is learned and then becomes perpetuated, or conserved.

[Let us now] deal with three of these enormously complex systems or arrangements of conservative loops. One is the human individual. Its physiology and neurology conserve body temperature, blood chemistry, the length and size and shape of organs during growth and embryology, and the rest of the body's characteristics. This is a system which conserves descriptive statements about the human being, body or soul. For the same is true of individual psychology, where learning occurs to conserve the opinions and components of the status quo.

Second, we deal with the society in which that individual lives – and that society is again a system of the same general kind. And third, we deal with the ecosystem, the natural biological surroundings of these human animals. Let me start from the natural ecosystems around man. An English oak wood, or a tropical forest, or a piece of desert, is a community of creatures. In the oak wood perhaps 1,000 species, perhaps more; in the tropical forest perhaps ten times that number of species live together.

I may say that very few have ever seen such an undisturbed system; there are not many of them left; they've mostly been messed up by *Homo sapiens* who either exterminated some species or introduced others which became weeds and pests, or altered the water supply, etc. We are rapidly, of course, destroying all the natural systems in the world, the balanced natural systems. We simply make them unbalanced – but still natural.

Be that as it may, those creatures and plants live together in a combination of competition and mutual dependency, and it is that combination that is the important thing to consider. Every species has a primary Malthusian capacity. Any species that does not, potentially, produce more young than the number of the population of the parental generation is out. They're doomed. It is absolutely necessary for every species and for every such system that its components have a potential positive gain in the population curve. But if every species has potential gain, it is then quite a trick to achieve equilibrium. All sorts of interactive balances and dependencies come into play, and it is these processes that have the sort of circuit structure that I have mentioned.

The Malthusian curve is exponential. It is the curve of population growth and it is not inappropriate to call this the population *explosion.*

You may regret that organisms have this explosive characteristic, but you may as well settle for it. The creatures that don't are out.

On the other hand, in a balanced ecological system whose underpinnings are of this nature, it is very clear that any monkeying with the system is likely to disrupt the equilibrium. Then the exponential curves will start to appear. Some plant will become a weed, some creatures will be exterminated, and the system as a *balanced* system is likely to fall to pieces.

What is true of the species that live together in a wood is also true of the groupings and sorts of people in a society, who are similarly in an uneasy balance of dependency and competition. And the same truth holds right inside you, where there is an uneasy physiological competition and mutual dependency among the organs, tissues, cells, and so on. Without this competition and dependency you would not be, because you cannot do without any of the competing organs and parts. If any of the parts did not have the expansive characteristics they would go out and you would go out, too. So that even in the body you have a liability. With improper disturbance of the system, the exponential curves appear. In a society, the same is true.

I think you have to assume that all important physiological or social change is in some degree a slipping of the system at some point along an exponential curve. The slippage may not go far, or it may go to disaster. But in principle if, say, you kill off the thrushes in a wood, certain components of the balance will run along exponential curves to a new stopping place.

In such slippage there is always danger – the possibility that some variable, e.g. population density, may reach such a value that further slippage is controlled by factors which are inherently harmful. If, for example, population is finally controlled by available food supply, the surviving individuals will be half starved and the food supply overgrazed, usually to a point of no return.

Now let me begin to talk about the individual organism. This entity is similar to the oak wood and its controls are represented in the *total* mind, which is perhaps only a reflection of the total body. But the system is segmented in various ways, so that the effects of something in your food life, shall we say, do not to totally alter your sex life and things in your sex life do not totally change your kinesic life and so on. There is a certain amount of compartmentalization which is no doubt a necessary economy. There is one compartmentalization which is in many ways mysterious but certainly of crucial importance in man's life. I refer to the 'semi-permeable' linkage between consciousness and the remainder of the total mind. A certain limited amount of information about what's happening in this larger part of the mind seems to be relayed to what we may call the screen of consciousness. But what gets to consciousness is selected; it is a systematic (not random) sampling of the rest.

Of course, the *whole* of the mind could not be reported in a part of the mind. This follows logically from the relationship between part and whole. The television screen does not give you total coverage or report of the events which occur in the whole television process; and this not merely because the viewers would not be interested in such a report, but because to report on any extra part of the total process would require extra circuitry. But to report on the events in this extra circuitry would require a still further addition of more circuitry and so on. Each additional step towards increased consciousness will take the system farther from total consciousness. To add a report on events in a given part of the machine will actually decrease the percentage of total events reported.

We therefore have to settle for very limited consciousness, and the question arises: How is the selecting done? On what principles does your mind select that which 'you' will be aware of? And, while not much is known of these principles, something is known, though the principles at work are often not themselves accessible to consciousness. First of all, much of the input is consciously scanned, but only after it has been processed by the totally unconscious process of perception. The sensory events are packaged into images and these images are then 'conscious'.

I, the conscious I, see an unconsciously edited version of a small percentage of what affects my retina. I am guided in my perception by *purposes*. I see who is attending, who is not, who is understanding, who is not, or at least I get a myth about this subject, which may be quite correct. I am interested in getting that myth as I talk. It is relevant to my purposes that you hear me.

What happens to the picture of a cybernetic system (oak wood or organism) when that picture is selectively drawn to answer only questions of purpose?

Consider the state of medicine today. It's called medical science. What happens is that doctors think it would be nice to get rid of polio, or typhoid, or cancer. So they devote research money and effort to focusing on these 'problems', or purposes. At a certain point Jonas Salk and others 'solve' the problem of polio. They discover a solution of bugs which you can give to children so that they don't get polio. This is the solution to the problem of polio. At this point, they stop putting large quantities of effort and money into the problem of polio and go on to the problem of cancer, or whatever it may be.

Medicine ends up, therefore, as a total science, whose structure is essentially that of a bag of tricks. Within this science there is extraordinarily little knowledge of the sort of things I'm talking about; that is, of the body as a systemically cybernetically organized self-corrective system. Its internal interdependencies are minimally understood. What has happened is that purpose has determined what will come under the inspection or consciousness of medical science.

If you allow purpose to organize that which comes under your conscious inspection, what you will get is a bag of tricks – some of them very valuable tricks. It is an extraordinary achievement that these tricks have been discovered; all that I don't argue. But still we do not know two penn'orth, really, about the total network system. Walter Cannon wrote a book on *The Wisdom of the Body*, but nobody has written a book on the wisdom of medical science, because wisdom is precisely the thing which it lacks. Wisdom I take to be the knowledge of the larger interactive system – that system which, if disturbed, is likely to generate exponential curves of change.

Consciousness operates in the same way as medicine in its sampling of the events and processes of the body and of what goes on in the total mind. It is organized in terms of purpose. It is a short-cut device to enable you to get quickly at what you want; not to act with maximum wisdom in order to live, but to follow the shortest logical or causal path to get what you want. [...]

On one hand, we have the systemic nature of individuals, the systemic nature of the culture in which they live and the systemic nature of the biological, ecological system around them; and, on the other, the curious twist in the individual's systemic nature, whereby consciousness is, almost of necessity, blinded to the systemic nature of the person. Purposive consciousness pulls out, from the total mind, sequences which do not have the loop structure characteristic of the whole systemic structure. If you follow the 'common sense' dictates of consciousness you become, effectively, greedy and unwise – again I use 'wisdom' as a word for recognition of and guidance by a knowledge of the total systemic creature.

Lack of systemic wisdom is always punished. We may say that the biological systems – the individual, the culture and the ecology – are partly living sustainers of their component cells or organisms. But the systems are nonetheless punishing of any species unwise enough to quarrel with its ecology.

Call the systemic forces 'God' if you will. [...]

Gregory Bateson, extract from *Steps to an Ecology of Mind* (Chicago: University of Chicago Press, 1972) 434–40.

Arne Naess
The Three Great Movements//1992

At the end of the twentieth century, we saw a convergence of three areas of self-destructiveness: the self-destructiveness of war, the self-destructiveness of exploitation and suppression among humans, and the self-destructiveness of the suppression of non-human beings and of the degradation of life conditions in general. The movement to eradicate wars has a long history as a global movement. The movement against abject poverty and cruel exploitation and domination is younger. The third movement is younger still. These are the great movements that require intense participation on the grassroots level far into the new century.

The supporters of the peace movement have always asked for policies that were often 'politically impossible' for governments to accept. The same applies to the second and third movements. But today the first two can at least point to people in power who declare strong sympathies with their radical points of view. Halvard Lange, a prominent supporter of stronger NATO forces, declared that at heart he was a pacifist (which made his wife whisper irreverently, 'Then I am a virgin'). Such publicly declared sympathy has probably not yet reached government level in support of the deep ecology movement.

The urgency of preserving nature for 'future generations', meaning 'future generations of humans' and not 'future generations of living beings', has won acclaim among power elites. What I, perhaps misleadingly, have called the 'shallow', 'reform' or 'non-deep' ecological movement *has* started to have an impact at government level. Environmental organizations are listened to, and their advice has occasionally been used in practice. But future generations of non-humans seem to be valued publicly only for the sake of future humans.

[By way of offering a definition] of the deep ecology movement, I find it difficult to do more than propose a tentative formulation of views that most supporters have in common. [...]

The realization of the [tasks required by this movement] requires significant changes in both rich and poor countries and affects social, economic, technical and lifestyle factors. Goals include the protection of the planet and its richness and diversity of life for its own sake. The specific urgency accorded to this third movement is due to the time factor: It is obvious that delays rapidly make the ecological crisis more difficult to overcome. Wait five years, and the process may take fifty years more. Such a nonlinear function of time does not restrict the other two movements.

What can be more urgent than the elimination of extreme poverty and suppression? We may answer that nothing can be more urgent. But whereas the general costs are roughly constant year after year, or increase linearly, the specific character of the ecological crisis makes the cost of reaching ecological sustainability increase exponentially.

Whether in civil or international war, the mentality created is that of almost complete indifference towards the destruction of nature. Destruction is even used as a weapon. To ask for mercy towards non-humans would in war be considered frivolous. This also holds to some extent even when the destruction caused by the gigantic military-industrial complex is placed increasingly under ecological scrutiny and is made known in wide circles.

Evidently the goals of the deep ecology movement cannot be reached without decisive victories of the peace movement. This should add to the motivation of people using much of their time and energy within the peace movement. Some have changed focus and are now active in the ecology movement, finding this comparable to a change of focus within a wider peace movement: work for peace with nature; end brutal invasions. But the change of focus undertaken by prominent peace activists such as E.F. Schumacher has not resulted in noticeable polemics about the relative importance of the two movements.

The many branches of the social justice movement have a more complex relation to the deep ecology movement. In the West, since the industrial revolution and at least through the twentieth century, labour was treated worse than cattle. For several hundred years, pollution at the workplace and in urban slums has damaged the health of the underprivileged, not the privileged.

A worker in the logging industry might have this to say about proposals to cease operations because of environmental problems: 'You speak of environmental degradation. *We* have suffered that for hundreds of years. You close down a factory because of poisons. But what are the consequences for you and what for us? The managers lose their jobs, but they take a long vacation in superb nature, and get new jobs. We increase the legions of the unemployed, we cannot move around easily with our families, we remain in an unhealthy environment, many of us lose our way of life, and our problems persist. You say the deep ecology movement asks for widening care so that non-human beings get more chance. But you should also support increased care for underprivileged humans.' It is right that deep ecology theorists, like the peace and social justice theorists and activists, talk publicly about these concerns. Their writings, if they write, reflect their specialities, and it is difficult to assess what they do privately without knowing them well. General conclusions about the various concerns of the supporters of the three movements are rather shaky.

It is an embarrassing scandal that the rich industrial nations do not use the urgency of work to be done to overcome the global ecological crisis as a basis for the significant reduction of unemployment. The jobs in this area are clearly more labour-intensive than those in industry.

Looking at philosophical 'schools' of the 1960s and later, we see that anarchism, Marxism, neo-Marxism, the Frankfurt school and hermeneutics have not felt at home with the tenets of the deep ecology movement – and not only because of the special terminology of its theoreticians. This is not the place to go into philosophical debates but in spite of different theoretical and terminological leanings, three groups – supporters of social ecology, eco-feminists and the deep ecology movement – co-operate well in praxis, learning from each other's specific activities. The frontier of work is long, and we need to express our appreciation of work done in different sectors from our own. The convergence of problems within the three great movements may be expected to increase, and their impact on policies to be correspondingly strengthened. [...]

It is not by chance that I have used the term *self* in these short characterizations of the lines of thinking, feeling and acting. The term suggested itself when I was trying out a conceptual unification of a normative system, with self-realization as the basic norm – expressed, inadequately of course, through a single phrase. For those who habitually look at the three global movements with the conceptualizations of the third movement in mind, concepts of ecosystems, not of human-environment, are central. The human self is then basically an ecological self, that is, a part of the ecosystems. [...]

Arne Naess, extract from 'The Three Great Movements' (1992), in *The Ecology of Wisdom: Writings of Arne Naess*, ed. Bill Devall and Alan Drengson (Berkeley: Counterpoint, 2008) 99–101.

Félix Guattari
The Three Ecologies//1989

[...] Throughout history and across the world existential cartographies founded on a conscious acceptance of certain 'existentializing' ruptures of meaning have sought refuge in art and religion. However, today the huge subjective void produced by the proliferating production of material and immaterial goods is becoming ever more absurd and increasingly irreparable and threatens the consistency of both individual and group existential Territories. While there no longer appears to be a cause-and-effect relationship between the growth in techno-scientific resources and the development of social and cultural progress, it seems clear that we are witnessing an irreversible erosion of the traditional mechanisms of social regulation. Faced with this situation, the most 'modernist' capitalist formations seem, in their own way, to be banking on a return to the past, however artificial, and on a reconstitution of ways of being that were familiar to our ancestors. We can see, for example, how certain hierarchical structures (having lost a significant part of their functional efficiency as a result, principally, of the computerization of information and organizational management) have become the object of an imaginary hypercathexis, at both upper and lower executive levels; in the example of Japan this hypercathexis occasionally verges on religious devotion. Similarly, we are witnessing a reinforcement of segregationist attitudes vis-à-vis immigrants, women, the young and the elderly. Such a rise in what we might call a subjective conservatism is not solely attributable to an intensification of social repression; it stems equally from a kind of existential contraction [*crispation*] involving all of the actors in the socius. Post-industrial capitalism, which I prefer to describe as Integrated World Capitalism (IWC), tends increasingly to decentre its sites of power, moving away from structures producing goods and services to structures producing signs, syntax and – in particular, through the control which it exercises over the media, advertising, opinion polls, etc. – subjectivity.

This evolution ought to make us reflect upon the ways in which earlier forms of capitalism operated, given that they too were not exempt from this same tendency towards the capitalization of subjective power, both at the level of the capitalist elites as well as among the proletariat. However, the true importance of this propensity within capitalism was never fully demonstrated, with the result that it was not properly appreciated by theoreticians of the workers' movement. I would propose grouping together four main semiotic regimes, the mechanisms [*instruments*] on which IWC is founded:

(1) Economic semiotics (monetary, financial, accounting and decision-making mechanisms);
(2) Juridical semiotics (title deeds, legislation and regulations of all kinds);
(3) Techno-scientific semiotics (plans, diagrams, programmes, studies, research, etc.);
(4) Semiotics of subjectification, of which some coincide with those already mentioned, but to which we should add many others, such as those relating to architecture, town planning, public facilities, etc.

We must acknowledge that models which claim to found a causal hierarchy between these semiotic regimes are well on their way to completely losing touch with reality. For example, it becomes increasingly difficult to maintain that economic semiotics and semiotics that work together towards the production of material goods occupy an infrastructural position in relation to juridical and ideological semiotics, as was postulated by Marxism. At present, IWC is all of a piece: productive–economic–subjective. And to return to the old scholastic categories, one might say that it follows at the same time from material, formal, efficient and final causes.

One of the key analytic problems confronted by social and mental ecology is the introjection of repressive power by the oppressed. The major difficulty here is the fact that the unions and the parties, which struggle, in principle, to defend the interests of the workers and the oppressed, reproduce in themselves the same pathogenic models that stifle all freedom of expression and innovation in their own ranks. Perhaps it will still be necessary for a lapse of time to ensue before the workers' movement recognizes that the economic-ecological vectors of circulation, distribution, communication, supervision and so on, are strictly situated on the same plane, from the point of view of the creation of surplus value, as labour that is directly incorporated into the production of material goods. In this regard, a dogmatic ignorance has been maintained by a number of theoreticians, which only serves to reinforce a workerism and a corporatism that have profoundly distorted and handicapped anti-capitalist movements of emancipation over the last few decades.

It is to be hoped that the development of the three types of eco-logical praxis outlined here will lead to a reframing and a recomposition of the goals of the emancipatory struggles. And let us hope that, in the context of the new 'deal' of the relation between capital and human activity, ecologists, feminists, anti-racists, etc., will make it an immediate major objective to target the modes of production of subjectivity, that is, of knowledge, culture, sensibility and sociability that come under an incorporeal value system at the root of the new productive assemblages.

Social ecology will have to work towards rebuilding human relations at every level of the socius. It should never lose sight of the fact that capitalist power has become delocalized and deterritorialized, both in extension, by extending its influence over the whole social, economic and cultural life of the planet, and in 'intension', by infiltrating the most unconscious subjective strata. In doing this it is no longer possible to claim to be opposed to capitalist power only from the outside, through trade unions and traditional politics. It is equally imperative to confront capitalism's effects in the domain of mental ecology in everyday life: individual, domestic, material, neighbourly, creative or one's personal ethics. Rather than looking for a stupefying and infantilizing consensus, it will be a question in the future of cultivating a dissensus and the singular production of existence. A capitalistic subjectivity is engendered through operators of all types and sizes, and is manufactured to protect existence from any intrusion of events that might disturb or disrupt public opinion. It demands that all singularity must be either evaded or crushed in specialist apparatuses and frames of reference.

Therefore, it endeavours to manage the worlds of childhood, love, art, as well as everything associated with anxiety, madness, pain, death, or a feeling of being lost in the Cosmos … IWC forms massive subjective aggregates from the most personal – one could even say intra-personal – existential givens, which it hooks up to ideas of race, nation, the professional workforce, competitive sports, a dominating masculinity [*virilité*], mass-media celebrity … Capitalistic subjectivity seeks to gain power by controlling and neutralizing the maximum number of existential refrains. It is intoxicated with and anaesthetized by a collective feeling of pseudo-eternity.

It seems to me that the new ecological practices will have to articulate themselves on these many tangled and heterogeneous fronts, their objective being processually to activate isolated and repressed singularities that are just turning in circles. (For example, a school class in which are applied the principles of the Freinet School aims to singularize the overall functioning through co-operative systems, assessment meetings, a newspaper, the pupils' freedom to organize their own work individually or in groups, etc.)

From this same perspective we will have to consider symptoms and incidents outside the norm as indices of a potential labour of subjectification. It seems to me essential to organize new micropolitical and microsocial practices, new solidarities, a new gentleness, together with new aesthetic and new analytic practices regarding the formation of the unconscious. It appears to me that this is the only possible way to get social and political practices back on their feet, working for humanity and not simply for a permanent re-equilibration of the capitalist semiotic universe. One might object that large-scale struggles are not necessarily in sync with ecological praxis and the micropolitics of desire, but that's the point: it is important not to homogenize various levels of practice or to make connections between them under some transcendental supervision, but instead to engage them in processes of heterogenesis. Feminists will never take a becoming-woman far enough, and there is no reason to demand that immigrants should renounce their nationalitarian belonging or the cultural traits that cling to their very being. Particular cultures should be left to deploy themselves in inventing other contracts of citizenship. Ways should be found to enable the singular, the exceptional, the rare, to coexist with a State structure that is the least burdensome possible.

Unlike Hegelian and Marxist dialectics, eco-logic no longer imposes a 'resolution' of opposites. In the domain of social ecology there will be times of struggle in which everyone will feel impelled to decide on common objectives and to act 'like little soldiers', by which I mean like good activists. But there will simultaneously be periods in which individual and collective subjectivities will 'pull out' without a thought for collective aims, and in which creative expression as such will take precedence. This new ecosophical logic – and I want to emphasize this point – resembles the manner in which an artist may be led to alter a work after the intrusion of some accidental detail, an event-incident that suddenly makes the initial project bifurcate, making it drift [*dériver*] far from its previous path, however certain it had once appeared to be. There is a proverb 'the exception proves the rule', but the exception can just as easily deflect the rule, or even recreate it.

Environmental ecology, as it exists today, has barely begun to prefigure the generalized ecology that I advocate here, the aim of which will be radically to decentre social struggles and ways of coming to one's own psyche. Current ecological movements certainly have merit, but in truth I think that the overall ecosophical question is too important to be left to some of its usual archaizers and folklorists, who sometimes deliberately refuse any large-scale political involvement. Ecology must stop being associated with the image of a small nature-loving minority or with qualified specialists. Ecology in my sense questions the whole of subjectivity and capitalistic power formations, whose sweeping progress cannot be guaranteed to continue as it has for the past decade.

The present ongoing crisis, both financial and economic, could not only lend an important upheaval of the social status quo and the mass-media imaginary that underlies it, but certain themes promoted by neo-liberalists – such as flexible labour, deregulation, etc. – could perfectly well backfire on them.

I stress once again that the choice is no longer simply between blind fixation to old State-bureaucratic supervision and generalized welfare on the one hand, and a despairing and cynical surrender to 'yuppie' ideology on the other. All the indications suggest that the productivity gains engendered by current technological revolutions will inscribe themselves on a curve of logarithmic growth. Henceforth it is a question of knowing whether the new ecological operators and the new ecosophical assemblages of enunciation will succeed in channelling these gains in less absurd, less dead-ended directions than those of Integrated World Capitalism.

The principle common to the three ecologies is this: each of the existential Territories with which they confront us is not given as an in-itself [*en-soi*], closed in on itself, but instead as a for-itself [*pour-soi*] that is precarious, finite, finitized, singular, singularized, capable of bifurcating into stratified and deathly repetitions or of opening up processually from a praxis that enables it to be made 'habitable' by a human project. It is this praxic opening-out which constitutes the essence of 'eco'-art. It subsumes all existing ways of domesticating existential Territories and is concerned with intimate modes of being, the body, the environment or large contextual ensembles relating to ethnic groups, the nation, or even the general rights of humanity. Having said this, it is not a question of establishing universal rules as a guide to this praxis, but on the contrary of setting forth the principle antinomies between the ecosophical levels, or, if you prefer, between the three ecological visions, the three discriminating lenses under discussion here.

The principle specific to mental ecology is that its approach to existential Territories derives from a pre-objectal and pre-persona logic of the son that Freud has described as being a 'primary process'. One could call this the logic of the 'included middle', in which black and white are indistinct, where the beautiful coexists with the ugly, the inside with the outside, the 'good' object with the 'bad' … In the particular case of the ecology of the phantasm, each attempt to locate it cartographically requires the drafting of an expressive framework that is both singular and, more precisely, singularized. Gregory Bateson has clearly shown that what he calls 'the ecology of ideas' cannot be contained within the domain of the psychology of the individual, but organizes itself into systems or 'minds', the boundaries of which no longer coincide with the participant individuals. But I part company with Bateson when he treats action and enunciation as mere parts of an ecological subsystem 'context'. I myself consider that existential taking on of context is always brought about by a praxis which is established in the rupture of the systemic 'pretext'. There is no overall hierarchy for locating and localizing the components of enunciation at a given level. They are composed of heterogeneous elements that take on a mutual consistency and persistence as they cross the thresholds that constitute one world at the expense of another. The operators of this crystallization are fragments of a-signifying chains of the type that Schlegel likens to works of art. ('A fragment like a miniature work of art must be totally detached from the surrounding world and closed on itself like a hedgehog'.)

Félix Guattari, extract from *Les trois écologies* (Paris: Éditions Galilée, 1989); trans. Ian Pindar, *The Three Ecologies* (New York and London: Continuum, 2005) 31–6.

Peter Halley
Nature and Culture//1983

Just a decade ago, having 'soul' was said to be the cure for the alienation with which consciousness in the industrialized world was plagued. In the mechanized, repressed, bourgeois world, it was argued, people had been stripped of their vitality, spontaneity and emotionality. Thus, an utterance that had 'soul', that was endowed with spirituality, could be said to play a role in returning humankind to its oneness with nature, to its 'essence'.

Today, however, thinking about these issues has changed, at least in the art world. Ideas like 'soul' and spirituality, are viewed by many as a means by which bourgeois culture has consolidated its position by denying its historicity. To say that a work of art is spiritual is to attribute to it universal, timeless value. It also suggests that the society which encourages and validates works with such attributes is itself timelessly and universally valid.

This radical and sudden transformation of opinion itself provokes examination. Such transformed judgements are the result of a tidal wave of intellectual change that has washed over the art world in the present decade. An art practice that had been dominant since the Second World War has been completely swept away and replaced by another.

The practice of art from World War II to the end of the last decade was dominated by ideas derived from phenomenology, existentialism and Jungian transcendentalism. The post-war period attributed to modernism a vanguard, heroic role, not in the political sense, but in the sense that it claimed that art was capable of reuniting humans with some lost essence and that art was able, as well, to release hidden, heretofore unaccomplished potentialities in the human being.

A history of art was written from this point of view. It confirmed trans-historically the validity of the work of 'masters' from other cultures and other historical periods, not simply to confirm a standard of formal values, but because formal quality was the sign by which the transcendental character of the individual master's consciousness could be apprehended. A canon of modern masters was also fashioned. Matisse and Brancusi were upheld for the magician-like quality of their subjective gestures and their embodiment of the role of the patient, transcendent craftsman; Mondrian was revered for the purity of his phenomenological investigation; Klee for the sincerity and ingenuousness of his personal vision-quest.

Along with the search for the integrated and spiritual in the art of the European culture, a canon of the primitive was continued from European modernism. This interest in the primitive was premised on the belief that in the cultures of tribal peoples evidence could be found of the possibility of a situation in which the whole human being was integrated with nature.

This attitude towards the primitive first surfaces in Abstract Expressionism, in Barnett Newman's appreciation of the terror of the primitive and in the influence that indigenous American cultures had on Clyfford Still and Jackson Pollock. Then, in Pollock there is the suggestion that the artefact could be replaced by action in 'real time', a suggestion that would be taken up a decade later in the work of an entire generation of conceptual, performance and process artists who believed that the tribal experience of real-time art was the key to overcoming the deadening effect of the bourgeois art object.

The post-war era was also a period of an art of nature – a period in which the artist sought unification with some lost or undiscovered absolutes, whether achieved through meditative serenity, the probing of the Jungian universal unconscious, or acts of reunification with the earth itself.

It is a period of landscape, from the landscape-derived imagery of Abstract Expressionism, which was continued in the work of the Colour Field painters (Kenneth Noland, Jules Olitski, et al.), to its final culmination in the earth art movement which sought literally to return consciousness to its primordial mother, Earth.

Even manifestations that at first seem to contradict this reading of the period on closer examination can be seen to confirm it. Pop art, which had the potential radically to alter the course of this history, was contained by the simple strategy of dismissing it as fun. Within this epoch the Pop artists were isolated and without successors. (Only now has Pop art become an influence on another generation of artists.) The efforts of the formalist artists were likewise misinterpreted because of the dominant needs of the era. To the work of true formalist artists like Frank Stella and Donald Judd was attributed 'presence', which thereby transcendentalized it. Conversely, many other so-called formalist artists were influenced at least as much by Eastern mysticism as by formalist ideas.

Reigning over this entire era, one finds the philosophical tenets of phenomenology and existentialism. The art of this period is overwhelmingly concerned with the situation of the individual as a perceiving and deciding entity. But before one can dismiss the production of this epoch as merely a typical manifestation of late industrialism concerned with preserving the mythic importance of the individual and of some absolute nature upon which the individual can act, one must remember that this era was formed and determined by another historical event, whose influence must be considered separately from the smooth progression of the stages of the development of capital.

If the art of this period can be seen as positing a relationship between the individual and nature, it is perhaps because World War II constituted an event that acted upon those who experienced it as nature. This mammoth event, although certainly caused by social forces, eventually evolved, for a considerable portion of the world's people, into a phenomenon not very different from a devastating flood or fire. World War II constituted a 'natural disaster' in so far as it tore asunder the seamless web of signs that constitutes modern civilization. It left countless persons in a situation in which they were faced not with the codes that their societies had invented for them but rather with an unintended hole in the 'empire of signs'.

One has only to look at the tenets of Sartrean existentialism, which advocates so many of the same values as Abstract Expressionism, to realize the extent to which this experience influenced the era. For Sartre, as for Abstract Expressionists, responsibility, action, 'good faith' and the problem of inventing meaning and morality were the basic issues. It is as if to say that in the codeless world that war on such a scale had created, a world in which the usual laws of market and class – the mechanics of the bourgeois universe as it should be – were in abeyance, philosophy and art should be simply about the possible actions and decisions that a human being who has been stripped of his social role can undertake.

Why then, at the end of the 1970s, did this transcendentalist, phenomeno-logically-oriented approach which had been dominant for thirty years abruptly disappear to be replaced by a new practice that looks exclusively to the mass media for its repertory of images, that rejects the phenomenology of art-making as pretentious and mandarin, that interprets language as a closed set without reference to extra-human reality? Why did a new practice emerge, that substitutes for phenomenological study a fascination with sociological and political reality, that rejects the positivism of both the physical and social sciences, and replaces the cult of originality with myriad variations on the theme or repetition?

And how and why, around 1980, did a group of French texts loosely referred to as post-structuralist or structuralist, which includes works written from ten to twenty years earlier by Roland Barthes, Michel Foucault, Jacques Derrida, and Jean Baudrillard, suddenly gain favour in the intellectual climate of the art world, influencing both artists and theorists and at the same time heralding and effecting the sudden vanquishing of nature from this world of culture?

To start with, it is impossible not to recognize that the generation of artists responsible for this upheaval is the first to be born after World War II and that, conversely, the significant figures whose work was formed by the experience of the war have gradually disappeared. Consequently, the existentialist values of the World War II generation have faded away, while the younger generation which (in the Western world, at least) has never experienced such a situation, in which all the rules are found inapplicable, has become fixated on rules, that is, on language.

This reading might suggest that Europe, which was far more devastated by the war than the United States, should remain intellectually affected by it longer, whereas not even a decade after the war ended the structuralist movement was already under way there. This perhaps only indicates how strong an intellectual force Marxism was in Europe that structuralism, which is so much a Marxian way of thinking, could so quickly evolve there in the wake of the war experience. Or perhaps, unless one would seek an explanation in a formalist theory that connects the development of intellectual trends to the necessary lag in the translation of crucial texts, or that explains artistic change by the inevitable entropy of intellectual movements, one must turn to a discussion of socio-economic factors which links cultural change to events in the development of industrial society and of capitalism. From this point of view, structuralism and the new art both reflect a transition from an industrial to a post-industrial society; from a society of expanding markets to a society of stagnant growth in which wealth is more redistributed than created; from a culture in which production, innovation and individualism are mythologized in the name of creativity to a society that stresses the manipulation of what already exists, be it capital or cultural signs. This is the culture that structuralism describes or which can at the time be said to create structuralism. The conditions of such a post-industrial society have existed in Europe since the end of World War II, when the first structuralist texts appeared there. In the United States, the conditions of post-industrialism have only appeared in the last few years, in the wake of Vietnam (with the curb it imposed on American colonial ambitions), and of the oil crisis of the 1970s, which effectively brought to an end the growth of the American economy. Along with the arrival of post-industrial conditions, a new structuralist-oriented art practice has appeared in the United States.

The advent of post-industrialism has also seemed to make obsolete the very concept of nature, giving rise to a critique of the reign of nature in art. If the industrial period represents the era in which nature was viewed as real, society can today be seen as entering an era in which bourgeois culture is severing its bond with this nature and completing the process by which it has established its own mode of thought, its own consciousness, as referent. Increasingly, the important 'others' of the industrial period have been eliminated – wilderness is bracketed by law, while tribal and folk modes of social organization have been almost completely assimilated (there remains only the difficult question of the unconscious).

Baudrillard, in particular, has advocated a historicization of the idea of nature. He describes the 'triumph of nature' in the industrial period as a historical occurrence:

Nature appeared truly as an essence in all its glory under the sign of the *principle of production*. This separation also involves the *principle of signification*. Under the objective stamp of Science, Technology and Production, Nature becomes the great Signified, the great Referent. It is ideally charged with 'reality'; it becomes Reality.[1]

Bourgeois culture is increasingly seizing the opportunity to 'simulate' (in Baudrillard's terminology) the crucial powers that were assigned to nature's dominion – the power of thought, repeated in the computer, which 'realizes' bourgeois dualism; the ability to create life, accomplished chemically and mechanically; and the ability to create space itself in the binary circuitry of computer-animation devices. Thus the circle of bourgeois thought is finally completed; the bourgeois world is made to refer back only to itself. Recently even the human heart, perhaps the most natural of objects in the old order, has been reconstituted according to the thought processes of bourgeois consciousness.

Advertising's recent appropriation of the vocabularies of nature and post-war modernism makes apparent the extent of this change, which is a triumph of the market over nature. That beer, detergent and make-up are now called 'natural' is significant. Today the name 'Nature Valley' refers to a kind of breakfast cereal; cigarettes have been given such transcendentalist labels as 'True', 'Light' and 'Now'.

Yet a number of troubling questions are provoked by recent structuralist art practice. First, there is the question of how artists can address the world of the simulacrum. If indeed the post-industrialist world is characterized by signs that simulate rather than represent, how can an artist communicate this situation? Is it possible to represent a simulation? If not, it only remains for the artist to engage in the practice of simulation himself of herself. But by so doing, an uncertain situation is set up. The practice of simulation by the artist can be seen as an endorsement of the culture of simulacra. But one wonders if such an endorsement is desirable if, as Marxist critics believe, post-industrial culture constitutes a further level of social alienation. Artists who subscribe to a serious structuralist practice still seem to be in the process of answering this question. But, as Hal Foster has pointed out, the work of the so-called neo-expressionist artists clearly validates the new social conditions by its simulation of the modernist notion of the masterpiece.[2]

Fredric Jameson has observed that cultural analysis is today dominated by two separate trends. On one hand, there is the theory of the simulacrum, as developed by Baudrillard. On the other, there is the work of Michel Foucault, which sees contemporary culture not as a shimmering surface of autonomous signs, but as a place in which the technologies of surveillance, normalization and categorization have ever broadening control over social life.[3] In contrast to Baudrillard's vision of the detached signifier, Foucault finds hidden behind the various signifiers of contemporary society the veiled signified of power, in the form of the consolidation of class position. One questions why artists and art theorists today have been attracted so exclusively to Baudrillard's rather than to Foucault's interpretation of social relationships. One wonders if perhaps Baudrillard's brilliant world of surfaces is not more seductive than Foucault's bleak excavation of the spaces of regimentation. And one wonders if artist and audience, seduced by this shimmering world, have not been deflected away from the investigation of crucial issues about society's structure.

Finally one finds oneself turning away reluctantly from poststructuralism's promise – its potential for sweeping away the mythologies of so many deceptive humanisms – to a consideration of what negative results it may engender. For, ultimately, structuralism, whether Baudrillard's, Foucault's or Barthes', cannot be separated from certain misinterpretations to which it inherently gives rise. To misinterpret structuralism is to arrive at a single reality, the reality of power – not the power with which one class controls another, but the single remaining power to understand and manipulate the codes.

Currently on television there is an advertisement for an investment services company admonishing the viewer that 'some investments require discipline, some require courage'. Clearly this advertisement addresses the potential 'investor' as if he or she were a kind of warrior needing the traditional martial traits. Here, as in so many sectors of contemporary society, including perhaps the present art world, the successful manipulation of the codes to gain social power is treated as if it were a life and death matter. To acknowledge only the existence of language has created an unfortunate limitation on the range of actions that are thought to make sense.

The final image that emerges from these reflections is the image of destruction. One thinks of the Second World War, that 'natural disaster' brought about by social players, and one shudders at imagining the torrent of destruction that may be unwittingly released by the inhabitants of our own empire of signs if, in their struggles to gain power over the codes, they unleash forces beyond everyone's controlling.

1   Jean Baudrillard, *The Mirror of Production* (St Louis: Telos Press, 1975).

2   Hal Foster, 'Between Modernism and the Media', *Art in America*, vol 70, no. 6 (June 1982).

3   Fredric Jameson, *The Political Unconscious* (Ithaca, New York: Cornell University Press, 1981).

Peter Halley, 'Nature and Culture', *Arts Magazine* (September 1983); reprinted in Peter Halley, *Collected Essays 1981–87* (Zürich: Bruno Bischofsberger, 1988) 61–73.

Trevor Paglen
Experimental Geography//2008

[…] Geography's major theoretical underpinnings come from two related ideas: materialism and the production of space.

In the philosophical tradition, materialism is the simple idea that the world is made out of 'stuff', and that moreover, the world is only made out of 'stuff'. All phenomena, then, from atmospheric dynamics to Jackson Pollock paintings, arise out of the interactions of materials in the world. In the western tradition, philosophical materialism goes back to ancient Greek philosophers like Democritus, Anaxagoras and Epicurus, whose conceptions of reality differed sharply from Plato's metaphysics. Later philosophers like Thomas Hobbes, David Hume, Ludwig Feuerbach and Karl Marx would develop materialist philosophies in contradistinction to Cartesian dualism and German idealism. Methodologically, materialism suggests an empirical (although not necessarily positivistic) approach to understanding the world. In the contemporary intellectual climate, a materialist approach takes relationality for granted, but an analytic approach that insists on 'stuff' can be a powerful way of circumventing or tempering the quasi-solipsistic tendencies found in some strains of vulgar poststructuralism.

Geography's second overarching axiom has to do with what we generally call 'the production of space'. Although the idea of the 'production of space' is usually attributed to the geographer-philosopher Henri Lefebvre, whose 1974 book *La Production de l'espace* introduced the term to large numbers of people, the ideas animating Lefebvre's work have a much longer history. Like materialism, the production of space is a relatively easy, even obvious, idea, but it has profound implications. In a nutshell, the production of space says that humans create the world around them. In other words, the human condition is characterized by a feedback loop between human activity and our material surroundings. In this view, space is not a container for human activities to take place within, but is actively 'produced' through human activity. The spaces humans produce, in turn, set powerful constraints upon subsequent activity. […]

Contemporary geography's theoretical and methodological axioms don't have to stay within any disciplinary boundaries. One can apply them to just about anything. Just as physical geographers can implicitly use the idea of production of space when they inquire into the relationship between human carbon emissions and receding Antarctic ice shelves, or when human geographers investigate the relationships between tourism and Tanzanian nature preserves, geography's axioms can guide all sorts of practice and inquiry, including art and culture. A geographic approach to art, however, would look quite different from most conventional art history and criticism. The difference in approach would arise from the ways in which various disciplines rely on different underlying conceptions of the world. A geographer looking into art would begin with very different premises from those of an art critic.

To speak very generally, the conceptual framework organizing much art history and criticism is one of 'reading culture', where questions and problems of representation (and their consequences) are of primary concern. In the traditional model, the critic's task is to describe, elaborate upon, explain, interpret, evaluate and critique pre-given cultural works. In a certain sense, the art critic's role is to act as a discerning consumer of culture. There's nothing wrong at all with this, but this model of art criticism must (again, in a broad sense) tacitly assume an ontology of 'art' in order to have an intelligible starting point for a reading, critique or discussion. A good geographer, however, might use her discipline's analytic axioms to approach the problem of 'art' in a decidedly different way.

Instead of asking 'What is art?' or 'Is this art successful?' a good geographer might ask questions along the lines of 'How is this space called "art" produced?' In other words, what are the specific historical, economic, cultural and discursive conjunctions that come together to form something called 'art' and moreover, to produce a space that we colloquially know as an 'art world'? The geographic question is not 'What is art' but 'How is art?' From a critical geographic perspective, the notion of a free-standing work of art would be seen as the fetishistic effect of a production process. Instead of approaching art from the vantage point of a consumer, a critical geographer might reframe the question of art in terms of spatial practice.

We can take this line of thinking even further. Instead of using geographic axioms to come up with an alternative 'interpretive' approach to art, we can use them in a normative sense. Whether we're geographers, artists, writers, curators, critics or anyone else, we can use geographic axioms self-reflexively to inform our own production.

If we accept Marx's argument that a fundamental characteristic of human existence is 'the production of material life itself' (that humans produce their own existence in dialectical relation to the rest of the world), and, following Lefebvre (and Marx) that production is a fundamentally spatial practice, then cultural production (like all production) is a spatial practice. [...]

[I]f one takes the production of space seriously, the concept applies not only to 'objects' of study or criticism, but to the ways one's own actions participate in the production of space. Geography, then, is not just a method of inquiry, but necessarily entails the production of a space of inquiry. Geographers might study the production of space, but through that study, they're also producing space. Put simply, geographers don't just study geography, they create geographies. [...]

Experimental geography means practices that take on the production of space in a self-reflexive way, practices which recognize that cultural production and the production of space cannot be separated from each other, and that cultural and intellectual production is a spatial practice. Moreover, experimental geography means not only seeing the production of space as an ontological condition, but actively experimenting with the production of space as an integral part of one's own practice. If human activities are inextricably spatial, then new forms of freedom and democracy can only emerge in dialectical relation to the production of new spaces. I deliberately use one of modernism's keywords, 'experimental', for two reasons. First is to acknowledge and affirm the modernist notion that things can be better, that humans are capable of improving their own conditions, to keep cynicism and defeatism at arm's length. Moreover, experimentation means production without guarantees, and producing new forms of space certainly comes without guarantees. Space is not deterministic, and the production of new spaces isn't easy. [...]

Experimental geography expands Walter Benjamin's call [in 'The Author as Producer'] for cultural workers to move beyond 'critique' as an end in itself and to take up a 'position' within the politics of lived experience. Following Benjamin, experimental geography takes for granted the fact that there can be no 'outside' of politics, because there can be no 'outside' to the production of space (and the production of space is, ipso facto, political). Moreover, experimental geography is a call to take seriously but ultimately move beyond cultural theories that equate new enunciations and new subjectivities as sufficient political ends in themselves. When decoupled from the production of new spaces, they are far too easily assimilated into the endless cycles of destruction and reconstitution characterizing cultural neoliberalism, a repetition Benjamin dubbed 'hell'.

The task of experimental geography, then, is to seize the opportunities that present themselves in the spatial practices of culture. To move beyond critical reflection, critique alone, and political 'attitudes', into the realm of practice. To experiment with creating new spaces, new ways of being. [...]

Trevor Paglen, extracts from 'Experimental Geography: From Cultural Production to the Production of Space', in *Experimental Geography: Radical Approaches to Landscape, Cartography and Urbanism*, ed. Nato Thompson (Brooklyn: Melville House, 2008) 30–33.

Claire Bishop, Lynne Cooke, Tim Griffin, Pierre Huyghe, Pamela M. Lee, Rirkrit Tiravanija, Andrea Zittel
Remote Possibilities: Land Art's Changing Terrain//2005

Tim Griffin A number of artists have recently executed high-profile projects in remote places – 'remote', at least, from traditional art-world centres. We can count three individuals participating today among them: Pierre and his recent voyage to Antarctica, Rirkrit and the Land in Thailand, and Andrea with her *High Desert Test Sites* near Joshua Tree. Realizing, of course, that there are significant differences among these projects, working in a 'remote' location seems to be a broader trend (think also of projects by Carsten Höller, Tacita Dean and Matthew Barney, among others). This development demands some comparison to work made by previous generations, such as the Land art of Robert Smithson and Michael Heizer, on the one hand, and the travels of artists like Bas Jan Ader or Hamish Fulton on the other. Is there any way that we can begin to characterize this way of working today, if only very broadly, while bearing these historical precedents in mind?

Claire Bishop To generalize perhaps too wildly, I think that a main difference between the Land artists of the late 1960s and 1970s and artists today can be characterized in terms of the medium with which they're engaged. If the precursors can be framed within an expanded field of sculpture, today's artists are working within an expanded cross-disciplinary field more likely to involve research as a geographer, social worker, anthropologist, activist or experimental architect. That said, there is a clear continuity in some of the projects you mention in terms of the lure of the remote.

But I think we may still need to differentiate between artists for whom the aesthetics of the remote landscape remains important (such as Matthew Barney and possibly Pierre) and those artists who engage critically with the social and political discourses that mark that landscape. The Center for Land Use Interpretation (CLUI) is a good example of the latter.

Pamela M. Lee My sense is that some of the artists discussed in these terms – CLUI, to follow Claire's lead, would be the prototype – might be 'reading' the earlier generation in a way that is closer to the Land artists' original thinking than the primary criticism was. With over thirty years of historical hindsight, it has become abundantly clear that the impulse to work in remote locations was less about a 'return to the land' as such – a kind of aesthetic nativism – than a critical engagement with the terms of artistic mediation, whether organized around institutions or forms of media.

Bishop I agree, Pamela. But there's no denying the gorgeousness of the landscape backdrops in those earlier works and the way in which the individual is set in relation to epic expanses. I'm thinking in particular of those photographs of Walter De Maria lying on the ground beside his *Mile Long Drawing* (1968), or the tiny person standing among Nancy Holt's *Sun Tunnels* (1973–76).

The question about mediation, however, makes me recall that the emergence of Land and installation art go hand in hand through the sixties. Both are grounded in the authenticity of one's first-hand experience of a site. So I wonder if we should also differentiate between contemporary and historical Land art on the basis of that famous 'indoor-outdoor' dialectic articulated by Smithson – and consider whether the 'indoor' itself has changed in recent decades with the rise of installation art. For example, Olafur Eliasson is one artist who deals with the paradoxical way in which such firsthand experiences (especially that of nature) are always already mediated (by ideas of the sublime or the 'uncontaminated'). You don't need to travel to a remote location to experience his exquisite fake sunsets or waterfalls. But it is telling that while Eliasson is at pains to reveal the mechanisms behind it, his work is nevertheless criticized for being too attractive or oversize.

Lee I think it's worth pursuing the lingering appeal to 'aesthetics' in this art, given that forms of artistic mediation are central *topoi* around which this work is organized, in both contemporary and historical iterations. In fact, the residual sublimity for which Eliasson's work is often criticized is continuous with many of the debates played out around Land art in the sixties; the technology has doubtless undergone radical change, but the rhetoric hangs on. Then, as now, the mechanisms supporting the production of the work were much in evidence, too. Smithson's non-site, however unequivalent with his Land art, necessarily revealed both social and historical influences swirling around the actuality of his 'objects'. Perhaps one of the historical legacies of this work has to do with our (not so) latent attachment to the aesthetic: that the 'remote' might stand as code for the 'aesthetic'. In which case, maybe we haven't travelled so far after all.

Cooke Could the criticism of those works by Eliasson that are monumental in scale or budget have to do with their lack of the kind of irony or self-conscious wryness one finds in, say, Tacita Dean's deadpan audio piece *Trying to Find the Spiral Jetty* (1997)? Do the lack of self-reflection and absence of an ironizing modesty of means in work currently presented in the institution, which nevertheless draws directly on these sixties precedents, indicate an indifference to the site/non-site dialectic, Smithson's most crucial gambit, rather than a substantive reworking of it?

Pierre Huyghe In my case, the issue of the 'remote' place is not exactly the point. The movement that brings you to the outside is as important as the outside itself. It's a question of displacement. What's interesting is how you create this conceptual displacement, the journey that brings you to this elsewhere, not the destination itself. I'm less concerned about place than the production of situations and complex, heterogeneous territories.

Our journey to Antarctica had nothing to do with going far away per se. A boat is a temporary habitat moving towards the unpredictable, a collective movement, a social time. Then it becomes about how you translate that experience. The displacement is in the constant renegotiations that take place between the people engaged in the journey. You can think of Foucault's idea of the heterotopia as a kind of counterplace, the place that's outside all other places but also includes them. And that could be found anywhere – in the middle of the city, at the hospital, in a museum. Going somewhere like Antarctica is an attempt to produce a place without pre-existing protocol, a no-knowledge zone. It might be easier to find this in a place that's not overcrowded with meaning, rules, culture, even longitude and latitude.

Lee Pierre, I know we're in agreement about the 'remote', even if we are coming from different places. (From my end, much of this would have to do with the critique of exteriority – and the values of immanence – taken up by much writing on globalization.) Here, though, I want to address the reception of this work through aesthetic terms because, alas, that is often the way it has been characterized. Lynne is right on the mark when she points to the ways in which today's artists sustain some degree of historical reflection about their projects, thereby relieving them, at least partially, of the problem of aesthetics.

Bishop Pam, I think your earlier point is brilliant: The remote is definitely coded as the aesthetic, and to my mind this is more interesting than discussions about the 'exotic' or the 'local'. But I would also want to defend the aesthetic. Smithson's work has a distinct aesthetic, for example, although it works entirely against those conventions of landscape found on calendars and postcards – making you read decrepit industrial interventions alongside the semi-spoiled nature. In a different key, and bearing in mind the 'social turn' of much recent contemporary art, we could think of Francis Alÿs' *When Faith Moves Mountains* (2002), which he describes as a 'land art for the landless'. Like Smithson, Alÿs undercuts a gorgeous landscape through human intervention: five hundred volunteers engaged in the Sisyphean task of moving a massive sand dune by four inches. Perhaps ironically, the work is distributed in the form of a postcard. It also exists as a video and (less verifiably) as an orally disseminated urban myth.

Andrea Zittel I have to admit to feeling like an oddball in this discussion so far, because I don't really consider *High Desert Test Sites* (*HDTS*) a remote project, and I've wondered if Rirkrit thinks similarly about the Land. My first interest in moving to the desert was in finding the most direct and cohesive way to present my own work. I wanted to create a forum that could integrate the locations of cultural or functional reference, the site of production, and the final site for viewing into a single location. But I was also drawn to the desert because it is the ultimate symbol of the 'frontier' – though in an expanded sense, as a space where lack of structure creates gaps in which innovation or change can happen. In this sense, you could say that the upheaval in Europe after World War I involved social and political frontiers, which set the stage for the Bauhaus and other utopian fantasies.

What I probably knew before *HDTS* and have now experienced first-hand is that geographical frontiers (at least in the United States) are a quickly disappearing entity. Life speeds up, distances shrink and populations swell … eventually settling all open territories. So for me it's interesting to see what other kinds of frontiers can still exist. Maybe the documentary *Dogtown and Z-Boys* (2001) describes a kind of frontier in Venice Beach in the seventies, for example, and I often wonder what an analogous 'frontier' could be in the arts. Maybe CLUI has found a new territory in which to operate, another kind of frontier, because they have created a fuzzy space running parallel to mainstream art (yes, we are all pretty much mainstream) that is still open for invention.

Rirkrit Tiravanija To clarify something about the Land, it is actually a collaborative undertaking, in the same way that Pierre's trip to Antarctica was. Last September, in fact, the Land became a foundation. Officially, I am the chair of the board but only voluntarily. The other board members are Kamin Lertchaiprasert, a Thai artist with whom I created the Land, and Uthit Atimana, another artist who is also a professor and the director of new-media art at Chiang Mai University. Kamin and I joined up roughly seven years ago, each of us having his own very different idea about cultivating a piece of land that would be utilized as a point of convergence. One thing we agreed on was that we didn't want to label the place. We've never even wanted to make it part of the sphere of art – although now we are unable to avoid that discussion, and perhaps we should admit that we are artists, as are most of the participants.

Regarding my own interests there, it's significant that I had previously been in a discussion with Pierre, as well as Dominique Gonzalez-Foerster, Philippe Parreno, Liam Gillick, Carsten Höller and Jorge Pardo about finding a place, a house, that could be a meeting point and rest stop away from our routines. Most of us at that time were very nomadic in work and life, and I think there was a need for some distance from the circuitry of the art world – to have a thinking 'site'. But even as I say that, I think it's nonsense to label artists 'nomadic' or say that they are travelling in an international art circuit today. The issue of nomadism has been with the artist even before Duchamp or Max Ernst moved to New York or Gauguin went to the South Pacific: artists are mobile by habit or, perhaps, desire. What's different about the present landscape, I think, is what constitutes the exterior. The Land is concerned primarily not with positive/negative, solid/liquid, mass-scale nature/culture, flux/non-flux, site/non-site dichotomies but rather with the presence of activities – with local and not-local, with living conditions. When Pierre took his trip to Antarctica, he didn't go alone to make his work, he invited other artists along to make their own work or collaborate. When Matthew made his project in Brazil, it was for Carnival. Today, the exterior is about the social.

Bishop Rirkrit, I completely agree with you that today the exterior lies in the social, in that so many artists posit the latter as the only authentic point of resistance to capital. But I wonder if you could comment on the idea of 'remoteness' that Tim mentioned in the introduction. Am I right to understand that the Land is close to the university in Chiang Mai and therefore not remotely 'remote' in the sense we are framing it?

Tiravanija That's right. The Land is twenty minutes outside of Chiang Mai, a provincial city, which is about 450 miles from Bangkok, and so it's no longer a remote place. Many people from the West have been there to work on projects or just to visit. Even so, the distance opens up possibilities.

Griffin Pierre, you've been to the Land. How would you describe working there?

Huyghe When Rirkrit asked me to come, I went there having in mind this garden where you would grow a community. There are two things that the Land is missing – an administrative building for the foundation and a meditation hall. So, I'm thinking about these needs. You can't erase the idea of the local. You need to be corrupted by the context but without forgetting that you're not from it.

Rirkrit has built a platform that could become a tool for the people there. In that sense, you can sort of eliminate the problem of exoticism, since exoticism is often a problem of representation. By attaching a use value to the project, you also start to get around the problem of representation and enter into a kind of post-representational situation. Any fiction has to produce a reality. That may in a certain way relate to the film that Philippe Parreno made there, which has a very fictional aspect to it – almost like a science-fiction film. He didn't want it to be simply a report.

Bishop Pierre is pointing to another difference between this project and its precursors of the sixties and seventies. There is a functional motive behind the Land, as there is with Andrea's *Test Sites*: These are pavilions and units to be used by a specific community.

Tiravanija Yes, in fact, the Land in itself is just a land, a levelled field to be acted on, and we request that this action be in the sphere of the everyday. Which is to say that we do not encourage earthworks unless we can eat, drink or live from them. At this point we are more interested in sustainable infrastructure than outdoor sculpture.

Griffin So clearly the idea of use value is central to the project of the Land. One thing that is emerging in this conversation, which bears remarking on, is that many of these projects involve a social or collaborative component, which would seem counter-intuitive given the traditional connotations of a solitary engagement (perhaps even a romantic one) with distant sites. But as Claire and others have pointed out, these social components do not preclude a romantic or aesthetic use of the figure of the landscape – which is true even of Pierre's Antarctic journey. Does this balance of the social and the aesthetic meaningfully distinguish recent projects from those of the sixties and seventies? [...]

[I] wonder whether the 'social' aspect of these works necessarily relates to the collaborative, communal connotations of that word; or are there examples of work today that engage with site in a more specifically critical way?

Bishop To twist that question and refer to artists outside the United States: We've already mentioned Alÿs' project in Lima, but I'd like to bring up Jennifer Allora and Guillermo Calzadilla's work on the island of Vieques, Puerto Rico – a location that from my European perspective fulfils the criterion of 'remoteness' but that has been integral to US military strategy. Their engagement with this island is similar to CLUI's interest in land use but is played out in a way that productively merges activism (assisting local campaigns against use of the island as a bombing range) with artistic actions and videos. And so their practice is socially collaborative but not in the sense of forming an artists' retreat or experimental community. For example, in *Land Mark (Foot Prints)* (2001–2), demonstrators could have their slogans put onto the soles of trainers, which left marks on the island sand; these formed counter-representations of the site's function and were in turn photographed by the artists. While it would be overestimating their work to compare it to *Spiral Jetty*'s conceptual density and decentred objecthood (Earthwork, article, film ...), Allora and Calzadilla do present a politically informed yet poetic angle on many of the subjects of our discussion: artistic mediation, critical engagement with a site, global politics, scale and sublimity, the temporality of art versus that of pragmatic action.

Lee I'd like to pick up on a point raised by Rirkrit having to do with the problematics of the 'local' implicitly addressed by much of this work versus the terms thought to be opposed to it, the global or the nomadic. Just a few years ago, when Lucy Lippard published *The Lure of the Local* (1997), that old sixties mantra 'Think globally, act locally' still retained a certain political (read: activist) currency. These days, however, I doubt that we are so innocent about the virtues of artistic 'locality'. By the same token, I suspect some of us participating in this roundtable assume a rather jaundiced attitude about the relationship between travel and work. A colleague of mine recently told me about a new genre of literary theory called 'eco-criticism'. I'm not in any position to represent this movement accurately, but I gather one of its tasks is to undo that opposition between the local and the remote (or global) and, along with it, to uncover the ideological underpinnings that sponsor that binary. This would be one way to put pressure on the notion that we can escape the art-world circuitry – or at least challenge the language by which we engage it. Perhaps this is where Pierre's notion of the fictive dimension of a project like Philippe's film at the Land enters the picture. [...]

Tim Griffin (chair), et al., extracts from 'Remote Possibilities: A Roundtable Discussion on Land Art's Changing Terrain', *Artforum* (Summer 2005) 289–95.

Helen & Newton Harrison
On Ecocivility//2009

From a Corbusien vision to any vast apartment building
to the 2000 foot tall structure in Dubai
Big Box Buildings are places
where each person enters at the bottom
and first by rapid elevation
then by traversing
a non-windowed hallway
reaches a mostly modest
sometimes opulent

public or private living or working space
These behaviours
repeated millions of times
normalize the social alienation
of Big Box Buildings
where the nature of the structure itself
determines that a community and/or a civil society
cannot take form in the populations within them
The loss of social capital is profound
Here we design a new structure
and a new use of space
based on an as yet untested premise
a complex synthesis of
normal elements in everyday life
placed in an unexpected relationship
basically a vertically designed small town
following the definition of complex systems
but behaving as any small town might
with the help of two interlocking forms
that comprise this urban ecosystem
The first is a vertical promenade
perhaps four blocks long
with side streets
The work of this promenade
is to host an activity and to be a place
a stage on which people in a community meet and mix
It is a leisurely meeting and mixing
having different purposiveness and tempo
from daily activities in a workplace
And like any promenade
it is marked by people
physically tuning their walking
to a common movement and rhythm
as is typical in all urban ecologies
This is a basic homeostatic
or self-regulating mechanism
by which the community as a whole
maintains awareness of the well-being
of the individuals who comprise it
and by which the sense of community

is reaffirmed collectively
It is an arena
in which the communal drama is publicly enacted
Even the funicular
which acts as transport
shares the leisurely pace
contributing to
the experience of constancy and change
defining self and group in the context of society and time
In fact this is the urban metabolism at work
As in any small town
the ways to traverse it are many
On foot
on a rapid elevator
or a funicular and occasionally on an escalator
Streets vary between 15 and 20 feet wide
and everybody is within 5 to 10 minutes
in physical time
of anyone anywhere and anyplace
Traversing it becomes an adventure
in diversity of experience
Internal flexibility permits evolution
and over time new patterns will emerge
which may generate new permissions
to improvise new relationships
between people and people
people and place
place and place

Helen & Newton Harrison, 'On Ecocivility' (2009) (theharrisonstudio.net)

Tomás Saraceno
In Conversation with Stefano Boeri and Hans Ulrich Obrist//2005

[Boeri and Obrist for *Domus* magazine] *Do you have a problem with gravity?*

[Saraceno] Whoa, no idea. I think Cedric Price was once asked a similar question. Fortunately, we don't have problems, only opportunities. I like the idea that a problem can become an opportunity, a problem as the driving force behind developing something new. In your question there is half of the answer: gravity is a physical psycho-social relationship.

Tell us about your Air-Port-City project.

My idea for an Air-Port-City is to create platforms or habitable cells made up of cities that float in the air. These change form and join together like clouds. This freedom of movement is borrowed from the orderly structure of airports, and it allows for the creation of the first international city. Airports are divided by 'air-side' and 'land-side'; on the 'air-side' you are under the jurisdiction of international law. Your every action is judged according to international norms. Air-Port-City is like a flying airport; you will be able legally to travel across the world while taking advantage of airport regulations. This structure seeks to challenge today's political, social, cultural and military restrictions in an attempt to re-establish new concepts of synergy.

Cells made up of cities?

Up in the sky there will be this cloud, a habitable platform that floats in the air, changing form and merging with other platforms just as clouds do. It will fly through the atmosphere pushed by the winds, both local and global, in an attempt to equalize the (social) temperature and differences in pressure. It will be a sustainable and mobile migration. These aerial cities will be in a permanent state of transformation, similar to nomadic cities. After all, gypsies never go back to the same place, simply because the place is constantly changing.

Is it a flying utopia?

Air-Port-City is like a huge kinetic structure that works towards a real economic transformation. Moving from a personal 'belief' to a collective one is the first step in the realization of this idea. After the unification of Europe, a 'europeanafroamericanasianoceaniasfydsdf' will be created. Like continental drift at the beginning of the world, the new cities will search for their positions in the air in order to find their place in the universe. From cirrocumulus to cirrocumuluscity! It provides feedback so as to enable a faster process of communication, capable of imagining more elastic and dynamic border rules (political, geographical, etc.) for a new space/cyberspace.

And what about your flying gardens?

Flying gardens are part of the Air-Port-City family. These spatial and temporal characteristics are needed for a sustainable occupation, a necessary invasion made up of plants, humans and animals. The geographic range of most plant and animal species is limited by climatic factors and any shift will have an impact on the organisms living there. Climate changes faster than plants can disperse to new, more suitable areas. A flying garden (think of it as multiple Amazons in transcontinental flight) with 62 different cities joined in the air will generate a spherical shape; the interior of the sphere will enclose enough air to lift the city and its flight will depend on solar energy. There will be 'airplants' from the genus Tillandsia. Native to South America and Africa, these are true air plants: they derive all their nutrition from the air, imbibing rain and dew and whatever nutrients the air brings to them through their leaf tissues. There are no roots for water and nutrient uptake so they are quite air-sufficient.

Who are your heroes?

It's difficult to identify just one hero. Maybe it's better to have many. Unfortunately, some cultures still need to identify with individual heroes. Here is my pick: 'Tensegrity' sculptural structures invented by the artist Kenneth Snelson that were later taken up by R. Buckminster Fuller, who went on to develop his own theory.

Your work deals with natural processes, as well as with dreams of transgravitation and elevation. What is your link to science? Do you have dialogues with scientists?

I will try to answer this by talking about aerogel. A year ago, with the help of engineers and lawyers, I took advantage of an application of a material called aerogel, which has been used in spacecraft. These vehicles use a gas that is lighter than air to rise up: a mix of helium and hydrogen and other gases. Aerogel gives these vehicles the possibility of flying solely on solar energy. These vehicles are the more efficient alternatives for mobility in the future and for a possible 'colonization' of the sky. There will no longer be a need for airports and air pollution will cease; they will be efficient alternatives for new satellites and will create new possibilities for communication. This will allow for greater energy saving and give people not only data but also an incredible mobility, thus permitting a constant redefining of boundaries and of national, cultural and racial identities.

Tomás Saraceno, Stefano Boeri and Hans Ulrich Obrist, interview, *Domus*, no. 883 (July/August 2005).

Ingeborg Reichle
Art in the Age of Technoscience//2009

[...] Viewed from a certain distance, it appears that the closely watched demarcation line between art and science, which currently both sides are trying to break down, is a fairly recent phenomenon. Descriptions of attempts to overcome the two systems, which are conceived of as diametrically opposed, often employ terms such as 'transgression' or 'hybridity'. The underlying assumption is that art and science contradict one another because such very different epistemes are involved, therefore never the twain shall meet.

The division between the arts and sciences is a legacy of the Enlightenment and the nineteenth century; science began to base itself on the ideals of neutrality and objectivity, and art increasingly expressed itself in ways that invoked subjectivity and artistic genius. The claim of being objective led to a changed self-conception in the natural sciences, because the precision of their methods appeared to guarantee the liability and correctness of all findings. This also led to the rapprochement of disciplines that had formerly been separate, such as physics and mathematics. The avant-garde art movements of the twentieth century merely registered the existence of science: it had become an alien cultural domain for them and they saw no possibility to overcome this. Moreover, art was condemned to an endless cycle of self-referentiality.

The opposition between art and science found particular expression in science's claim of the universal validity and mathematical formulation of its findings, and in art's breaking of rules and lawless subversion that deliberately defied verification. In the instances where twentieth-century avant-gardes purportedly drew upon and cited science, art did not seriously engage with science but instead pursued a rigorous course of inversion: art attempted to visualize that which science suppressed, neglected or simply ignored. Marcel

Duchamp, for example, regarded the laws and subject matter of science as pure myths that were no more real than the rules of a game of chance.

Since the 1960s art appears to understand its field of activity as work on the cultural conditions of social processes; it no longer seeks to express the 'universal', but instead turns its attention to the exemplary and orients itself on interventions and concrete changes that it could possibly induce. Art has long operated with local and temporary strategies within a field of practices, which do not stop short of any context, including science and the laboratory. Like any other institution or subsystem of society, science and scientific research have also become a location and a subject of artistic reflection.

Due to this circumstance art has recently begun to include the word 'research' in its vocabulary and has introduced the term *artistic research*. This term shifts the focus to the linkage of art with other spheres of knowledge, theory, the discourses of art and its function; the performative element of contemporary art, and the artist as subject are foregrounded and the artwork or art object in its exhibition context are neglected. Today art is readily seen as an independent form of epistemic practice in order to break science's monopoly in scientific research methods. To this end artists who engage in experiments and research – and who reflect to a high degree their performative approach and the materials of their actions are contrasted with scientific researchers, who allegedly utilize the tools and semantization processes of scientific representation processes without reflecting on them and only too willingly obfuscate the complex and laborious process of knowledge acquisition.

By turning to content and methods from other disciplines and contexts artists are increasingly entering foreign territory where the rules are frequently in opposition to artistic approaches. In science practical research generally begins with the posing of a question which defines the problem to which answers are sought; this facilitates a target-oriented manner of proceeding. A further step is to break down the problem, usually into several discrete parts, which are investigated in parallel or consecutively. The choice of methods, which may lead to solving the problem, are usually left to the discretion of the researcher. The important thing is that the application of whatever methods are selected results in intersubjectively verifiable propositions concerning the facts of the case and that these are capable of being reproduced (under the same experimental conditions) at any time and the same results will be obtained. In science methods are not applied for their own sake but only with reference to a specific research problem, whereas in art, the utilization of a particular method is often an integral component of the concept of an artistically motivated project or its material result.

In contemporary art practice artists avail themselves of the most varied forms of articulation whereby the development of a method, or strict adherence to a foregiven method, can be part of an artistic form of expression. A 'methodical' manner of proceeding by an artist, however, is only rarely effective outside of his/her work or circle of influence. Thus in the case of artists who do turn to methodical procedures it is necessary to analyse their projects and artworks in depth.

If one examines the methods of production and operation in both art and science, many commonalities come to light: collecting, archiving, observing, speculating, abstracting, modelling, experimentally examining and using analogies and metaphors. Yet in spite of artistic and scientific practices seemingly not being far apart, for example, researching and experimenting, the ideal of knowledge in the natural sciences is viewed as empirical and objective and artistic creativity is devalorized as rather speculative and subjective. Although scientific experiments are conducted with the goal of achieving new knowledge in a methodical, systematic and verifiable manner, experimentation and research are understood as creative intellectual activities and thus an intuitive character is ascribed to them. At the same time the development of the modern natural sciences is replete with attempts to erase the traces of researchers' subjectivity, for example, by utilizing rigorous scientific methodology, technical apparatus and applying mathematical procedures. By contrast, art seems to have greater freedom to choose its forms of expression, which are not subject to the paradigms of rationality and causality. Yet many artists and groups of artists do proceed in a manner that is informed by system and empiricism and can in no way be understood as arbitrary or purely subjective. Paradoxically, exceptional scientific achievements that decisively contribute to new directions in science as well as artistic achievements are not often attributed to objective or systematic ways of proceeding, but instead to the creativity and visionary power of both scientists and artists. [...]

In recent years art has reflected on and interrogated the social reality of the laboratory in a variety of very different ways, but the sociocultural determination of the production of scientific facts has always been an integral part of the artistic approach to research fields such as molecular biology or tissue culture. Artists thematize in best avant-gardist manner the processes of scientific praxis and what science does not describe, what it leaves out. It is almost as though artists are following the dictum of Joseph Beuys by incessantly declaring the end of art. Nevertheless, art that is created in a scientific context or in forms of artistic research inevitably leads to academic and scientized art. By adapting and adopting scientific methods, processes and materials, art – whose audience has long since become nebulous and inaccessible – has embarked on a course with an uncertain outcome. On the one side art projects that present living sculptures or transgenic organisms in the context of an exhibition attract a great deal of attention and challenge both institutions and curators, but on the other art out of the laboratory is covered with so many layers of meaning that the reception of newer art trends, like bio art, is fraught with much misunderstanding. Ultimately, it is to be hoped that bridges will not only be built between two cultures and between science and art, but also between science and its technologies and our everyday life so that we are better prepared for the emergence of a biocybernetic humanity. [...]

Ingeborg Reichle, extract from *Art in the Age of Technoscience: Genetic Engineering, Robotics and Artificial Life in Contemporary Art* (Berlin and New York: Springer Verlag, 2009) 213–16.

Oliver Grau
The History of Telepresence: Automata, Illusion and Rejecting the Body//2000

[...] Telepresence combines the contents of three archetypal areas of thought: automation, virtual illusion and a non-physical vision of the self. These notions collide in the concept of telepresence, which enables the user to be present in three different places at the same time: a) in the spatio-temporal location determined by the user's body, b) by means of teleperception in the simulated, virtual image space (the point to which attempts in art history have led so far to obtain Virtual Reality), and c) by means of teleaction in the place where, for example, a robot is situated, directed by one's own movement and providing orientation through its sensors.

The media-induced epistemology of telepresence seems to be a paradox. Telepresence is indeed a mediated perspective that surmounts great dimensions; however, perception will soon be enriched in the virtual environment. The so-called 'lesser senses' will be amended (feeling, smell and even taste), thereby eradicating the abstracting and term-generating function of distance. The threefold nature of telepresence raises fundamental questions in telepistemology, questions about how distance affects our capacity for knowledge and discovery. Aesthetic theories since the eighteenth century have seen distance as a precondition of reflection, self discovery, and the experiencing of art and nature. This is distance understood primarily as the accrual of overview and not, in a more ordinary sense, as physical separation. In his intellectual collaboration with Ernst Cassirer,[1] Aby Warburg stressed the intellectual, awareness-raising power of distance in his *Mmemosyne Atlas*.[2] The result of this physical and psychological distancing from the phenomenon is a conceptual space (*Denkraum*) – the precondition for awareness of an object distinct from the conscious subject. It seemed to him that this was already threatened at the beginning of our century by the sudden proximity created by the telegraph.[3] This idea was inherited and expanded in the theories of aesthetic distance offered by Theodor Adorno,[4] Hans Jonas[5] and Michel Serres.[6]

Telepresence is not, however, always seen as a barrier to reflection and self-discovery. In contrast to Warburg stands Paul Valéry, whose 'The Conquest of Ubiquity' predicted long-distance transmission of sense-experiences. A kind of spiritual father of McLuhan, Valéry envisioned an art medium that, like electricity or tap water,[7] could be available everywhere to relay polysensual stimuli:

> Works will attain a kind of ubiquity. Reacting on our call, works of art will obediently present themselves anywhere at any time. They will cease to exist only in themselves, but will be present anywhere, wherever there is someone and a suitable set of equipment … We [will] find it completely natural … to receive these extremely swift mutable images and oscillations out of which our sensual organs … will make up all that we know. I do not know if there has ever been a philosopher who dreamed up a company specializing in the free home delivery of sensually perceptible reality.[8]

If we did not know that these comments were written in 1928, they could be describing contemporary net-based telepresence. It seems as though soon a fusion of all the senses with a virtual image machine will produce a compelling illusion of intimate bodily closeness for the spatially distant observer. In the animated image, the observer is electronically present at light-speed, via robot, possibly at several locations simultaneously. Telepresence is transforming the classical perception of space, which had been linked primarily to physical location. The immediate local subject of experience is superseded by the locationless, ubiquitous telerobotics-user. Distance as Cassirer described it is giving way to Valéry's notion of visual and tactile experience provided on demand anywhere, anytime.

Today we are on the threshold of change with regard to a location-oriented concept of persons. Telepresence has far-reaching consequences for work, culture, law and politics. However, there is hope for a global shift in consciousness. Impetus for this was formulated a few years ago with the Gaia-perspective. The telepresence installation *T-Vision* by ART+COM (1995–99) attempted to visualize this by aesthetic means. The entire face of the earth was generated out of topographical data and satellite images. Using a level of detail to manage scene complexity, the work presents a model of the earth as seen from a million kilometres above its surface, or at the level of a desktop in Berlin.[9] It's a bit like Eric Davis described it: 'Spinning the earth, you feel like a god; plunging toward its surface, like a falling angel.'[10] Simon Penny's *Traces* (1999) is still a work in progress, but it promises to take an important step towards an art of telepresence. *Traces* is a project for three networked CAVES [Cave Automatic Virtual Environments] in Tokyo, Bonn and Chicago. Users see (or will see) large virtual spaces, hear spatially distributed sound, and experience vibrations through the floor. The user interacts with gossamer traces that have movements and volumes, but are translucent and ephemeral. Each CAVE will use stereo cameras to construct real-time body maps of its inhabitants. Following Penny's concept, the interaction will take the form of real-time collaborative sculpturing with light, created through dancing with telematic partners.[11] Consequently, *Traces* will give users the opportunity to experience a dispersed body and to interact with traces of other remote bodies. The division of body and mind is not only easily traced back to the dualistic conception of human beings, but also to the Gnostic tradition of devaluing corporeality. According to this conception, the spirit is simulated to an increasing extent, whereas the body is restrained in its function of getting sensual knowledge of the world, generally by tactile experiences through the skin.[12] The experience conveyed by machines replaces the real body, and with it embodied experience. By networking various technobodies, telepresence makes possible a multitude of spaces of experience and bodies. Those might even be set up to provide the user with logically inconsistent experiences. The ability to move with and through different bodies intensifies this paradox.

The desire to overcome physical distance, to project ourselves outside the constraints of our own physical bodies, has always been a powerful motivation for both art and technology. It has spurred us to develop extraordinary robotic and telecommunication technologies, and to conceive of technologies that are more extraordinary still. It has inspired art that strives to bring about what the technology itself could not realize. Telerobotics and the Internet mark the latest stage in this development, a union of fact and fiction that is both technological and artistic.

1   [footnote 41 in source] Cassirer, *Individuum und Kosmos* (1927) (Darmstadt: Wissenschaftliche Buchgesellschaft, 1963) 179.

2   [42] Warburg, 'Einleitung zum Mnemosyne-Atlas', ed. Ilsebill Barta Fliedl and Christoph Geismar (Vienna, 1991) 171–3. Erwin Panosfky emphasized the central function of perspective for the construction of the ego and personal space. 'Die Perspektive als Symbolische Form', *Verüffentlichungen der Bibliothek Warburg* (Berlin: Teubner, 1927) 287.

3   [43] Warburg, *Images from the Region of the Pueblo Indians of North America* (1923) (Ithaca: Cornell University Press, 1995 [1923]).

4   [44] Adorno wrote: 'Distance is what nearness to a work's substance requires first. In the Kantian term of indifference, which demands an aesthetic behaviour that does not seize the object, does not devour it, this is noted. ... Distance, concerning the phenomenon, transcends the mere

existence of a work of art; its total nearness would be its total integration.' (trans. Oliver Grau) Adorno: *Ästhetische Theorie* (Frankfurt am Main: Suhrkamp, 1973) 460.

5 [45] Jonas, *Der Adel des Sehens. Eine Untersuchung zur Phänomenologie der Sinne* (1954), in *Organismus und Freiheit. Ansätze zu einer philosophischen Biologie* (Göttingen: Vandenhoeck & Ruprecht, 1973) 198–219.

6 [46] Serres points out that only in the fixed artwork whose elements the onlooker 'sets into motion' does the spatial configuration become a vivid sensuous event. Serres, Carpaccio: *Ästhetische Zugänge* (Reinbek: Rowohlt, 1981) 152.

7 [47] Valéry, 'Die Emberung der Allgegenwärtigkeit', *Über Kunst* (Frankfurt am Main, 1973) 47 (trans. Oliver Grau).

8 [48] Ibid.

9 [49] www.artcom.de/projects/t_vision/welcome.en

10 [50] Davis, *Techgnosis: Myth, Magic + Mysticism in the Age of Information* (New York: Harmony Books, 1998) 305.

11 [51] http://imk.gmd.de/docs/ww/mars/proj1_4.mhtml

12 [52] Regarding a cultural history of the skin: Claudia Benthien, *Hau: Literaturgeschichte – Körperbilder – Grenzdiskurse* (Reinbek: Rowohlt, 1999).

Oliver Grau, extract from 'The History of Telepresence: Automata, Illusion and Rejecting the Body', in *The Robot in the Garden: Telerobotics and Telepistemology in the Age of the Internet*, ed. Ken Goldberg (Cambridge, Massachusetts: The MIT Press, 2000) 239–43.

Donna Haraway
A Cyborg Manifesto//1985

This [text] is an effort to build an ironic political myth faithful to feminism, socialism and materialism. Perhaps more faithful as blasphemy is faithful, than as reverent worship and identification. Blasphemy has always seemed to require taking things very seriously. I know no better stance to adopt from within the secular-religious, evangelical traditions of United States politics, including the politics of socialist feminism. Blasphemy protects one from the moral majority within, while still insisting on the need for community. Blasphemy is not apostasy. Irony is about contradictions that do not resolve into larger wholes, even dialectically, about the tension of holding incompatible things together because both or all are necessary and true. Irony is about humour and serious play. It is also a rhetorical strategy and a political method, one I would like to see more honoured within socialist-feminism. At the centre of my ironic faith, my blasphemy, is the image of the cyborg.

A cyborg is a cybernetic organism, a hybrid of machine and organism, a creature of social reality as well as a creature of fiction. Social reality is lived social relations, our most important political construction, a world-changing fiction. The international women's movements have constructed 'women's experience', as well as uncovered or discovered this crucial collective object. This experience is a fiction and fact of the most crucial, political kind. Liberation rests on the construction of the consciousness, the imaginative apprehension, of oppression, and so of possibility. The cyborg is a matter of fiction and lived experience that changes what counts as women's experience in the late twentieth century. This is a struggle over life and death, but the boundary between science fiction and social reality is an optical illusion.

Contemporary science fiction is full of cyborgs – creatures simultaneously animal and machine, who populate worlds ambiguously natural and crafted. Modern medicine is also full of cyborgs, of couplings between organism and machine, each conceived as coded devices, in an intimacy and with a power that was not generated in the history of sexuality. Cyborg 'sex' restores some of the lovely replicative baroque of ferns and invertebrates (such nice organic prophylactics against heterosexism). Cyborg replication is uncoupled from organic reproduction. Modern production seems like a dream of cyborg colonization work, a dream that makes the nightmare of Taylorism seem idyllic. And modern war is a cyborg orgy, coded by C3I, command-control communication intelligence, an $84 billion item in 1984's US defence budget. I am making an argument for the cyborg as a fiction mapping our social and bodily reality and as an imaginative resource suggesting some very fruitful couplings. Michel Foucault's biopolitics is a flaccid premonition of cyborg politics, a very open field.

By the late twentieth century, our time, a mythic time, we are all chimeras, theorized and fabricated hybrids of machine and organism; in short, we are cyborgs. The cyborg is our ontology; it gives us our politics. The cyborg is a condensed image of both imagination and material reality, the two joined centres structuring any possibility of historical transformation. In the traditions of 'Western' science and politics - the tradition of racist, male-dominant capitalism; the tradition of progress; the tradition of the appropriation of nature as resource for the productions of culture; the tradition of reproduction of the self from the reflections of the other – the relation between organism and machine has been a border war. The stakes in the border war have been the territories of production, reproduction and imagination. This [text] is an argument for pleasure in the confusion of boundaries and for responsibility in their construction. It is also an effort to contribute to socialist-feminist culture and theory in a postmodernist, non-naturalist mode and in the utopian tradition of imagining a world without gender, which is perhaps a world without genesis, but maybe also a world without end. The cyborg incarnation is outside salvation history. Nor does it mark time on an Oedipal calendar, attempting to heal the terrible cleavages of gender in an oral symbiotic utopia or post-Oedipal apocalypse. As Zoë Sofoulis argues in her unpublished manuscript on Jacques Lacan, Melanie Klein and nuclear culture, 'Lacklein', the most terrible and perhaps the most promising monsters in cyborg worlds are embodied in non-Oedipal narratives with a different logic of repression, which we need to understand for our survival.

The cyborg is a creature in a post-gender world; it has no truck with bisexuality pre-Oedipal symbiosis, unalienated labour, or other seductions to organic wholeness through a final appropriation of all the powers of the parts into a higher unity. In a sense, the cyborg has no origin story in the Western sense – a final irony since the cyborg is also the awful apocalyptic telos of the 'West's' escalating dominations of abstract individuation, an ultimate self untied at last from all dependency, a man in space. An origin story in the 'Western', humanist sense depends on the myth of original unity, fullness, bliss and terror, represented by the phallic mother from whom all humans must separate, the task of individual development and of history, the twin potent myths inscribed most powerfully for us in psychoanalysis and Marxism. Hilary Klein has argued that both Marxism and psychoanalysis, in their concepts of labour and of individuation and gender formation, depend on the plot of original unity out of which difference must be produced and enlisted in a drama of escalating domination of woman/nature. The cyborg skips the step of original unity, of identification with nature in the Western sense. This is its illegitimate promise that might lead to subversion of its teleology as star wars.

The cyborg is resolutely committed to partiality, irony, intimacy and perversity. It is oppositional, utopian and completely without innocence. No longer structured by the polarity of public and private, the cyborg defines a technological polis based partly on a revolution of social relations in the *oikos*, the household. Nature and culture are reworked; the one can no longer be the resource for appropriation or incorporation by the other. The relationships for forming wholes from parts, including those of polarity and hierarchical domination, are at issue in the cyborg world. Unlike the hopes of Frankenstein's monster, the cyborg does not expect its father to save it through a restoration of the garden; that is, through the fabrication of a heterosexual mate, through its completion in a finished whole, a city and cosmos. The cyborg does not dream of community on the model of the organic family, this time without the Oedipal project. The cyborg would not recognize the Garden of Eden; it is not made of mud and cannot dream of returning to dust. Perhaps that is why I want to see if cyborgs can subvert the apocalypse of returning to nuclear dust in the manic compulsion to name the Enemy. Cyborgs are not reverent; they do not re-member the cosmos. They are wary of holism, but needy for connection – they seem to have a natural feel for united front politics, but without the vanguard party. The main trouble with cyborgs, of course, is that they are the illegitimate offspring of militarism and patriarchal capitalism, not to mention state socialism. But illegitimate offspring are often exceedingly unfaithful to their origins. Their fathers, after all, are inessential.

I will return to the science fiction of cyborgs, but now I want to signal three crucial boundary breakdowns that make the following political-fictional (political-scientific) analysis possible. By the late twentieth century in United States scientific culture, the boundary between human and animal is thoroughly breached. The last beachheads of uniqueness have been polluted if not turned into amusement parks – language, tool, use, social behaviour, mental events, nothing really convincingly settles the separation of human and animal. And many people no longer feel the need for such a separation; indeed, many branches of feminist culture affirm the pleasure of connection of human and other living creatures. Movements for animal rights are not irrational denials of human uniqueness; they are a clear-sighted recognition of connection across the discredited breach of nature and culture. Biology and evolutionary theory over the last two centuries have simultaneously produced modern organisms as objects of knowledge and reduced the line between humans and animals to a faint trace re-etched in ideological struggle or professional disputes between life and social science. Within this framework, teaching modern Christian creationism should be fought as a form of child abuse.

Biological-determinist ideology is only one position opened up in scientific culture for arguing the meanings of human animality. There is much room for radical political people to contest the meanings of the breached boundary. The cyborg appears in myth precisely where the boundary between human and animal is transgressed. Far from signalling a walling off of people from other living beings, cyborgs signal disturbingly and pleasurably tight coupling. Bestiality has a new status in this cycle of marriage exchange.

The second leaky distinction is between animal-human (organism) and machine. Pre-cybernetic machines could be haunted; there was always the spectre of the ghost in the machine. This dualism structured the dialogue between materialism and idealism that was settled by a dialectical progeny, called spirit or history, according to taste. But basically machines were not self-moving, self-designing, autonomous. They could not achieve man's dream, only mock it. They were not man, an author to himself, but only a caricature of that masculinist reproductive dream. To think they were otherwise was paranoid.

Now we are not so sure. Late twentieth-century machines have made thoroughly ambiguous the difference between natural and artificial, mind and body, self-developing and externally designed, and many other distinctions that used to apply to organisms and machines. Our machines are disturbingly lively, and we ourselves frighteningly inert.

Technological determination is only one ideological space opened up by the reconceptions of machine and organism as coded texts through which we engage in the play of writing and reading the world. 'Textualization' of everything in poststructuralist, postmodernist theory has been damned by Marxists and socialist feminists for its utopian disregard for the lived relations of domination that ground the 'play' of arbitrary reading. It is certainly true that postmodernist strategies, like my cyborg myth, subvert myriad organic wholes (for example, the poem, the primitive culture, the biological organism). In short, the certainty of what counts as nature – a source of insight and promise of innocence – is undermined, probably fatally. The transcendent authorization of interpretation is lost, and with it the ontology grounding 'Western' epistemology. But the alternative is not cynicism or faithlessness, that is, some version of abstract existence, like the accounts of technological determinism destroying 'man' by the 'machine' or 'meaningful political action' by the 'text'. Who cyborgs will be is a radical question; the answers are a matter of survival. Both chimpanzees and artefacts have politics, so why shouldn't we?

The third distinction is a subset of the second: the boundary between physical and non-physical is very imprecise for us. Pop physics books on the consequences of quantum theory and the indeterminacy principle are a kind of popular scientific equivalent to Harlequin romances as a marker of radical change in American white heterosexuality: they get it wrong, but they are on the right subject. Modern machines are quintessentially micro-electronic devices: they are everywhere and they are invisible. Modern machinery is an irreverent upstart god, mocking the Father's ubiquity and spirituality. The silicon chip is a surface for writing; it is etched in molecular scales disturbed only by atomic noise, the ultimate interference for nuclear scores. Writing, power and technology are old partners in Western stories of the origin of civilization, but miniaturization has changed our experience of mechanism. Miniaturization has turned out to be about power; small is not so much beautiful as pre-eminently dangerous, as in cruise missiles. Contrast the TV sets of the 1950s or the news cameras of the 1970s with the TV wrist bands or hand-sized video cameras now advertised. Our best machines are made of sunshine; they are all light and clean because they are nothing but signals, electromagnetic waves, a section of a spectrum, and these machines are eminently portable, mobile – a matter of immense human pain in Detroit and

Singapore. People are nowhere near so fluid, being both material and opaque. Cyborgs are ether, quintessence.

The ubiquity and invisibility of cyborgs is precisely why these sunshine-belt machines are so deadly. They are as hard to see politically as materially. They are about consciousness – or its simulation. They are floating signifiers moving in pickup trucks across Europe, blocked more effectively by the witch-weavings of the displaced and so unnatural Greenham women, who read the cyborg webs of power so very well, than by the militant labour of older masculinist politics, whose natural constituency needs defence jobs.

Ultimately the 'hardest' science is about the realm of greatest boundary confusion, the realm of pure number, pure spirit, C3I, cryptography, and the preservation of potent secrets. The new machines are so clean and light. Their engineers are sun-worshippers mediating a new scientific revolution associated with the night dream of post-industrial society. The diseases evoked by these clean machines are 'no more' than the minuscule coding changes of an antigen in the immune system, 'no more' than the experience of stress. The nimble fingers of 'Oriental' women, the old fascination of little Anglo-Saxon Victorian girls with doll's houses, women's enforced attention to the small take on quite new dimensions in this world. There might be a cyborg Alice taking account of these new dimensions. Ironically, it might be the unnatural cyborg women making chips in Asia and spiral dancing in Santa Rita jail whose constructed unities will guide effective oppositional strategies.

So my cyborg myth is about transgressed boundaries, potent fusions and dangerous possibilities which progressive people might explore as one pan of needed political work. One of my premises is that most American socialists and feminists see deepened dualisms of mind and body, animal and machine, idealism and materialism in the social practices, symbolic formulations, and physical artefacts associated with 'high technology' and scientific culture. From *One-Dimensional Man* (Marcuse, 1964) to *The Death of Nature* (Merchant, 1980), the analytic resources developed by progressives have insisted on the necessary domination of technics and recalled us to an imagined organic body to integrate our resistance. Another of my premises is that the need for unity of people trying to resist worldwide intensification of domination has never been more acute. But a slightly perverse shift of perspective might better enable us to contest for meanings, as well as for other forms of power and pleasure in technologically mediated societies. From one perspective, a cyborg world is about the final imposition of a grid of control on the planet, about the final abstraction embodied in a *Star Wars* apocalypse waged in the name of defence, about the final appropriation of women's bodies in a masculinist orgy of war (Sofia, 1984). From another perspective, a cyborg world might be about lived social and bodily realities in which people are not afraid of their joint kinship with animals and machines, not afraid of permanently partial identities and contradictory standpoints. The political struggle is to see from both perspectives at once because each reveals both dominations and possibilities unimaginable from the other vantage point. Single vision produces worse illusions than double vision or many-headed monsters. Cyborg unities are monstrous and illegitimate; in our present political circumstances, we could hardly hope for more potent myths for resistance and re-coupling. I like to imagine LAG, the Livermore Action Group [an eco protest direct action group of the early 1980s], as a kind of cyborg society, dedicated realistically to converting the laboratories that most fiercely embody and spew out the tools of technological apocalypse, and committed to building a political form that actually manages to hold together witches, engineers, elders, perverts, Christians, mothers and Leninists long enough to disarm the state. Fission Impossible is the name of the affinity group in my town. (Affinity: related not by blood but by choice, the appeal of one chemical nuclear group for another, avidity.)

Donna Haraway, 'A Cyborg Manifesto: Science, Technology and Socialist-Feminism in the Late Twentieth Century' (1985), in *Simians, Cyborgs and Women: The Reinvention of Nature* (London and New York: Routledge, 1991) 149–55. [footnotes not included].

Stelarc
From Psycho-Body to Cybersystems: Images as Post-Human Entities//1998

The body needs to be repositioned from the psycho realm of the biological to the cyber zone of the interface and extension – from genetic containment to electronic extrusion. Strategies towards the post-human are more about erasure than affirmation – an obsession no longer with self but an analysis of structure. Notions of species evolution and gender distinction are remapped and reconfigured in alternate hybridities of human-machine. Outmoded metaphysical distinctions of soul-body or mind-brain are superseded by concerns of body-species split, as the body is redesigned – diversifying in form and functions. Cyborg bodies are not simply wired and extended but also enhanced with implanted components. Invading technology eliminates skin as a significant site, an adequate interface or a barrier between public space and physiological tracts. The significance of the cyber may well reside in the act of the body shedding its skin. And as humans increasingly operate with surrogate bodies in remote spaces they function with increasingly intelligent and interactive images. The possibility of autonomous images generates an unexpected outcome of human-machine symbiosis. The post-human may well be manifested in the intelligent life form of autonomous images.

1. BEYOND AFFIRMATION INTO ERASURE: Can we re-evaluate the body without resorting to outmoded Platonic and Cartesian metaphysics? The old and often arbitrary psychoanalytical readings have been exhausted. Postmodern critiques generate a discourse of psychobabble that not so much reveals but entraps the body in the archetypical and allegorical. The obsession with the self, sexual difference and the symbolic begins to subside in cybersystems that monitor, map and modify the body. Increasing augmentation of the body and automation by transferring its functions to machines undermines notions of free agency and demystifies mind. CYBERSYSTEMS SPAWN ALTERNATE, HYBRID AND SURROGATE BODIES.

2. The MYTH OF INFORMATION: The information explosion is indicative of an evolutionary dead end. It may be the height of human civilization, but it is also the climax of its evolutionary experience. In our decadent biological phase, we indulge in the information as if this compensates for our genetic inadequacies. The INFORMATION IS THE PROSTHESIS THAT PROPS UP THE OBSOLETE BODY. Information gathering has become not only a meaningless ritual, but a deadly destructive paralysing process, preventing it from taking physical phylogenetic action. Information-gathering satisfies the body's outmoded Pleistocence programme. It is mentally seductive and seems biologically justified.

The cortex craves for information, but it can no longer contain and creatively process it all. How can a body subjectively and simultaneously grasp both nanoseconds and nebulae? THE CORTEX THAT CANNOT COPE RESORTS TO SPECIALIZATION. Specialization, once a manoeuvre methodically to collect information, now is a manifestation of information overloads. The role of information has changed. Once justified as a means of comprehending the world, it now generates a conflicting and contradictory, fleeting and fragmentary field of disconnected and undigested data. INFORMATION IS RADIATION. The most significant planetary pressure is no longer the gravitational pull, but the information thrust. The psycho-flowering of the human species has withered. We are in the twilight of our cerebral fantasies. The symbol has lost all power. The accumulation of information has lost all purpose. Memory results in mimicry. Reflection will not suffice. THE BODY MUST BURST FROM ITS BIOLOGICAL, CULTURAL, AND PLANETARY CONTAINMENT.

3. FREEDOM OF FORM: In this age of information overloads, what is significant is no longer freedom of ideas but rather freedom of form – freedom to modify and mutate the body. The question is not whether society will allow people

freedom of expression but whether the human species will allow the individuals to construct alternate genetic coding. THE FUNDAMENTAL FREEDOM IS FOR INDIVIDUALS TO DETERMINE THEIR OWN DNA DESTINY. Biological change becomes a matter of choice rather than chance. EVOLUTION BY THE INDIVIDUAL, FOR THE INDIVIDUAL. Medical technologies that monitor, map and modify the body also provide the means to manipulate the structure of the body. When we attach or implant prosthetic devices to prolong a person's life, we also create the potential to propel post-evolutionary development – PATCHED-UP PEOPLE ARE POST-EVOLUTIONARY EXPERIMENTS.

4. BIOTECH TERRAINS: The body now inhabits alien environments that conceal countless BODY PACEMAKERS – visual and acoustical cues that alert, activate, condition and control the body. Its circadian rhythms need to be augmented by artificial signals. Humans are now regulated in sync with swift, circulating rhythms of pulsing images. MORPHING IMAGES MAKE THE BODY OBSOLETE …

5. OBSOLETE BODY: It is time to question whether a bipedal, breathing body with binocular vision and a 1400cc brain is an adequate biological form. It cannot cope with the quantity, complexity and quality of information it has accumulated; it is intimidated by the precision, speed and power of technology and it is biologically ill-equipped to cope with its new extraterrestrial environment. The body is neither a very efficient nor a very durable structure. It malfunctions often and fatigues quickly; its performance is determined by its age. It is susceptible to disease and is doomed to a certain and early death. Its survival parameters are very slim. It can survive only weeks without food, days without water, and minutes without oxygen. The body's LACK OF MODULAR DESIGN and its overreactive immunological system make it difficult to replace malfunctioning organs. It might be the height of technological folly to consider the body obsolete in form and function: yet it might be the highest of human realizations. For it is only when the body becomes aware of its present position that it can map its post-evolutionary strategies. It is no longer a matter of perpetuating the human species by REPRODUCTION, but of enhancing male/female intercourse by human-machine interface. THE BODY IS OBSOLETE. We are at the end of philosophy and human physiology. Human thought recedes into the human past.

6. ABSENT BODIES: We mostly operate as Absent Bodies. That is because A BODY IS DESIGNED TO INTERFACE WITH ITS ENVIRONMENT – its sensors are open-to-the-world (compared to its inadequate internal surveillance system). The body's mobility and navigation in the world require this outward orientation. Its absence is augmented by the fact that the body functions habitually and automatically. AWARENESS IS OFTEN THAT WHICH OCCURS WHEN THE BODY MALFUNCTIONS. Reinforced by Cartesian convention, personal convenience and

neurophysiological design, people operate merely as minds, immersed in metaphysical fogs. The sociologist P.L. Berger made the distinction between 'having a body' and 'being a body'. AS SUPPOSED FREE AGENTS, THE CAPABILITIES OF BEING A BODY ARE CONSTRAINED BY HAVING A BODY. Our actions and ideas are essentially determined by our physiology. We are at the limits of philosophy, not only because we are at the limits of language. Philosophy is fundamentally grounded in our physiology ...

7. REDESIGNING THE BODY / REDEFINING WHAT IS HUMAN. It is no longer meaningful to see the body as a site for the psyche or the social, but rather as a structure to be monitored and modified; the body not as a subject but as an object – NOT AS AN OBJECT OF DESIRE BUT AS AN OBJECT FOR DESIGNING. The psycho-social period was characterized by the body circling itself, orbiting itself, illuminating and inspecting itself by physical prodding and metaphysical contemplation. But having confronted its image of obsolescence, the body is traumatized to split from the realm of subjectivity and consider the necessity of re-examining and possibly redesigning its very structure. ALTERING THE ARCHITECTURE OF THE BODY RESULTS IN ADJUSTING AND EXTENDING ITS AWARENESS OF THE WORLD. As an object, the body can be amplified and accelerated, attaining planetary escape velocity. It becomes a post-evolutionary projectile, departing and diversifying in form and function. [...]

Stelarc, extract from 'From Psycho-Body to Cybersystems: Images as Post-Human Entities' (1998), in *The Cybercultures Reader* (London and New York: Routledge, 2000) 560–62.

Tom McDonough
No Ghost//2004

[...] [For *No Ghost Just a Shell*, begun in 1999, Pierre Huyghe and Philippe Parreno] bought the digital files and copyright for AnnLee, a generic Japanese manga character, from a company that develops such stock figures for use in cartoons, advertisements, video games and the like. The inexpensive price of this purchase (around $400) is an indication of the simplicity of her 'identity', suitable for insertion into a given storyline as a minor figure, but lacking the more developed 'personality' of a narrative lead. In the operations of digital animation, she would have been used as a background character in a few frames, then been set aside forever. Huyghe and Parreno purchased AnnLee, undertook extensive retouching and three-dimensional development of this image, and produced several short videos in which it was provided with different 'personae.' Later the image was made available to other artists, before being permanently retired from use in 2002.

The rhetoric around this work has generally been one of emancipation. By acquiring the rights to this character, it is claimed, Huyghe and Parreno removed it from the commercial cycle, thereby freeing it from the ruthless economics of the *manga* industry. The computer code constituting the image of AnnLee is relentlessly humanized in this criticism so that, for example, it is seen as being 'brought to life' through its appropriation by these artists. They themselves, it should be noted, have participated in this naïve set of assumptions: 'The idea', Parreno has said, 'was to free a character that doesn't have any chance to produce a storyline. The expensive ones have everything and they don't need us [to be freed].'[1] Despite these claims, however, the logic of *No Ghost Just a Shell* is anything but redemptory, and what we witness in this collective work is less the transposition of the class struggle onto the plane of images than what Adorno once presciently termed the 'illusion of the absolute reality of the unreal.'[2] Indeed, the title itself provides us with a strong indication of just what attitude Huyghe and Parreno have adopted towards their purchased 'character'.

That title, as many have noted, is derived from a well-known *manga* film, *Ghost in the Shell* (1995), whose narrative revolves around an altogether conventional science-fiction trope: the uncertain line between the human and the inanimate as figured in the (not coincidentally female-gendered) cyborg.[3] Yet this particular plot line seems not to have particularly interested the artists. For AnnLee is no Eve of the future, and our experience of this figure contains none of the frisson of the uncanny that had motivated an earlier modernist fascination with the automaton or mannequin. (When a critic purported to see a flicker of humanity in its eyes, Huyghe scolded: 'Don't make it romantic.')[4] In other words, we should take the first half of the work's title quite literally: no ghost, no haunting, only 'a fictional character with a copyright designed by a company and proposed for sale. That's it', as Huyghe himself has AnnLee remind us in his film *Two Minutes Out of Time* (2000). What Huyghe and Parreno appear to be signalling here is the demise of one of the great figures of modern oppositional culture – the obsession with spectres and the phantasmagoric, the untimely and the unhomely, activated by the Surrealists some eighty years ago as the return of what bourgeois society resolutely had repressed. It is the uncanny itself whose critical force seems to have become exhausted.

Even the briefest comparison of AnnLee to that fascination with the mannequin so characteristic of Surrealism suffices to reveal the cultural transformation – indeed, the absolute historical break – that separates the present from that earlier moment of avant-garde contestation. The mannequin may be considered a 'veritable emblem of the sensibility of a whole age', as Fredric Jameson has observed:

> [the] supreme totem of the Surrealist transformation of life – in which the human body itself comes before us as a product, where the nagging awareness of another presence, as in the terror of the blue gaze that meets us from the doll's eyes, the secret premonition of a lifeless voice somehow about to address us, all figure emblematically the central discovery by Surrealism of the properties of the objects that surrounded us.[5]

Jameson goes on to specify the historical condition of these experiences of the uncanny as bound to an earlier moment of capitalist development – the passage from a liberal economy to one of cartels and monopolies – which had nevertheless not yet succeeded in fully industrializing or systematizing all of society, certainly not in France. At that moment, 'the properties of the objects' that made up the human milieu still consisted in their appearance as 'mysterious things', as objects in which the social character of human labour might yet make itself known in the manner of the return of the repressed, 'the nagging awareness' of which Jameson speaks, or what we should properly call in this context the revenant. What returned was indeed a premonition of the use value that capitalist production had been in the process of systematically destroying in favour of the commodity as pure value, as mere token of exchange. AnnLee exists at the other side of this divide; it is pure exchange value, 'a fictional character with a copyright … and proposed for sale. That's it.' To imagine that Huyghe and Parreno's purchase of the rights to its use somehow freed it from the commercial cycle is sheer fantasy – AnnLee was made for just this purpose. 'That's it': utterly without depth, and (wide eyes notwithstanding) incapable of sustaining the sort of libidinal investment that had made the Surrealist mannequin such a powerful allegorical figure of modernity.

The critical force of the spectral was linked ultimately to the project of rational enlightenment. The world of commodities might present itself as a phantasmagoria, alternately terrifying and seductive, but the mechanisms of such false appearance and illusion could be revealed for what they were; what Marx called the 'religion of everyday life' could be shown to be the product of mere human labour and the social relations between producers. Even the Surrealist interest in the uncanny was less a means of re-enchanting a rationalized world than of figuring the alienated labour that lay behind the false appearance of the commodity. In each case, the dispelling of mirages and hallucinations unveiled the human intercourse, the subjects, that had been occluded by capital. That critical project has been rendered obsolete by the transformations of capital itself; indeed, what has been called the contemporary 'immaterial labour' of post-Fordism has seen the conscription of the category of subjectivity itself into the relations of production. 'The prescription of tasks' along the assembly line, in which the worker was subject to the coordination of the various functions of production 'as simple command', has given way in the post-industrial economy to 'a prescription of subjectivities', in which the worker is expected to become a participating agent in processes of control, the handling of information and decision-making. 'The new slogan of Western societies', Maurizio Lazzarato has written in his account of this restructured worker, 'is that we should all "become subjects". Participative management is a technology of power, a technology for creating and controlling the "subjective processes".'[6] Subjectivity itself, in other words, has been put to work and, no less than economic value, the subject is now the product of the regime of immaterial labour. If this site was once considered a locus of potential resistance to capitalist production, or at least a space of inferiority not yet subject to the discipline of the workplace, today its colonization is complete.[7] AnnLee has not been 'freed' from the production of value by being imbued with an ephemeral 'subjectivity' – such individuality is the very condition of its existence as a commodity, and is the token of its isomorphic position to the capital relation.

'Don't make it romantic.' If AnnLee is not a ghost, what does it mean to describe the image as 'just a shell?' This phrase from the work's title, too, needs to be interrogated. It is tempting, of course, to read it as referring to the character as an empty sign, a kind of digital avatar that the various artists involved in this project could appropriate, just as certain crustaceans come to inhabit the vacant shells of other species. Such an interpretation presupposes in turn the replete subjectivity of those participants, who 'fill' the otherwise empty shell of the commodity form; as we have seen, however, subjectivity no longer constitutes some outside to the system of production, but has been wholly hollowed out and internalized to its logic. Moreover, this reading simply fails to correspond with our experience of the work. Huyghe and Parreno's digital animations of AnnLee do not strike the viewer as some advanced form of puppet-theatre; the artists are not hidden illusionists manipulating the phantasmagoria seen by the audience. Indeed, what is striking about these films is their quality of the inhuman, the utter absence of humanity from the scene. This is particularly clear in Huyghe's *Two Minutes Out of Time*, in which AnnLee appears before the viewer as some sort of alien, her buglike eyes – blank and slightly projecting – out of all proportion to the scale of her mouth and nose. Her skin is modelled in shades of grey, hardly distinct from the indeterminate backdrop against which she appears. Coupled with her narration, with its shifting sites of enunciation (she sometimes speaks from her own point of view, sometimes from that of the viewer), Huyghe seems determined to remove the image from any identification; it remains, in some sense, beyond recognition. In this light, a rather different connotation of the phrase 'just a shell' becomes apparent; in it, we may hear the echo of Sartre's account of the dehumanization of reality, what he called the 'petrification' of the human, in one influential strand of modern cultural production.

In his essay on the poetry of Francis Ponge, 'Man and Things', Sartre wrote of the former's assimilation of language to a kind of shell, a material envelope secreted by the individual as a protective carapace. Ponge, the philosopher wrote, imagined those shells emptied, as if 'after the disappearance of our species, in the hands of other species that look at them as we look at shells on the sand'.[8]

There was in fact a persistent necrological fantasy at work here in the form of an entropic scenario worthy of science fiction, whereby Ponge's ultimate wish was 'that this entire civilization should one day appear', in Sartre's words, 'as a vast necropolis of shells in the eyes of some higher ape ... who will distractedly leaf through these remains of our glory'.[9] *No Ghost Just a Shell* proposes an analogous project of separating the signifying object (images now, rather than language proper) from its anthropocentric context. Nowhere is this clearer than in Huyghe's film *One Million Kingdoms* (2001), in which AnnLee's voice maps out the very landscape through which the figure walks. That voice is an electronically altered version of that of Neil Armstong, derived from his transmissions from the first moon landing, and the vista produced by those sound waves is a barren lunar terrain. Here too the world is divested of any properly human significance, the voice separated from its speaker and transformed into a frozen panorama. AnnLee herself is reduced to a glowing blue outline, rendered as transparent – empty – while she rather dejectedly wanders across a grey moonscape of a patent artificiality (the digital animation here being notably crude). It is as if image and speech have become mere things among other things that might acquire their own meaning and resonance apart from any human use to which they may be put; 'thus eluding the man who has produced it', Sartre wrote of Ponge's language, 'the word becomes an absolute.'[10] It is in just this sense that AnnLee may be described as a veritable shell, and we viewers are placed in the curious position of that post-apocalyptic ape who looks down with curiosity on this petrified remain of an unknown civilization.

For Sartre, such a view entails an inversion of the a priori human perception of the world as a setting for purposeful intentions. Objects appear to us first as full of meaning, as instruments that refer us to human ends and intentions, and only later as things-in-themselves. '[I]n the Heideggerian world', Sartre explains, the existent is first *Zeug*, tool. To see in it *das Ding*, the temporo-spatial object, one must be willing to practice a neutralization upon oneself. One pauses, one embraces the project of suspending all projects, one adopts the posture of *nurverweilen bei ...*

Then the object, which is, in short, only a secondary aspect of the tool – an aspect that is founded in the last instance on usefulness – will appear …[11]

Ponge turned this Heideggerian distinction upside-down, so that the object existed first, 'in its inhuman solitude', and humanity came second as 'the object that transformed other objects into instruments'.[12] And so with AnnLee who, relegated to the lunar surface, tells us: 'I have become animated … not by a story with a plot, no … See, I'm not here for your amusement … You are here for mine!' AnnLee's removal from narrative is less an act of freeing this figure from the commercial constraints of its origin than one of stripping the image of its usefulness, its socialized significations, of seizing it at the very moment it is about to become an independent object. Of course, for Sartre such a displacement of the properly human significance of the world was a travesty, the pathetic dream of an 'inoffensive and radical catastrophe' that Ponge had shared with contemporaries like Blanchot or Bataille. Over a half century on, however, that catastrophe appears precisely to have overtaken us – not in the dramatic form supposed by Sartre, but as the gradual subsumption of the human subject to the logic of an integrated spectacle culture. Huyghe describes this world, one experienced no longer as 'hodological' space – as, that is, 'a complex organization of means and ends and projects, unveiled through the movement of my own adventures and desires' – but instead as entropic space, 'motionless space spread out before me', infinite and beyond meaning.[13] *No Ghost Just a Shell* does not appropriate the figure of AnnLee as a means, but, through a process of purification (of what Sartre called 'decrassage'), places it before us as an end in itself, strangely autonomous and independent of human will. […]

<hr>

1   [footnote 12 in source] Philippe Parreno quoted in Kendra Mayfield, 'Art Explores Cartoon as Commodity', *Wired* (14 December 2002).

2   [13] Theodor W. Adorno, *In Search of Wagner* (1937–8); trans. Rodney Livingstone (London: New Left Books, 1981) 90.

3   [14] For an account of this film, see Philip Nobel, 'Sign of the Times', *Artforum* (January 2003) 105–6.

4   [15] Ibid., 106.

5   [16] Fredric Jameson, *Marxism and Form* (Princeton: Princeton University Press, 1971) 104–5.

6   [17] Maurizio Lazzarato, 'Immaterial Labour', trans. Paul Colilli and Ed Emory, in *Radical Thought in Italy*, ed. Paolo Virno and Michael Hardt (Minneapolis: University of Minnesota Press, 1996) 135.

7   [18] On this subject, see also Herbert Marcuse's important essay 'The Obsolescence of the Freudian Concept of Man', in *Five Lectures*, trans. Jeremy J. Shapiro and Shierry M. Weber (Boston: Beacon Press, 1970). One should keep in mind, however, Hal Foster's caution that such a model of the shattering of the subject necessarily presupposes 'a prior moment or model in which the subject is whole and complete', and that such a concept is problematic, not least for the danger

it runs of nostalgically preserving 'the old pragmatic, patriarchal' bourgeois self – a charge to which the Frankfurt School, Marcuse included, is particularly susceptible. See Hal Foster, *Recodings* (Port Townsend, Washington: Bay Press, 1985) 132; 134.

8   [19] Jean-Paul Sartre, 'L'homme et les choses', in *Situations*, no. 1 (Paris: Éditions Gallimard, 1947) 252.

9   [20] Ibid., 287–8.

10   [21] Ibid., 252.

11   [22] Ibid., 257–8. Jameson has glossed this argument: 'For human reality, involved in its projects, each object is primarily a frozen project, an immobile imperative, a thing-to-be-used-in-a-certain-way – *zuhanden*, available, lying to hand in case of need', as opposed to the thing or object 'as *vorhanden*, as simply being there, as an entity with no evident relationship to myself'. Fredric Jameson, 'Three Methods in Sartre's Literary Criticism', in *Critical Essays on Jean-Paul Sartre*, ed. Robert Wilcocks (Boston: G.K. Hall, 1988) 104.

12   Sartre, 'L'homme et les choses', op. cit., 258.

Tom McDonough, extract from 'No Ghost', *October*, no. 110 (Fall 2004); reprinted in Tom McDonough, *The Beautiful Language of My Century: Reinventing the Language of Contestation in Postwar France, 1945–1968* (Cambridge, Massachusetts: The MIT Press, 2007) 180–89.

UMWELT, 2011
10.000 ANTS,
50 SPIDERS
UNIQUE
€110.000,00 (EX MWST)
(€117.700,00 INC. MWST @ 7,00%)

TEN THOUSAND ANTS OF THE FAMILY POLYRHACHLIS DIVES
ARE CO-INHABITING THE GALLERY SPACE WITH A GROUP OF FIFTY
DOMESTIC SPIDERS. ANTS AND SPIDERS ARE WALKING ON THE
FLOOR AND WALLS. WHILE THE ANTS FORM TRAILS OR DISPERSE
IN GROUPS THE SPIDERS REMAIN ALONE. SOME OF THE SPIDERS
INHABIT THE CORNERS OF THE ROOM,OTHERS ARE FREELY
WALKING AROUND.

Pierre Huyghe, *Umwelt* (Environment), 2011. 'Influants' exhibition inventory, Galerie Esther Schipper, Berlin

COGNITION AND CONSCIENCE

Roger Caillois
The Natural Fantastic//1971

[...] As opposed to fairy tales or to the Marvellous, which involves a world of enchantment, of constant metamorphoses and miracles where everything is always possible, I think the Fantastic presumes a well-ordered universe ruled by the immutable laws of physics, astronomy and chemistry. This world is one in which like causes produce like effects, and which consequently excludes the slightest chance of miracles. The fantastic appears as the disruption of a natural order that is deemed impossible to disturb. This natural order, not to say nature itself in the strong sense of the word, can be defined only as a form of regularity so fundamental that it is beyond the reach of any manipulation. By definition, it is so strong that human skill can modify it only by obeying it. It follows from this point of view that the fantastic can never be 'natural', for it is presented, on the contrary, as the inadmissible breach wrought in nature by some mysterious power that is specifically viewed as supernatural. It has to be imaginary, that is, a deliberate invention of the mind, which recognizes it as such. Therefore, the fantastic cannot exist, properly speaking: it cannot be part of nature, of the attested universe.

Yet common parlance allows that a landscape may seem fantastic, as frequently occurs where some erosion has carved out simulacra of towers, palaces or gigantic animals. Likewise, a tree or a flower may be termed fantastic (or the details of a flower, such as the passion flower, in which a certain naïve piety has long discerned the nails, hammer and lance of Christ's Crucifixion) and all anthropomorphic root such as the mandrake. And, so too, an insect (or one of its features, such as the skull pattern on the corselet of the *Acherontia atropos*), a fish, a bird, or a Saurian may all be termed fantastic, even though they are products of nature, if their appearance is so surprising, baffling or disquieting that it does not seem they could really be what they are.

Under these conditions, it is surely useful to try to define how animate or inanimate nature can give the impression of escaping its own norms, and even of mocking them outright. Rarity and strangeness here play a crucial role. For example, simply considering the world of vertebrates, alongside the animals that are the stuff of legend (sphinxes, chimeras, centaurs, mermaids, griffons, etc.), there exist animals, such as the unicorn, that natural science catalogued and described for a long time. Conversely, certain animals catalogued only quite recently actually do exist. Their morphology is so bizarre that an observer would readily judge them more thoroughly unreal and inadmissible than the legendary hybrids.

Of course, to name them 'fantastic' is a misuse of language, but a significant one. In any event, being subject myself – perhaps unwittingly – to the diffuse pressure exerted by language, I was induced to launch the idea (surprising, to say the least, especially to me) of the natural fantastic. I first used the term in connection with an insect from north-east Brazil, the lantern fly, and a North American mammal, the star-nosed mole or *Condylura*. These two animals' appearances made me resort to a category whose specious nature I could easily perceive. Quite obviously, these creatures were not fantastic because they were a part of nature. Just as obviously, they seemed fantastic, and even gave quite an exceptional sense of the fantastic: the tree-dwelling *homopteron*, on account of its frontal protuberance, which is almost as big as its body and deceptively suggests a crocodile's muzzle; and the subterranean vertebrate, on account of its snout, which sports a crown of twenty-two short tentacles of live pink flesh, all mobile, sensitive, and retractable, flaccid or tensed at will, and very vaguely like an intricate starfish or some horrible corolla.

In both cases, observers can hardly believe their own eyes and think themselves in the presence of nightmarish creatures that contradict reality more than they emerge from it. Upon consideration, the surprise effect is not caused by the same mechanism in the two cases. With the lantern fly, the disconcerting element results from the presence of a hollow and weird mask. This is the spitting image of the snout of some animal from which its flying bearer differs in all other respects and with which it could never in any way be confused, even in terms of size. The resemblance is stunning and seems inexplicable, in so far as it is indeed exact, striking, and, at the same time, useless. The undulating halo of the *Condylura* is terrifying, on the contrary, because it does not recall any known form and because it draws on dissimilar elements to compose a repugnant and novel entity.

One could give numerous examples of such phenomena and show that in each case, there is a certain mythology or specific fascination attached to the bizarre animal, whether this is a spider, octopus, bat, praying mantis or seahorse. [...]

Letters left adrift, terms without a lexicon, these boundary markers, whose aberrant arrangement does not correspond to any register or cadastral survey on the order of humanity, nonetheless figure among the indications that move it most, and me most obscurely. In the end, more or less alone, they guarantee me wagers and resources for the images of tenacious poetry. The network of surprising markers constitutes a secret and inexhaustible warranty, a sort of intellectual gold supporting all fiduciary transactions of the intellect and imagination.

In exchange for this repository (in so far as it accepts its reality) humanity is dispossessed of the ancient pre-eminence it briefly claimed as its own – an instant that is immemorial for it but very swift for geological time. Henceforth, man knows that he is neither alone nor a monarch. In the infinite game of Snakes and Ladders without a well, jail or fruitful stops, humankind is not a player – nor even the dice – but an almost passive counter that is moved from square to square in its turn, together with other reiterated emblems. Sometimes we are stopped by an image that disturbs us, an image reminding us of another or else holding out the promise of different ones. The return of the simulacrum lets us glimpse the tattered shreds of a concealed order we can barely reach, and never with certainty. Dazzled or enlightened, we try to understand and, at times, to expand the rules of a game we never asked to take part in, and that we are not allowed to renounce. [...]

Roger Caillois, extracts from transcript of the lecture 'Le Fantastique naturel' (1971); trans. Claudine Frank and Camille Nash, 'The Natural Fantastic', in *The Edge of Surrealism: A Roger Caillois Reader*, ed. Claudine Frank (Durham, North Carolina: Duke University Press, 2003) 349–51; 357.

Thomas Nagel
What is It Like to be a Bat?//1974

[...] Conscious experience is a widespread phenomenon. It occurs at many levels of animal life, though we cannot be sure of its presence in the simpler organisms, and it is very difficult to say in general what provides evidence of it. (Some extremists have been prepared to deny it even of mammals other than man.) No doubt it occurs in countless forms totally unimaginable to us, on other planets in other solar systems throughout the universe. But no matter how the form may vary, the fact that an organism has conscious experience *at all* means, basically, that there is something it is like to *be* that organism. There may be further implications about the form of the experience; there may even (though I doubt it) be implications about the behaviour of the organism. But fundamentally an organism has conscious mental states if and only if there is something that it is to *be* that organism– something it is like *for* the organism.

We may call this the subjective character of experience. It is not captured by any of the familiar, recently devised reductive analyses of the mental, for all of them are logically compatible with its absence. It is not analysable in terms of any explanatory system of functional states, or intentional states, since these could be ascribed to robots or automata that behaved like people though they experienced nothing. It is not analysable in terms of the causal role of experiences in relation to typical human behaviour – for similar reasons. I do not deny that conscious mental states and events cause behaviour, nor that they may be given functional characterizations. I deny only that this kind of thing exhausts their analysis. Any reductionist programme has to be based on an analysis of what is to be reduced. If the analysis leaves something out, the problem will be falsely posed. It is useless to base the defence of materialism on any analysis of mental phenomena that fails to deal explicitly with their subjective character. For there is no reason to suppose that a reduction which seems plausible when no attempt is made to account for consciousness can be extended to include consciousness. Without some idea, therefore, of what the subjective character of experience is, we cannot know what is required of physicalist theory.

While an account of the physical basis of mind must explain many things, this appears to be the most difficult. It is impossible to exclude the phenomenological features of experience from a reduction in the same way that one excludes the phenomenal features of an ordinary substance from a physical or chemical reduction of it – namely, by explaining them as effects on the minds of human observers. If physicalism is to be defended, the phenomenological features must themselves be given a physical account. But when we examine their subjective character it seems that such a result is impossible. The reason is that every subjective phenomenon is essentially connected with a single point of view, and it seems inevitable that an objective, physical theory will abandon that point of view.

Let me first try to state the issue somewhat more fully than by referring to the relation between the subjective and the objective, or between the *pour-soi* and the *en-soi*. This is far from easy. Facts about what it is like to be an X are very peculiar, so peculiar that some may be inclined to doubt their reality, or the significance of claims about them. To illustrate the connection between subjectivity and a point of view, and to make evident the importance of subjective features, it will help to explore the matter in relation to an example that brings out clearly the divergence between the two types of conception, subjective and objective.

I assume we all believe that bats have experience. After all, they are mammals, and there is no more doubt that they have experience than that mice or pigeons or whales have experience. I have chosen bats instead of wasps or flounders because if one travels too far down the phylogenetic tree, people gradually shed their faith that there is experience there at all. Bats, although more closely related to us than those other species, nevertheless present a range of activity and a sensory apparatus so different from ours that the problem I want to pose is exceptionally vivid (though it certainly could be raised with other species). Even without the benefit of philosophical reflection, anyone who has spent some time in an enclosed space with an excited bat knows what it is to encounter a fundamentally *alien* form of life.

I have said that the essence of the belief that bats have experience is that there is something that it is like to be a bat. Now we know that most bats (the *microchiroptera*, to be precise) perceive the external world primarily by sonar, or echolocation, detecting the reflections, from objects within range, of their own rapid, subtly modulated, high-frequency shrieks. Their brains are designed to correlate the outgoing impulses with the subsequent echoes, and the information thus acquired enables bats to make precise discriminations of distance, size, shape, motion and texture comparable to those we make by vision. But bat sonar, though clearly a form of perception, is not similar in its operation to any sense that we possess, and there is no reason to suppose that it is subjectively like anything we can experience or imagine. This appears to create difficulties for the notion of what it is like to be a bat. We must consider whether any method will permit us to extrapolate to the inner life of the bat from our own case, and if not, what alternative methods there may be for understanding the notion.

Our own experience provides the basic material for our imagination, whose range is therefore limited. It will not help to try to imagine that one has webbing on one's arms, which enables one to fly around at dusk and dawn catching insects in one's mouth; that one has very poor vision, and perceives the surrounding world by a system of reflected high-frequency sound signals; and that one spends the day hanging upside down by one's feet in an attic. In so far as I can imagine this (which is not very far), it tells me only what it would be like for *me* to behave as a bat behaves. But that is not the question. I want to know what it is like for a *bat* to be a bat. Yet if I try to imagine this, I am restricted to the resources of my own mind, and those resources are inadequate to the task. I cannot perform it either by imagining additions to my present experience, or by imagining segments gradually subtracted from it, or by imagining some combination of additions, subtractions and modifications.

To the extent that I could look and behave like a wasp or a bat without changing my fundamental structure, my experiences would not be anything like the experiences of those animals. On the other hand, it is doubtful that any meaning can be attached to the supposition that I should possess the internal neurophysiological constitution of a bat. Even if I could by gradual degrees be transformed into a bat, nothing in my present constitution enables me to imagine what the experiences of such a future stage of myself thus metamorphosed would be like. The best evidence would come from the experiences of bats, if we only knew what they were like.

So if extrapolation from our own case is involved in the idea of what it is like to be a bat, the extrapolation must be incompletable. We cannot form more than a schematic conception of what it is like. For example, we may ascribe general types of experience on the basis of the animal's structure and behaviour. Thus we describe bat sonar as a form of three-dimensional forward perception; we believe that bats feel some versions of pain, fear, hunger and lust, and that they have other, more familiar types of perception besides sonar. But we believe that these experiences also have in each case a specific subjective character, which it is beyond our ability to conceive. And if there's conscious life elsewhere in the universe, it is likely that some of it will not be describable even in the most general experiential terms available to us. (The problem is not confined to exotic cases, however, for it exists between one person and another. The subjective character of the experience of deaf and blind people from birth is not accessible to me, for example, nor presumably is mine to them. This does not prevent us each from believing that the other's experience has such a subjective character.)

If anyone is inclined to deny that we can believe in the existence of facts like this whose exact nature we cannot possibly conceive, he or she should reflect that in contemplating the bats we are in much the same position that intelligent bats or Martians would occupy if they tried to form a conception of what it was like to be us. The structure of their own minds might make it impossible for them to succeed, but we know they would be wrong to conclude that there is not anything precise that it is like to be us: that only certain general types of mental state could be ascribed to us (perhaps perception and appetite would be concepts common to us both; perhaps not). We know they would be wrong to draw such a sceptical conclusion because we know what it is like to be us. And we know that while it includes an enormous amount of variation and complexity, and while we do not possess the vocabulary to describe it adequately, its subjective character is highly specific, and in some respects describable in terms that can be understood only by creatures like us. The fact that we cannot expect ever to accommodate in our language a detailed description of Martian or bat phenomenology should not lead us to dismiss as meaningless the claim that bats and Martians have experiences fully comparable in richness of detail to our own. It would be fine if someone were to develop concepts and a theory that enabled us to think about those things; but such an understanding may be permanently denied to us by the limits of our nature. And to deny the reality or logical significance of what we can never describe or understand is the crudest form of cognitive dissonance.

Thomas Nagel, extract from 'What is it Like to Be a Bat?', *Philosophical Review*, LXXXIII (October 1974) 435–50.

Jacques Derrida
The Animal That Therefore I Am//1997

Since time, therefore.

Since so long ago, can we say that the animal has been looking at us?

What animal? The other.

I often ask myself, just to see, *who I am* – and who I am (following) at the moment when, caught naked, in silence, by the gaze of an animal, for example, the eyes of a cat, I have trouble, yes, a bad time, overcoming my embarrassment.

Whence this malaise?

I have trouble repressing a reflex of shame. Trouble keeping silent within me a protest against the indecency. Against the impropriety [*malséance*] that can come of finding oneself naked, one's sex exposed, stark naked before a cat that looks at you without moving, just to see. The impropriety of a certain animal nude before the other animal, from that point on one might call it a kind of *animalséance*: the single, incomparable and original experience of the impropriety that would come from appearing in truth naked, in front of the insistent gaze of the animal, a benevolent or pitiless gaze, surprised or cognizant. The gaze of a seer, a visionary or extra-lucid blind one. It is as if I were ashamed, therefore, naked in front of this cat, but also ashamed for being ashamed. A reflected shame, the mirror of a shame ashamed of itself, a shame that is at the same time specular, unjustifiable and unavowable. At the optical centre of this reflection would appear this thing – and in my eyes the focus of this incomparable experience – that is called nudity. And about which it is believed that it is proper to man, that is to say, foreign to animals, naked as they are, or so it is thought, without the slightest consciousness of being so. […]

Ashamed of what and before whom? Ashamed of being as naked as a beast. It is generally thought, although none of the philosophers I am about to examine [in further texts] actually mentions it, that the property unique to animals, what in the last instance distinguishes them from man, is their being naked without knowing it. Not being naked therefore, not having knowledge of their nudity, in short, without consciousness of good and evil.

From that point on, naked without knowing it, animals would not be, in truth, naked.

They wouldn't be naked because they are naked. In principle, with the exception of man, no animal has ever thought to dress itself. Clothing would be proper to man, one of the 'properties' of man. 'Dressing oneself' would be inseparable from all the other figures of what is 'proper to man', even if one talks about it less than speech or reason, the *logos*, history, laughing, mourning, burial, the gift, etc. (The list of 'what is proper to man' always forms a configuration, from the first moment. For that very reason, it can never be limited to a single trait and it is never closed; structurally speaking it can attract a non-finite number of other concepts, beginning with the concept of a concept.)

The animal, therefore, is not naked because it is naked. It doesn't feel its own nudity. There is no nudity 'in nature'. There is only the sentiment, the affect, the (conscious or unconscious) experience of *existing* in nakedness. Because it is naked, without existing in nakedness, the animal neither feels nor sees itself naked. And therefore it isn't naked. At least that is what is thought. For man it would be the opposite, and clothing derives from technics. We would therefore have to think shame and technicity together, as the same 'subject'. And evil and history, and work, and so many other things that go along with it. Man would be the only one to have invented a garment to cover his sex. He would be a man only to the extent that he was able to be naked, that is to say, to be ashamed, to know himself to be ashamed because he is no longer naked. And knowing *himself* would mean knowing himself to be ashamed. On the other hand, because the animal is naked without consciousness of being naked, it is thought that modesty remains as foreign to it as does immodesty. As does the knowledge of self that is involved in that.

What is shame if one can be modest only by remaining immodest, and vice versa? Man could never be naked any more because he has the sense of nakedness, that is to say, of modesty or shame. The animal would be *in* non-nudity because it is nude, and man *in* nudity to the extent that he is no longer nude. There we encounter a difference, a time or *contretemps* between two *nudities without nudity*. This *contretemps* has only just begun giving us trouble or doing us harm [*mal*] in the area of the knowledge of good and evil.

Before the cat that looks at me naked, would I be ashamed *like* a beast that no longer has the sense of its nudity? Or, on the contrary, *like* a man who retains the sense of his nudity? Who am I, therefore? Who is it that I am (following)? Whom should this be asked of if not of the other? And perhaps of the cat itself?

I must immediately make it clear, the cat I am talking about is a real cat, truly, believe me, *a little cat*. It isn't the figure of a cat. It doesn't silently enter the bedroom as an allegory for all the cats on the earth, the felines that traverse our myths and religions, literature and fables. [...]

If I say 'it is a real cat' that sees me naked, this is in order to mark its unsubstitutable singularity. When it responds to its name (whatever 'respond' means, and that will be our question), it doesn't do so as the exemplar of a species called 'cat', even less so of an 'animal' genus or kingdom. It is true that I identify it as a male or female cat. But even before that identification, it comes to me as *this* irreplaceable living being that one day enters my space, into this place where it can encounter me, see me, even see me naked. Nothing can ever rob me of the certainty that what we have here is an existence that refuses to be conceptualized [*rebelle à tout concept*]. And a mortal existence, for from the moment that it has a name, its name survives it. It signs its potential disappearance. Mine also, and that disappearance, from this moment to that, *fort/da*, is announced each time that, with or without nakedness, one of us leaves the room.

But I must immediately emphasize the fact that this shame that is ashamed of itself is more intense when I am not alone with the pussycat in the room. Then I am no longer sure before whom I am so numbed with shame. In fact, is one ever alone with a cat? Or with anyone at all? Is this cat a third [*tiers*]? Or another in a face-to-face duel? These questions will return much later. In such moments, on the edge of the thing, in the imminence of the best or the worst, when anything can happen, where I can die of shame or pleasure, I no longer know in whose or in what direction to throw myself. Rather than chasing it away, chasing the cat away, I am in a hurry, yes, in a hurry to have it appear otherwise. I hasten to cover the obscenity of the event, in short, to cover myself. One thought alone keeps me spellbound: dress myself, even a little, or, which amounts to the same thing, run away – as if I were chasing myself out of the room – bite myself, therefore, bite my tongue, for example, at the very moment when I ask myself 'Who?' But '*Who therefore?*' For I no longer know who, therefore, I am (following) or who it is I am chasing, who is following me or hunting me. Who comes before and who is after whom? I no longer know which end my head is. Madness: 'We're all mad here. I'm mad. You're mad.' I no longer know how to respond, or even to respond to the question that compels me or asks me who I am (following) or after whom I am (following), but am so as I am running [*et suis ainsi en train de courir*].

To follow and to be after will not only be the question, and the question of what we call the animal. We shall discover in the follow-through the question of the question, that which begins by wondering what *to respond* means and whether an animal (but which one?) ever replies in its own name. And by wondering whether one can answer for what 'I am (following)' means when that seems to necessitate an 'I am in as much as I am *alongside* [*après*] the animal'. Being *after*, being *alongside*, being near [*près*] would appear as different modes of being, indeed of *being-with*. With the animal. But, in spite of appearances, it isn't certain that these modes of being come to modify a preestablished being, even less a primitive 'I am'. In any case, they express a certain order of *being-huddled-together* [*être-serré*] (which is what the etymological root, *pressu*, indicates, whence follow the words *près*, *auprès*, *après*), the being-pressed, the being-with as being strictly attached, bound, enchained, being-under-pressure, compressed. impressed, repressed, pressed-against according to the stronger or weaker stricture of what always remains pressing. In what sense of the neighbour [*prochain*] (which is not necessarily that of a biblical or Graeco-Latin tradition) should I say that I am close or *next* to the animal, and that I am (following) it, and in what type or order of pressure? Being-with it in the sense of being-close-to-it? Being-alongside-it? Being-after-it? *Being-after-it* in the sense of the hunt, training, or taming, *being-after-it* in the sense of a succession or inheritance? In all cases, if I am (following) *after* it, the animal therefore comes before me, earlier than me (*früher* is Kant's word regarding the animal, and Kant will be one of our witnesses to come). The animal is there before me, there next to me, there in front of me – I who am (following) after it. And also, therefore, since it is before me, it is behind me. It surrounds me. And from the vantage of this being-there-before-me it can allow itself to be looked at, no doubt, but also – something that philosophy perhaps forgets, perhaps being this calculated forgetting itself – it can look at me. It has its point of view regarding me. The point of view of the absolute other, and nothing will have ever given me more food for thinking through this absolute alterity of the neighbour or of the next(-door) than these moments when I see myself seen naked under the gaze of a cat.

Jacques Derrida, extracts from *L'Animal que donc je suis* (manuscript 1997); trans. David Wills, *The Animal That Therefore I Am* (New York: Fordham University Press, 2008) 3–6; 9–11.

Giorgio Agamben
The Open: Man and Animal//2002

[...] For anyone undertaking a genealogical study of the concept of 'life' in our culture, one of the first and most instructive observations to be made is that the concept never gets defined as such. And yet, this thing that remains indeterminate gets articulated and divided time and time again through a series of caesurae and oppositions that invest it with a decisive strategic function in domains as apparently distant as philosophy, theology, politics and – only later – medicine and biology. That is to say, everything happens as if, in our culture, life were *what cannot be defined, yet precisely for this reason, must be ceaselessly articulated and divided*.

In the history of Western philosophy, this strategic articulation of the concept of life has a foundational moment. It is the moment in *De anima* when, from among the various senses of the term 'to live', Aristotle isolates the most general and separable one.

It is through life that what has soul in it (*l'animale*) differs from what has not (*l'inanimato*). Now this term 'to live' has more than one sense, and provided anyone alone of these is found in a thing we say that the thing is living – viz. thinking, sensation, local movement and rest, or movement in the sense of nutrition, decay and growth. Hence we think of all species of plants also as living, for they are observed to possess in themselves a principle and potentiality through which they grow and decay in opposite directions ... This principle can be separated from the others, but not they from it – in mortal beings at least. The fact is obvious in plants; for it is the only psychic potentiality (*potenza dell'anima*) they possess. Thus, it is through this principle that life belongs to living things. ... By nutritive power (*threptikon*) we mean that part of the soul which is common also to plants.

It is important to observe that Aristotle in no way defines what life is; he limits himself to breaking it down, by isolating the nutritive function, in order then to rearticulate it in a series of distinct and correlated faculties or potentialities (nutrition, sensation, thought). Here we see at work that principle of foundation which constitutes the strategic device par excellence of Aristotle's thought. It consists in reformulating every question concerning 'what something is' as a question concerning 'through what (*dia ti*) something belongs to another thing'. To ask why a certain being is called living means to seek out the foundation by which living belongs to this being. That is to say, among the various senses of the term 'to live', one must be separated from the others and settle to the bottom, becoming the principle by which life can be attributed to a certain being. In other words, what has been separated and divided (in this case nutritive life), what a sort of *divide et impera* – allows the construction of the unity of life as the hierarchical articulation of a series of functional faculties and oppositions.

The isolation of nutritive life (which the ancient commentators will already call vegetative) constitutes in every sense a fundamental event for Western science. When Bichat, many centuries later, in his *recherches physiologiques sur la vie et la mort*, distinguishes between 'animal life', which is defined by its relation to an external world, and 'organic life', which is nothing other than a habitual succession of assimilation and excretion', it is again Aristotle's nutritive life that marks out the obscure background from which the life of the higher animals get separated. According to Bichat, it is as if two 'animals' lived together in every higher organism: *l'animal existent au-dedans* – whose life, which Bichat defines as 'organic', is merely the repetition of, so to speak, blind and unconscious functions (the circulation of blood, respiration, assimilation, excretion, etc.) – and *l'animal existent au-dehours* – whose life, for Bichat the only one that merits the name of 'animal', is defined through its relation to the external world. In man, these two animals live together, but they do not coincide; the internal animal's (*animale-di-dentro*) organic life begins in the foetus before animal life does, and in ageing and in the final death throes it survives the death of the external animal (*animale-di-fouri*).

It is hardly necessary to mention the strategic importance that the identification of this split between the functions of vegetative life and the functions of relational life has had in the history of modern medicine. The successes of modern surgery and anaesthesia are founded upon, among other things, just the possibility of dividing and, at the same time, articulating Bichat's two animals. And as Foucault has shown, when the modern State, starting in the seventeenth century, began to include the care of the population's life as one of its essential tasks, thus transforming its politics into bio-politics, it was primarily by means of a progressive generalization and redefinition of the concept of vegetative life (now coinciding with the biological heritage of the nation) that the State would carry out its new vocation. And still today, in discussions about the definition *ex lege* of the criteria for clinical death, it is a further identification of this bare life – detached from any brain activity and, so to speak, from any subject – which decides whether a certain body can be considered alive or must be abandoned to the extreme vicissitude of transplantation.

The division of life into vegetal and relational, organic and animal, animal and human, therefore passes first of all as a mobile border within living man, and without this intimate caesura the very decision of what is human and what is not would probably not be possible. It is not possible to oppose man to other living things, and at the same time to organize the complex – and not always edifying – economy of relations between men and animals, only because something like an animal life has been separated within man, only because his distance and proximity to the animal have been measured and recognized first of all in the closest and most intimate place.

But if this is true, if caesura between the human and the animal passes first of all within man, then it is the very question of man – and of 'humanism' – that must be posed in a new way. In our culture, man has always been thought of as the articulation and conjunction of a body and a soul, of a living thing and a *logos*, of a natural (or animal) element and a supernatural or social or divine element. We must learn instead to think of man as what results from the incongruity of these two elements, and investigate not the metaphysical mystery of conjunction, but rather the practical and political mystery of separation. What is man, if he is always the place – and, at the same time, the result – of ceaseless divisions and caesurae? It is more urgent to work on these divisions, to ask in what way – within man – has man been separated from non-man, and the animal from the human, than it is to take positions on the great issues, on so-called human rights and values. And perhaps even the most luminous sphere of our relations with the divine depends, in some way, on that darker one which separates us from the animal.

Giorgio Agamben, extract from *L'Aperto: l'uomo e l'animale* (Turin: Bollati Boringhieri, 2002); trans. Kevin Atell, *The Open: Man and Animal* (Stanford: Stanford University Press, 2004) 13–16.

Alan Sonfist
In Conversation with Robert Rosenblum//1990

Alan Sonfist The idea of digging up the past to bring it into the present is exactly what my art is about. I see myself as a visual archaeologist. The research that I do is extensive: the New York City sculpture *Time Landscape*, which I started in 1965, took ten years. I searched through old Dutch records of lumber supplies and read accounts of walks to their favourite streams. From that I was able to get an idea of how the city looked prior to man's interventions. The idea of uncovering the multiple histories of an area and incorporating them into an artwork set in a contemporary environment is integral to my artwork, and has been from the beginning.

Robert Rosenblum So is it really a sort of natural history equivalent to art history? The whole tenor of the past ten, twenty years is to reconstruct the historical past, to dig it out, and make it look as if it were resurrected. You are doing that in terms of what was here before we were. There seems to be a parallel there.

Sonfist All my art deals with the primal experience of creation in the land. A good example is the *Circles of Time* (1986–89) at the Villa Celle in Tuscany. There, to enter the main part of the sculpture, you must go through a tunnel in the earth and rediscover our geological past. What I have created is a circle, rippling in waves of rock, each concentric circle representing a layer of time, as with the growth of a hardwood tree. This is a visualization of the upper and lower strata of the Tuscan hills. As one walks out of this ring, one enters a ring of laurel representing the Greeks, who introduced the tree to Italy. One then goes through an opening which is close to the ground, and there you can feel and smell the Etruscan herbs. Then the passage rises, opening to view bronze castings of endangered and extinct trees, which mimic and represent the Greek and Roman heroes of ancient sculpture. In the centre of the circle is the virginal forest of Italy, that which existed before human intervention. Finally, to complete the histories of the land, I have represented its contemporary use by a ring of olive trees and wheat.

Rosenblum One of the things that I wonder about, since this includes not only your geological strata in regression, is your regression to primitive states of being. How do you fit that in? I mean, the pieces where you were caged in the zoo, and where you ran through the woods imitating an animal?

Sonfist I would say that, as humans we are all part of the environment. That is a primary revelation in my art. The earth artists, for instance, went out into the desert to work: my art is to rediscover my own part in the city. I grew up in New York. The roots of my caged-animal performance are here, especially in my childhood trips to the Bronx Zoo. Somtimes I would sneak into those environments, right into the cages with the animals.

Rosenblum What are the species? I'm trying to think of how you could get in.

Sonfist Mostly I visited the wolves, antelope and deer. Since I was a child, the animals would walk right up to me. They were very curious. Sometimes I would just jump the fence, go into the trees and play. So the actual past is where my animal fantasies came from. It relates to archaeology, because it's almost like I'm unearthing my own childhood experiences. When I grew up in the city, I lived next to one of the last original New York forests in the Bronx, which has since been destroyed.

Rosenblum It seems like an ideal situation. A combination of both private and personal history, your own regression to our past, and also public history, because your experience is part of a general communal one. I am always curious about the proportion of science to poetry, if they can be separated. That is, how much actual work do you do in terms of research in order to find the truth about geological, botanical developments wherever you are working. Is it imaginary? I mean, what is the proportion of fact to fiction?

Sonfist In New York City I have created several forests. Each one has its own unique vegetation which I get from a history of each sculpture site. In Dallas, I have traced the history of the Trinity River, so that it could be reconstructed into a functional waterway. The city is using this environmental sculpture as part of its master plan. I have also traced the historical streams of New York and proposed that a bronze line be set in the concrete, marking the courses they once traversed. During Earth Day in 1970, I marked off the natural boundary of

New York to show where the island naturally ended before its boundary was expanded by humans.

Rosenblum Have any of the official historians of New York, whether involved in social history or natural history, been concerned with your work?

Sonfist Yes. After the sculpture in New York was created, several historians from around the city called to compliment me on the site. In the natural forests, I am not creating a true ecological model but a romantic one. My goal is to uncover the primary struggle of nature: between life and death. The human interaction is also a part of the historical time forest. It is like a palette. I see it as a layering out of the facts, be they natural cycles, ecological models or pure history; then I make the aesthetic decisions.

Rosenblum It is like reconstructing Darwin. Have you ever thought of doing environments with animals?

Sonfist When plans to reconstruct the Central Park Zoo were taking shape, I proposed to New York City officials that they create an environment with animals indigenous to Manhattan, such as deer, fozes and raccoons. It would be different from a typical zoo that has exotic animals. This is another concept of archaeological layering of the city environment. In Dallas, I proposed to create islands that would present primal forests, each with animals indigenous to the unique vegetation of that island. With contemporary evolution, the animals native to the city have become unfamiliar. Can you imagine walking down Spring Street and seeing a fox? Yet there are five ocelots in the Central Park zoo.

Rosenblum It is the most thrilling irony to turn the least natural of cities to its natural origins. It almost seems impossible to get from the present to the past. But obviously you work between the layers, and New York is the perfect place. The perfect city to do it in.

Sonfist As an art centre, New York is unique, but actually all cities have obliterated their natural past. They have built layers and layers of human habitation on top of it. It is only in the last twenty years that New York has rediscovered its historical buildings. In my work the city's historical nature can also become a functional monument to the fabric of community. [...]

Alan Sonfist and Robert Rosenblum, extract from 'Interview with the Artist' (Brookfield, New York: Hillwood Art Museum, 1990); reprinted in *Nature: The End of Art* (Florence: Gli Ori, 2004) 8–10.

Mark Dion and Alexis Rockman
In Conversation//1991

Mark Dion The idea of both of us working collaboratively on a project may surprise some people. Our work represents opposite positions in terms of presentational methods. Yet we are both fascinated by this issue of r-selected species [such as weeds, insects or small rodents whose chief defence against unstable environments is rapid reproduction rather than adaptation]. I imagine this is because these animals and plants have a direct relationship to the theme of extinction – the focus of both of our practices for several years. I'm certain that you share my view that the loss of biodiversity is a critically underestimated ecological issue. For some time now we have known that life is based on complex webs of interrelationships. By destroying elements within those interrelationships we reduce our options for the future and threaten to disrupt the natural processes that keep the life-cycle going. Just how many pieces from the puzzle can you remove before you lose the picture?

Alexis Rockman Of course no one knows, and it's hard to decide what the picture is or was. Our relationship to this issue is based upon late twentieth-century conceptions, and the closest thing we have to a laboratory is the introduction of Europeans into the 'New World' in 1492. There is every indication that the track record for dealing with native peoples and species of plants and animals is atrocious. I view the r-selected species as symptomatic of Western intolerance and arrogance. It's surprising to think that most of the species synonymous with American history were deliberately introduced by Europeans. The horse, the pig and cattle all outcompeted the indigenous species. There is, of course, an even darker side to the equation. With the Europeans came a host of freeloading inquiline species: rats, roaches, pigeons, European sparrows. It's like the return of the repressed; no matter how controlled or controlling, there is always a fly in the ointment. This reminds me of the movie *Creepshow* where the protagonist quarantines himself in his modernist box penthouse and the water bugs still find a way to come up through the drain.

Dion You're right when you suggest that the European invasion of the Americas presents a test case for the introduction of r-selected species. The Europeanization of the 'New World' ecosystems was well underway by 1500, and by 1550, North and South American flora and fauna were irrevocably altered. In the same way that we can never piece together a clear picture of pre-Columbian cultures before the disease, ethnocide and genocide perpetrated by the Europeans, we also will never know exactly what and how many plant and animal species (in particular, birds and reptiles) were driven to extinction during the first one hundred years of the European conquest.

Rockman Back to the question of our involvement with ecological issues … There are several differences regarding the way in which we approach such problems. You seem to come to them from a more clinical, methodological position wherein you generate a revisionist 'official story' of natural history in a pseudo-documentary format. My position is more about ambivalence. I see these organisms as symptomatic of our own arrogance and vulnerability, these symbolically marginalized species are considered ruthless and out of control. But this perception is really symptomatic of our inability to control nature. I admire their power and adaptability.

Dion You've touched on exactly what makes these organisms so detestable in our culture. These creatures are constant reminders of our part in the biological contract. They remind us that, like all animals, we are implicated in a set of relations with other animals, that we do not benefit from some of those relationships. The modernist cube, which you referred to earlier, is an example of the denial of the biological contract. It is the environment without nature. In the same way that our culture does not acknowledge shit, distances itself from the production of food or denies the processes of ageing, these animals remind us that we too are animals – and therefore mortal. You mentioned that my approach is related to documentary. I view my practice as closely akin to documentary. In the 1960s, documentary film was dissected and then reinvented. And in the 1970s the use of photodocumentary was examined. I'm interested in a different site for the production of truth – the pedagogical institution of the museum. Since, like you, my main interest is the question of the representation of nature, it is the natural history, ethnographic and history museums – as well as the zoological and botanical parks – that interest me. These are fascinating institutions because they represent a society's 'official story', all the conventions and assumptions of what gets to stand for nature at a particular time for a particular group of people. [...]

Rockman Although we share an enthusiasm for the traditional language of natural history representations, the differences in our methods are quite radical. You tend to use the format of the installation to collect and reframe taxidermic specimens, signs, didactic diagrams and other elements in order to construct an engaging framework of investigation and information. I use empirical studies of botanical and zoological illustrations and the great mural cycles depicting the natural world, produced during the early part of the century, as primary models […]

Dion I think we both have an interest in challenging institutional forms of knowledge, representation and information. The natural history museum, as a cultural construct, often remains under the spell of an ideology of pure scientific objectivity, even though scientists such as Stephen Jay Gould and Robert Barker represent clear departures from this tradition. Anyone interested in working within these institutions soon finds a lack of tolerance for anything but the most authoritarian method of presentation. Metaphor, irony, humour and self-reflexivity are all strategies outside their notion of how information should be organized. The exhibition of science imagines its expression existing outside the realms of politics and popular culture. Yet quite recently there have been some encouraging signs of change within the institutional framework. But as artists, we have a certain advantage over the conventional methods, because we are not necessarily inclined to accept the notion that scientific discourse should be isolated; also, we are not obliged to produce logical equations that add up in an entirely rational manner. I'm convinced that our method of organizing information can be much more compelling and challenging. For me, making a point is the easy part of a project – it's just the beginning. […]

Mark Dion and Alexis Rockman, extract from conversation, *Journal of Contemporary Art* (Spring/ Summer, 1991); reprinted in *Concrete Jungle* (Middletown, Connecticut: Ezra and Cecile Zikha Gallery, Wesleyan University, 1993) 6–8.

Andrew Ross
In Conversation with Mark Dion//1996

Mark Dion In your recent writing, you discuss a certain suspicion of pleasure and excess found within the Green movement (from the asceticism of Thoreau to Jimmy Carter's sweater, to the limit-to-growth arguments of today). Yet, sometimes when I read your characterizations of environmentalists, I don't recognize who you are speaking about. If there is one thing that unites the various individuals I know involved in eco-activism, it is the intense pleasure they derive from nature. Regardless of whether they are bird watchers, conservation biologists, city parks planners, urban gardeners, social ecologists or vacant lot naturalists, many different people have become politicized through a passionate pleasure derived from their interaction with the natural world. None of these people are essentialists or purists in their understanding of what gets to stand for Nature. Perhaps because you are admittedly not a nature-lover, you sometimes underplay the political potential generated by the pleasure that motivates these individuals?

Andrew Ross Yes and no. My arguments are in no way directed at or against the pleasure people take in natural environments, but rather at the advocacy of sacrifice and collective self-denial urged by many environmentalist polemics in the movement. Many of these polemics do appeal to guilt and self-reform in the Puritan mould, and have a limited, local meaning (i.e. the Northern tier of countries). When I suggest that Green politics has to offer more in the way of social fulfilment than coercive self-limitation, I am drawing attention to the uses that have been made, historically, of manufactured scarcity to impose austerity on vulnerable populations.

The rage for limitation often has dangerous social consequences, and in many cases is underscored by neo-Malthusian currents that run strong in certain quarters of the Green movement. By now, you would think that most people would be aware of the eugenic connotations of the arguments about overpopulation, or that the concept of 'wilderness preservation' only makes sense in Northern countries where purification has often depended upon a powerful link between social Darwinism and ideas about the natural order. The American practice of evacuating indigenous peoples in order to create wilderness is now being exported to those parts of the non-Western world where eco-tourism is beginning to flourish.

On the other hand, the pleasure people take in nature is far from innocent, and not unrelated to some of these concerns. This is why it's a little dodgy to build a politics solely upon pleasure, although a politics without pleasure is not worth having. When I say that I am not a nature-lover, I mean that I don't have any of the bona fide credentials conventionally required of environmentalist writers. I get my quota of countryside trips, but I don't hike on trails regularly. I don't live in the Adirondacks, like nature writer Bill McKibben (although if everyone followed his example there wouldn't be an Adirondacks), and my leisure time is not driven by the pursuit of nature. I say that upfront to preempt being called on it, although saying it always partially undercuts any authority one might claim to speak about environmental matters. Quite frankly, I am just as much interested in urban ecology, and in the kinds of questions relating to environmental justice that are not ordinarily associated with trees, rivers and mountains.

Dion You and I use a kind of shorthand. When we say 'the Greens', we are talking about a social movement roughly called environmentalism. It has its own complex history and ideology, both left and right, which includes aspects of ecology (the science of the study of living organism's relation to their non-living environment) and conservation (the notion that the natural world must be wisely managed in order to continue to exist). But maybe we don't mean exactly the same thing. For example, I was just in Europe and had a difficult time explaining how the animal rights movement, which supports individual animal welfare, differs from conservation biology's stress on biodiversity, or the rights of animal species. Who are the Greens to you, and how is it possible to lump them all together?

Ross I'm not sure that there's significantly more disagreement, or lack of common ground, among environmentally-minded people than in other social movements, but it often feels that way. Nature, after all, is the consummate people-pleaser – it is serviceable to anyone who wants to speak in its name (viz. the Wise Use movement, which borrowed the moniker of early century Conservationists in order to camouflage their backlash campaigns with Green rhetoric). Nature can always be wheeled in to ventriloquize support for a social claim about environmental matters. It's more difficult to do that within social movements of disenfranchised peoples. They have their own voices, after all, which Nature lacks. This is the fundamental problem of Green politics. Nature cannot speak for itself, but everyone else is all too willing to do the job. Now this perception is often caricatured and sleazily dismissed as a belief that the natural world is entirely socially constructed and doesn't really exist. In fact, it's a very important point to acknowledge, and goes a long way to explaining the difficulties you allude to in your question.

Dion One of the most invaluable aspects of your writing is a relentless scrutiny of the more sinister flaws in the history of America's environmental movement. You have examined its relation to eugenics, its pervasive social Darwinism, its obsession with self-denial and scarcity and its anti-urbanism and machismo. A number of ecological organizations and environmental studies programmes maintain a deeply romantic relationship to this grimly chequered past. Of course, there are other models. After all, for every gun-toting, neocolonial, patriarchal conservationist like Teddy Roosevelt, there is a socially insightful ecologist, compelled to translate science into environmental activism, like Rachel Carson. But, why is serious eco-criticism such a late bloomer?

Ross There has always been a body of criticism devoted to nature writing, landscape art and wilderness appreciation. By 'serious', I assume that you mean a critical approach that does not take Nature for granted, but interrogates its representation. Well, most of the reasons have to do with the distance between environmentalism and other social movements related to race, gender and sexuality. First, environmentalism has been pursued under the aegis of scientific authority, so there has been a tradition of deference to natural, as opposed to social or cultural criteria in building a critical body of ethics. It has taken a while for cultural critics to catch up, and there's still a long way to go. Second, the other social movements I mentioned developed schools of cultural criticism that are largely based upon 'liberating' unheard voices in literature or history or art. Movements in critical writing have been the point of entry for identity politics on the part of women, queer, postcolonial and minority thinkers. This was accompanied by a certain degree of empowerment and representation in public life. As I said before, Green politics does not necessarily carry this liberatory air. By this criterion, of course, the predominantly white, middle-class stewardship of the ecology movement does not make it a great candidate for the empowerment of marginalized persons or communities, at least, not in the pastoral mode of its perceived stereotype. Another major difference is that cultural critics do not respond well to narratives of self-restraint. More often they favour a hermeneutic that uncovers that which is hidden. Liberating the voice of the planet doesn't count in the same way. More attention to urban ecology and environmental justice will change this view.

Dion Some have characterized your critique of the Greens as too harsh. Clearly you would not waste so much energy on the environmental movement if you didn't think it had some powerful potential.

Ross My criticisms are strategic rather than constitutional, and they emerge out of the tensions within the ecology movement that are well-known: basically, the antagonism between social justice and wilderness wings of the movement. If my criticisms are a little zealous at times, it's because I do think that ecological consciousness is one of the most important bulwarks against the ravages of capitalism, at all levels – economic, political, cultural. And the value of Green politics is that there is little that cannot and should not be subsumed under its banner. To limit the definition of ecological concerns to one sector of our political life is to balkanize our ability to respond in a concerted fashion, or to think in terms of coalitions. Look at 'quality of life' issues in the cities. Where do you draw the line between issues that relate to toxic dumping, or the location of incinerators, and those that relate to the uneven distribution of resources like education, housing, parks, transportation and clinics? All of these factors affect our environment, not just the former. […]

Mark Dion and Andrew Ross, extract from conversation in Dion and Alexis Rockman, eds, *Concrete Jungle: A Pop Media Investigation of Death and Survival in Urban Ecosystems* (New York: Juno Books, 1996) 6–10.

herman de vries
the world we live in is a revelation//1992

the world we live in is a revelation that can be 'read', experienced. everything we experience or are able to experience is significant for itself and for everything. we can find this significance everywhere around us. but as plastics, cars, computers and ice cream have in the first place significance for our human life and culture, plants, trees, birds flying, earth and the streams of water are of more general significance, because they form part of our primary reality, nature. that many of us do not know anything anymore of this primary reality is dramatic, makes life poor, makes culture poor, but does not change the actuality of its primarity.

around our house is only a small garden. many plants grow there of many species and all kinds of insects abound around and between. but the richness of it is only seen by her or him who can see. i collected from all the different species in this little garden one leaf and mounted them on the surface of paper. a multitude of forms became visible in 'forms from the garden'.

there are artists who use natural materials. they create with natural materials or take them into their work. not me. the difference is that they use natural materials – i only present them. i have nothing to add, nothing to change, only to respect – because of the revelatory character of everything in the natural world. here i find my identity. when i look and see a grass, a tree, a stream, it becomes part of my identity, inner and outer world unite. my food becomes me – i become my food. all and everything that is material shows at the same time its transcendence. physics and metaphysics are one.

to be all ways to be to be to be ways all to be to be to be.

once i published a book: *i am what i am – flora incorporata.* it contains the names of all the species of plants that i remembered to have taken in me. as food, for healing, for change of mind, for free insights, such as peyote, psilocybe, datura. they cleansed my view, cleansed my senses, made me free to see.

as a child i had a deep mystic feeling for nature. sometimes in a quiet spot in the dunes on the coast of holland, i undressed myself and pressed my body to the earth and felt a great joy. or, as a little boy, i fixed my eyes on the endless rolling waves of the sea and fell into a light trance. later, i did scientific work for two institutes for research in nature. i studied the geographic distribution of small mammals, i studied the food of water rats, i studied the food habits of weasels and wild cats – but i was never so close any more. taking psychedelics liberated my view of many conditions and the old relationship was renewed.

in the early sixties i exhibited my work in zero context. we liberated seeing by stripping away all the unneeded, and zero remained. this position is still mine – the facts i show now (since 1970) are no longer empty white surfaces or randomly distributed elements but 'real works' from nature. my studio is about 200 km² around and always there where i am.

in 1972 i wrote on a walk in our vast forests:

my poetry is the world
i write it every day
i rewrite it every day
i see it every day
i read it every day
i eat it every day
i sleep it every day

the world is my chance
it changes me every day
my chance is my poetry

this line of thought is still guiding me now. i have nothing to say: it is all here. art is not definable. every definition of it is a limitation. but for me it has to do with the formulation of consciousness or with the process of becoming conscious. this consciousness i see happening around me in nature and i show what i have seen happening, what i have seen being.

this and no thing
here and everywhere
all

herman de vries, 'the world we live in is a revelation' (eschenau, october 1992), in herman de vries, *to be* (Stuttgart, 1995) 156–8.

Bonnie Sherk
Crossroads Community: The Farm//1977

It seems that some clues to our possible, positive survival as a species can be found by involving ourselves in the human creative process (art) and by re-examining our place as human creatures in relation to other life forms, and by understanding and communicating with those life systems and forms in a more sensitive and conscious way. Very generally, people of our civilization tend to be extremely presumptuous and naïve about their relationship to the universe. Some symptoms of this adolescence are racism and sexism; renovating much of the earth with concrete and basing our modern lives on confused computer categories and bureaucratic ballgames; insensitivities to native intelligences of plants, animals and children; mass disregard and disrespect for the uniqueness of individuals; bias against feeling states; and the overwhelming greed, waste and territorialism of huge numbers of people, corporations and governments. If we are to continue on this planet and grow as conscious beings we must attain a more spiritual and ecological balance within ourselves and among larger groups and nations. How can we do this?

Each of us has the potential for discovery and may have solutions for these grave problems. If we can learn to trust and share, and relax and flow, we will be able to receive the magic which surrounds us every moment and which we are.

In my own life I have striven to understand and act on these issues and qualities, which to me are connected to the essence of being. I have experienced through art and the observation of natural processes the wholeness of life and the interconnectedness of different states of being/knowing/loving. The creation of art is akin to the spirit and attitude of country in its logic of wholeness and process. Everything found in the country is implicit in the city. Urban environments today, however, due in part to technological excesses, fragment our spaces and lives so that we have difficulty experiencing whole systems. This fragmentation guides us towards the disintegration of our personalities and the loss of our identities.

As an artist, I have tried to expand the concept of art to include and even be life, and to make visible connections among different aesthetics, styles and systems of knowledge. The most recent and devotional vehicle for this coming together is a multicultural, agricultural collaborative artwork called *Crossroads Community (the farm)*, or more simply, *The Farm*. This life-scale environmental, performance sculpture, which is also a non-profit public trust, and a collage of local, State and Federal sources, exists at a multitude of levels, including cartoon, metaphor, contradiction and action.

Physically, *The Farm* is a series of simultaneous community gathering spaces: a farmhouse with earthy, funky and elegant environments; a theatre and rehearsal space for different artforms; a school without walls; a library; a darkroom; unusual gardens; an indoor/outdoor environment for humans and other animals; and a future cafe, tea room and nutrition/healing centre. Within these places many people of different ages, backrounds and colours come and go, participating in and creating a variety of programmes which richly mix with the life processes of plants and animals. All of these life elements are integrated and relate holistically, with fascinating interfaces. It is these interfaces which may indeed be the sources of emerging new artforms,

The Farm, as a life frame, is particularly unusual, however, because it juxtaposes, symbolically and actually, a technological monolith with an art/farm/life complex. Crossroads Community sits adjacent to a major freeway interchange on its southern side, where four high need neighbourhoods and three creeks converge.

On its northern boundaries, *The Farm* edges on a 5.5 acre open space of land which the City of San Francisco has just acquired for a neighbourhood park. (*The Farm* was instrumental in calling attention to the availability of this land and convincing the City to buy it.)

Part of *The Farm*'s dream is to uncover the natural resources of the earth, like the water which flows underneath, and to recycle the concrete which currently covers the land to create rolling hillsides, meadows, gardens, windmills, ponds, play and performing spaces, etc. This lush, green environment would connect *The Farm* with the public elementary school that borders the future park on the north.

The potential for this project, which involves the creative integrity of its surrounding neighbours and school children is astounding as a model for other places and as a possible series of solutions for the many urban errors specific to this site. Another aspect for the future is to blur the boundaries between land parcels and act on new possibilities for fluid interchange.

The most critical difficulty for *The Farm*, at present, is to make an unresponsive and frightened establishment receptive to a Gift that is a tribute to humanity and a celebration of magic.

Bonnie Sherk, 'Crossroads Community (The Farm)', Center for Critical Inquiry Position Paper, 1st International Symposium, San Francisco Art Institute (November 1977).

Joseph Beuys
7,000 Oaks: Conversation with Richard Demarco//1982

Joseph Beuys [*7,000 Oaks*] puts a kind of line under my so-called spatial doings in so-called environments. I want it principally to mark the finish of this kind of work. I wish to go more and more outside, to be among the problems of nature and problems of human beings in their working places. This will be a regenerative activity; it will be a therapy for all of the problems we are standing before … That is my general aim. I proposed this to Rudi Fuchs when he invited me to participate in Documenta. I said that I would not like to go again inside buildings to participate in the setting up of so-called artworks. I wished to go completely outside and to make a symbolic start for my enterprise of regenerating the life of humankind within the body of society and to prepare a positive future in this context.

I think the tree is an element of regeneration which in itself is a concept of time. The oak is especially so because it is a slowly growing tree with a kind of really solid heartwood. It has always been a form of sculpture, a symbol for this planet ever since the Druids, who are called after the oak: Druid means oak. They used their oaks to define their holy places. I can see such a use as representing the really progressive character of the idea of understanding art, when it is related to the life of humankind within the social body in the future. The tree planting enterprise provides a very simple but radical possibility for this when we start with the 7,000 oaks.

Demarco Why seven thousand, Joseph?

Beuys I think that is a kind of proportion and dimension, firstly because the seven represents a very old rule for planting trees. You know that from already existing places and towns. In America there is a very big town called Seven Oaks, also in England at Sevenoaks. You see that seven as a number is organically, in a way, related to such an enterprise and it matches also the seventh Documenta. I said that seven trees is a very small ornament. Seventy is not bringing us to the idea of what I call in German *Verwaldung*. It suggests making the world a big forest, making towns and environments, forest-like. Seventy would not signify the idea. Seven hundred again was still not enough. So I felt 7,000 was something I could do in the present time for which I could take the responsibility to fulfil as a first step. So 7,000 oaks will be a very strong visible result in 300 years. So you can see the dimension of time. […]

I see it as a first step because this enterprise will stay forever and I think I see coming the need for such enterprises: tree planting enterprises and tree planting organizations, and for this the Free International University is a good body. [...]

Demarco It is a sadness isn't it, in our time, that it is the United States which is growing rockets, and nuclear weaponry, rather than trees. Now you will make this statement to counterbalance this, in the middle of Kassel. Can you describe this enterprise more precisely.

Beuys I will start in very difficult places in the centre of the town. There the places are very difficult because there are already coatings of asphalt and stone slabs with infrastructures of electrical things and the German Post Office. In the centre of the town the planting of trees is most necessary for the people that live there within an urban context. There the planting of the trees will also be most expensive. The whole thing I guess will cost about three million Deutschmarks. [...]

I have received already help for the start of this thing, so for this year I have enough money to buy the stones because every tree is marked with a basalt stone. It's a natural form which need not be worked on as a sculpture or by stone masons. The stone is similar to what you will find in the basalt columns of the Giant's Causeway, but more triangular in shape with five, six, or seven angles or irregular angled stones which come from the volcanos ...

Demarco Will they come from the volcanos around Kassel?

Beuys It is very organic because this nearest volcano to Kassel is only thirty kilometres from the centre of the town. It is very natural to take the stone to the place where I will plant the trees. [...]

I planted the first symbolic tree in the centre of the Friedrichsplatz. This is on the axis of the main building for the Documenta exhibitions and on the right side of this tree there is one stone already deposited. When the last of the 7,000 stones will disappear from this place it will say that the last of the 7,000 oaks is planted. That will be maybe in three years. [...]

Demarco Can you tell me, Joseph, just before we finish, how this tree project will allow you to continue your work on a new and wider dimension ... this is a new dimension ... it is a new step for you.

Beuys It is a new step in this working with trees. It is not a real new dimension in the whole concept of the metamorphosis of everything on this earth and of the metamorphosis of the understanding of art. It is about the metamorphosis of the social body in itself to bring it to a new social order for the future in comparison with the existing private capitalistic system and state centralized communistic system. It has a lot to do with a new quality of time. There is another dimension of time involved, so it has a lot to do with the new understanding of the human being in itself.

It has to make clear a reasonable, practical anthropology. It is also a spiritual necessity which we have to view in relation to this permanent performance. This will enable it to reach to the heart of the existing systems – especially to the heart of economics – since the wider understanding of art is related to everybody's creative ability. It makes it very clear and understandable to everybody that the capital of the world is not money, as we understand it, but capital is the human ability for creativity, freedom and self-determination in all their working places ... This idea would lead to a neutralization of capital and would mean that money is no longer a commodity in the economy. Money is a bill for law, for rights and duties you know ... it will be as real, and will lead to a democratic bank system ...

Demarco It will, in fact, bring employment ...

Beuys In fact it will organically prohibit every kind of unemployment, and organically it will stop inflation and deflation. This is because it deals with the rules of organic money-flow. This makes clear that all these interpretations of the future, especially the interpretations of time, have a lot to do with a new understanding of the human being as a spiritual being. If you have the spirit in focus, you have also another concept of time ... you see time on earth as a physical reality. It takes place in space so it is the space/time relation which Einstein is speaking about. This already gives a kind of allusion to another dimension, but I think this other dimension is something we have still to detect ... When I say we have still to detect it, it has already been detected. It is there as one dimension in my work which I show [in the gallery]. This is the warmth quality ...

Demarco The quality of warmth.

Beuys The quality of warmth. This dimension is, in fact another dimension that has nothing to do with the space and time relation. It is another dimension which comes to exist in a place and which goes away again. This is a very interesting aspect of physics, since until now most physicists were not prepared to deal with the theory of warmth. Thermodynamics was always very complicated stuff.

Love is the most creative and matter-transforming power. You see in this context it is very simply expressed. Now it is not shown in very interesting diagrams, which one could also bring to this discussion ... But to promote this interest for all these necessities to the real anthropology, and not this fashionable way of speaking about anthropology ... in this relationship I start with the most simple looking activity, but it is a most powerful activity; it is planting trees.

Joseph Beuys and Richard Demarco, extracts from 'Interview with Richard Demarco', in *Energy Plan for the Western Man* (New York: Four Walls Eight Windows, 1990) 109–16.

Robert Morris
Notes on Art as/and Land Reclamation//1979

[...] Although site-specific works have been produced now for over a decade, their sponsorship has been erratic and the budgets generally below what is required for truly ambitious works. There has certainly been no one source of sponsorship: various museums, private individuals, international exhibitions, local communities – these and others have from time to time made site works possible, but often just barely. The works sponsored have more often than not been temporary. But now on the horizon there is potential for widespread sponsorship of outdoor earth and site-specific works. Local, state, federal and industrial funding is on tap. The key that fits the lock to the bank is 'land reclamation'. Art functioning as land reclamation has a potential sponsorship in millions of dollars and a possible location over hundreds of thousands of acres throughout the country.

A number of issues, or perhaps pseudo- or non-issues, are raised by this possible ménage à trois between art, government and industry. One of these is not an issue, and that is the objection to art's 'serving' as land reclamation, that it would somehow lose its 'freedom' in so doing. Art has always served. Sometimes the service has been visible – service to a patron, or to a governmental propaganda campaign. Sometimes the service is less visible, as when art meshes with and reinforces commodity consumption or remains 'abstract' while fulfilling a government commission. Context can also be read as service; it binds the political load of any work of art. In a deeper way, however, context is content. The issue of art as land reclamation is of course blurred by appeals by industry to the 'public need' for more natural resources, and thus more mines and environmental entropy that need cleaning up. Although minerals have been mined and used since the end of the Stone Age, the present-day escalation of mineral requirements and the energy needed for accelerating production is not so much an index of public need as of corporate administration. In a complex society, where everything is interconnected, it is not possible to decide which commodity, therefore which technology, therefore which resource, therefore which mine is essential and therefore worthy of reclamation. It might then seem that to practice art as land reclamation is to promote the continuing acceleration of the resource-energy-commodity-consumption cycle, as reclamation – defined aesthetically, economically, geophysically – functions to make acceptable original acts of resource extraction.

In so far as site works participate in art as land reclamation, they would seem to have no choice but to serve a public-relations function for mining interests in particular and the accelerating technological-consumerist programme in general. Participation, however, would seem to be no different from exhibition in any art gallery, which ipso facto participates in the commodity structure. None of the historical monumental works known today would have been made if the artists had refused to work (many, of course, had no option to refuse) because of either questionable sponsorship or disagreement with the ends to which the art was used. It is an illusion that artists have ever had anything to say about the functions of their works.

Although my project at Johnson Pit No. 30 in King County, Washington,[1] is to my knowledge the first instance of the hiring of an artist to produce art billed as land reclamation, the idea is far from new. The coal industry has in fact given the aesthetics of reclamation some attention: 'While aesthetics is a frequent subject of discussion among reclamation officials, regulatory agencies and environmentalists, aesthetic quality and the criteria and standards by which it is evaluated seem to be one of the least understood facets of surface mining.' [Nicholas Chironis, *Coal Age Operating Handbook of Surface Mining* (New York: Coal Age Mining Information Services, 1978)] [This handbook] notes a research effort (source of funding not given) centred at the University of Massachusetts involving the engineering firm of Skelly and Loy and two University of Massachusetts faculty members, Robert Mallary, a designer and sculptor, and Ervin Zube, who deals with the 'psychology of landscape assessment'. Although the overwhelming local feeling regarding reclamation, according to this research effort, is to 'return it to the previous contour', in Appalachia one of the prevailing surface mining techniques involves the removal of the tops of mountains. The major thrust of the group's 'systems approach' is aimed at dealing with reclamation that retains the flattened mountains of such sites. The research group notes with no trace of irony that 'operators at mountain-top removal mine sites are tending to favour this flat-top approach'. (Why wouldn't they, since it would be virtually impossible to rebuild the tops of mountains?) The group has proposed such striking aesthetic formulations as the following: 'Leav[ing] a few strategically located portions of the site untouched and unmined'. Such approaches are obviously nothing but coal-mining public relations.

What would *not* function as public relations, as any aesthetic effort made during or after mining operations functions to make the operations more acceptable to the public? Such aesthetic efforts are incapable of signalling any protest against the escalating use of non-renewable minerals and energy sources. What, one wonders, could be done for the Kennecott Bingham site, the ultimate site-specific work of such raging, ambiguous energy, so redolent with formal power and social threat, that no existing earthwork should even be compared to it? It should stand unregenerate as a powerful monument to a one-day non-existent resource. Other sites come to mind as well: those in Butte, Montana; the abandoned quarry at Marble, Colorado; some of the Vermont granite quarries; and a few of the deep-shaft coal and diamond mines qualify as significant monuments of the twentieth century. Are their implications any less sinister than those of the Great Pyramids? All great monuments celebrate the leading faith of the age – or, in retrospect, the prevailing idiocy. In one form or another, technology has produced the monuments of the twentieth century: the mines, the rocket assembly buildings so vast that weather forms inside, the Four Corners Power Complex, the dams of the 1930s, the linear and circulator accelerators of the 1950s and 1960s, the radiotelescope arrays of the 1960s and 1970s, and soon, the tunnel complex for the new MX missile. All these structures are testimony to faith in science and technology, the practice of which has brought the world to a point of crisis that nobody knows how to resolve. Art's greatest efforts are by comparison very definitely epiphenomena. Until now there could be no comparison. But the terms change when the US Bureau of Mines contributes to an artist's reclaiming the land. Art must then stand accused of contributing its energy to forces that are patently, cumulatively destructive.

Or is art beyond good and evil? It can and does flourish in the worst moral climates. Perhaps because it is amoral, it can deal with all manner of social extremes. It is an enterprise whose nature invites the investigation of extremes. Art erodes whatever seeks to contain and use it and inevitably seeps into the most contradictory recesses, touches the most repressed nerve, finds and sustains the contradictory without effort. Art has always been a very destructive force, the best example being its constant capacity to self-destruct, as in the sinking of modernism once it became a set of established rules that rationalized procedure, a lifestyle. Art has always been dependent upon and served one set of forces or another with little regard for the morality of those forces (pharoah, pope, nobility, capitalism). It makes little difference what forces make use of art. Art is always propaganda – for someone. History, which is always *someone's* history, invariably attempts to neutralize art (according to someone's history, Speer was a better artist than Géricault). Artists who deeply believe in social causes most often make the worst art.

If the only rule is that art must use whatever uses it, then one should not be put off by the generally high level of idiocy, politics and propaganda attached to public monuments – especially if one is in the business of erecting them. Should the government/industry sponsorship of art as land reclamation be enthusiastically welcomed by artists? Every large strip mine could support an artist in residence. Flattened mountain tops await the aesthetic touch. Dank and noxious acres of spoil piles cry out for some redeeming sculptural shape. Bottomless industrial pits yawn for creative filling – or deepening. There must be crews out there, straining and tense in the seats of their D-8 Caterpillars, waiting for that confident artist to stride over the ravaged ground and give the command. 'Gentlemen, start your engines, and let us definitively conclude the twentieth century.'

1   [*Untitled* (1979), an earthwork on a 3.7-acre site, formerly a sand and gravel pit abandoned in the 1940s. 'The work consists of a series of descending concentric slopes and benches located in the central part of the site. A hill-form rises on the lower third of the site. A parking lot is located at the top of the site. The entire site, graded and ungraded areas, is to be cleared of trees and planted in rye grass. I have employed a method of terracing which has been used in ancient times as well as the present. Such a method has produced sites of such widely varying context and purpose as palaces and strip-mines, highway embankments and mountainside cultivation. Persian and Moghul gardens were terraced as were the vast amphitheatres of Muyu-uray in Peru. Entire mountains in China have been terraced for erosion control and agriculture. The terrace is basically a cut and fill operation. The earth is removed in one place and piled in another.' – Robert Morris, in *Earthworks: Land Reclamation as Sculpture* (Seattle: Seattle Art Museum, 1979) 27.]

Robert Morris extract from 'Notes on Art as/and Land Reclamation', revised version of paper for the symposium 'Earthworks/Land Reclamation as Sculpture' (31 July 1979), *October*, vol. 12 (Spring 1980); reprinted in *Continuous Project Altered Daily: The Writings of Robert Morris* (Cambridge, Massachusetts: The MIT Press, 1993) 225–30 [original footnotes not included].

Mel Chin
In Conversation with Fareed Armaly and Ute Meta Bauer//1997

[Fareed Armaly and Ute Meta Bauer for *Georgia Magazine*] *Your two major projects that involved intense collaboration are* Revival Field *(1990–93) and* In the Name of the Place, *the [project for which you created the] GALA Committee. Let's begin with a discussion of* Revival Field, *which is important to see as a working methodological shift, linked to your first museum exhibition.*

[Mel Chin] *Revival Field* became an important research project as well as a sculpture. The revived ecological system that is created from sculpting away toxins from millions of tons of polluted earth – that is the 'aesthetic product'. Something that has potential for death or injury because of chemical and industrial practices is brought back to life using something that is found naturally – that is the sculpture. Its development has to be traced back to a decision I made after my first museum exhibition in 1989 at the Hirshhorn Museum in Washington DC.

I made there an extensive work called *The Operation of the Sun through the Cult of the Hand*, a study of alchemy from Greek and Chinese sources, linking everything from Joseph Needham's *Science and Civilization in China* to texts from ancient Alexandria. I was looking beyond Duchamp to explore the linking of material, form and linguistics. I was also trying to expose a relationship between Greek and Chinese thought, and the process by which transmission of ideas occurs. It was a fundamental work for me, partly as a reinvestigation of the term alchemy, described as an artistic process, but more as a way of mining and transforming information. A major factor was that all these were objects made by hand.

I remember being in an elevator, questioning myself, asking 'What do you love more than anything else Mel?', and a voice said, 'I love to make things with my hands', with a mind of course to continue to craft these kinds of unusual objects. And then another voice said 'OK – Stop!!' So I listened, I just stopped. After spending all this energy on my first museum exhibition, I really quit making artwork. I felt it was part of the alchemical process that the exhibition had investigated: when the fire has just started, you have to initiate something else – a transmutative process.

I did all kinds of jobs at the time – carpentry, art handling or whatever – it didn't matter. I partly felt I had to do it that way because the support wasn't there. It made more free time available for research though. I didn't make work but would just to go to libraries. I stumbled upon one article that struck me, written by Terence McKenna, a famous Psilocybe expert, in the *Whole Earth Review* in the fall of 1989. He described using the plant Datura as a method of cleaning heavy metals from the earth. I was struck by the poetic aspects of this possibility and I started studying Datura and its properties, but I found there was no case for it. I became dedicated to finding a scientist who really knew about this subject.

This turned out to be Dr Rufus Chaney, a research scientist from the US Department of Agriculture (USDA), whose passion was these specific plants that can remove toxins from the soil. Interestingly, he had to put his research aside due to the conservative political agenda during the 1980s. I mentioned to him McKenna's idea of cleaning up metals with Datura and he said 'that plant will get you high but it won't pick up any heavy metals; but if you want to pick up heavy metals I've got the plants.' He suggested reading material for me to better understand the technical language and background of what are termed 'hyper-accumulator' plants, which can pull metals out of the soil into their stems and leaves. Therefore this idea of cleansing the soil using plants seemed more and more possible to me. Chaney had explained that for the project to be scientific, a replicated field test needed to be done at a randomly selected site with toxic contamination somewhere in the world. The plants have to prove that they can pull up the metals. So I began to restructure my concept around these plants, and to create a revival field that would be able to provide data for the three years required for a field test. I suggested to Dr Chaney that since the USDA, the EPA (Environmental Protection Agency) and the other branches of government that are assigned to protect the environment are not going to do the testing, perhaps we can reinvent this piece as a shared field – an art project that would meet the needs of a scientific experiment.

Revival Field is a project that clearly involves collaboration, although that word was not available in the scientific field when we began – we had to call it co-operation. Dr Chaney was not officially able to work with me on a collective basis because he could not receive money and he could not give me money. I would be responsible for finding funding and a site, which led to a whole series of operations. It's easy enough to find a contaminated site, but it took months of negotiations with lawyers, waste management officials, the polluters themselves and city governments. I was on the phone every day for about a year talking to the EPA, and a lot of routes ended with an absolute 'no'. You can tell people you may have a solution for cleaning up their soil and they will tell you to your face that you are opening a can of worms. Negotiating: that was my artwork for many years.

So Revival Field was not about finding the universal 'green' cure. In fact, you drew upon ecology as a first experiment towards shaping your notion of new interrelated fields in art practice – in the tradition of alchemy, mixing the fields of science and art.

Well, *Revival Field* was not just a technical activity to grow plants, or an idea to save the earth or a clean-up process for everything. We understand a plant as a living organism held by primary forces – sun, water, soil – in an easy three-part relationship. But in the real world there are secondary, tertiary and quaternary relationships that make up a complex life that is always at the edge of chaos, at least that's the way it is always described. And in that definition of the ecology of relationships, life cannot be a two-dimensional mandala, it has to be extended into a shape that keeps changing, spinning, moving, stopping, moving backwards and bottlenecking in time because of many blocks. An idea floating through this continuum is constantly affected by changes in the political structure and economic structures, and it exists in a post-Newtonian space which is curving and moving around. These attitudes are all part of what it takes to have an idea exist in the world.

There is also a generational aspect to time, and importantly, a generational transfer of ideas. It has been ten years since *Revival Field* was first planned. Within the art world perhaps there is an understanding of the formal structure of an experiment that was done. There has also been progress in the field of green remediation, and I am so excited about that. Some day there may be a landscape that had once been a dangerous place to live, or could not be farmed because of its contamination, which has been cleaned and made usable by plants. In that case, who cares whether it is art or science? It is something that has occurred in the world which makes it more than it was. And I feel that the so-called 'sculpture' will be completed at that time.

Mel Chin, Fareed Armaly and Ute Meta Bauer, extract from interview in *Georgia Magazine* (Athens, Georgia, USA: University of Georgia, June 1997).

Mary Mattingly
In Conversation with Shane Danaher//2010

[…] *Shane Danaher* With *Waterpod* (2006–9, a floating, sculptural eco-habitat), *Wearable Home* (a series begun in 2001) and several of your other projects it seems as if you're blurring the line between 'art' and 'experimental engineering'. I was curious about your opinion on what constitutes an 'artist' at this point in history and what role artists should be playing in our world.

Mary Mattingly I think that the in-between spaces are one of the most interesting areas of art today, and they are clear ways for art to intervene in society. While I'm interested in the history of art, I am not interested in repeating history. I know that I am full of contradictions but I like using spaces that are not prepared for art to instigate, and spaces that are prepared for art to tell stories about evolution and ideas.

Danaher Your art is obviously very much intertwined with activism. Is this something you see as a personal choice or is it something you think should be a goal of artists in general? In your opinion, is there such a thing as art without a political subtext?

Mattingly The act of making art is infused with political subtext, and activism. Art is an agitation to the status-quo space and artists are agitators. Art is a freedom and opportunity to improve socio-political shortages in a society. It's hard to ignore the world surrounding us. As a human, if we are political then as an artist we should be political. I believe that a person's life and art should reflect one another.

Danaher In your *Wearable Home* series you've mentioned how one of your goals with the project was to create a 'general look de-emphasizing self and re-emphasizing everything else'. Seeing as art is for so many people a work, a self-actualization, how do you balance this view of the artist as an individual achiever with the stated goal of the artist being the exact opposite of that?

Mattingly I am interested in community. The *Wearable Home* is designed looking at uniforms around the world. It is designed to depict a dystopic future, but one that humans are swiftly approaching, and there is a safety in being part of a group, being identical to a friend and an enemy. Theories behind uniforms usually have to do with striving for a deeper consciousness. The idea is that people would spend less time focusing on appearance and more time focusing on questions about life and the worlds around us or, with the *Wearable Home*, more time focusing on survival and play.

But to respond to these ideas as being the antithesis of artists today, I think that there is a general understanding that artists are committed to a life of study and re-examination that is less based on personal appearance than most of society. But it is true, people in our culture in general spend a lot of time and energy attempting to be different, and our culture encourages that, largely to sell more products. There can be an infinite amount of things to sell if individuals are exponentially in process of differentiating themselves from one another and expressing uniqueness through products instead of ideas.

Danaher It seems that from most angles *Waterpod* was regarded as a success. Could you talk a little bit about what surprised you most about the project and any areas that you would have changed in retrospect? I know there were some more *Waterpod* concepts floating around; are you planning any other iterations of the project?

Mattingly The planning process for the *Waterpod* felt endless and demanded my total attention for a solid year before we launched. With a new request and demand daily from one agency or another, the only way to adapt to the situation was just to focus on completing one small step at a time.

Knowing that there was so much to do before it could be realized, I could not really take time or a step back from my position as organizer to consider what the reality would be like if it was achieved, because that reality was always so far away. So when we moved on to the *Waterpod* this past June, I didn't really have any preconceptions about what it would be like. I had hopes, and imagined many different scenarios, and none of them prepared me for the incredible kindness, engagement of many communities, and the welcoming aspects of the project. Nothing prepared me for life under a microscope either. In a way I hadn't really imagined, the *Waterpod* was an endurance project and a performance, but coupled with a place for scientific data collection for appropriate technologies. At times I imagined that it felt like the Biosphere II must have felt, but really it was so different from that. It was truly a living sculpture, influenced by every person that set foot on board. Being in New York, each neighbourhood is extremely different, and the *Waterpod* was docked in a different neighbourhood every two weeks. Because people move here from all over the world, the interactions that took place on the *Waterpod* were very rich and instigated a lot of unexpected meetings and collaborations. People left inspired, and I think empowered.

Danaher You mentioned some of the problems you had with the red tape surrounding *Waterpod* and I was curious about what the reactions of New York City officials were once they learned about the project. Do you feel like they took something away from the experience as well?

Mattingly I think so. None of the agencies we worked with knew exactly how to permit a project like the *Waterpod*, because it fell somewhere between public art on land (being attached to a pier at most times), an event space, and a boat. So we all learned about all of the nuances in permits and codes between different city departments. Some agencies were worried because they thought our budget was unrealistic, so I think that they were nicely surprised to see a project of that scale, and requiring a lot of surrounding infrastructure, pulled off for a minimal amount of money, and I think that they really saw different communities pulling together to help the project succeed, from the company that towed the *Waterpod* from pier to pier, to our legal counsel, to the many talented people who volunteered their time and knowledge.

Danaher It seems like you're drawn to the idea of utopianism in an era where it feels like many people have simply given up on the concept. Do you think utopian ideas are still worth exploring and why?

Mattingly Utopia, like a boat, is a placeless place and a vestige of our imagination. I am interested in utopias as a concept, and accept that to attempt to create a utopic space is a romantic and nostalgic idea that stems from literature more than reality, because in reality a utopic space cannot be sustained due to human nature. The *Waterpod* was somewhere between real and imaginary and I imagined it as a constantly changing space, which is maybe the only way to sustain a utopic environment. Although these are intriguing concepts, I'm more interested in the reality of heterotopias, and am much more worried about the fate of humanity than about creating a utopia. I believe we can create some kind of personal-bubble utopias, and the artist-worker is an action that embeds a thread of necessary utopian points of view into society. […]

Danaher I'm curious about your idea of art as 'using spaces that are not prepared for art to instigate'. You mentioned also that your upcoming photography project deals with the idea of place. Could you tell me what it is about the idea of location that attracts you?

Mattingly I'm interested in boundaries that we have as individuals or as communities, towns and countries. I'm also interested in systems of control, from value systems to political systems. Distorting boundaries between places and combining different geographies has this effect of distorting our spatial memories and expands our ability to imagine why and how this could be. Places are also metaphors of states of being, and a place that is a collage or cut-up of a post-industrial society, although it is altered as I create it, is true to my own state of mind, and I imagine the state of mind of many other people living in this spatio-temporal reality. [...]

Danaher There's a lot of concern in your work about the future of humanity and I was curious about what, at this point, you see as a cause for hope.

Mattingly Growing up with parents who were children of the Great Depression, my family reused everything. I have a habit of saving things, and since I move around often, I'm careful about acquiring things. Ten years ago, I saw the excess in people's habits as a lot greater than I believe it is now, in the USA. I witness people's resourcefulness more and more, and I see people in the city wanting to connect with nature. I see so many inspirational role models in people today at every age. I also see the increasing levelling of technology as a truly remarkable marker of this time and place in history. Technological advances can be made very quickly now that so many more people have the tools to discover and create. The acceleration rate of technology is both frightening and exciting. [...]

Mary Mattingly and Shane Danaher, extracts from interview, *Rough Copy* (2010) (http://roughcopymag. wordpress.com)

Brandon Ballengée
In Conversation with Tim Chamberlain//2009

Tim Chamberlain How do you see the role of artist facilitating your ideas of 'wildlife conservation'?

Brandon Ballengée Being an artist allows me to bring the information I find in nature to a wide audience. My belief is that art can contribute to society through inspiration, engagement and direct action. As an artist my practice facilitates activism, amateur biological studies and communication about ecological phenomena to the public. Through this transdisciplinary technique, the model I employ is proactive environmental stewardship. While conducting primary research biological laboratory and field studies I utilize scientific methodologies and standards. As activism, the involvement of local students and the public in these studies (*Eco-Actions*) is essential. Together we investigate and 'experience' ecosystems – the goal is to inspire people to learn more about their local ecology and play an active role in protecting it. […]

Chamberlain Should art be didactic?

Ballengée No, otherwise it falls into pure communication or a kind of mono-interpretative illustration. Though art can teach and deliver messages, being open to interpretation is fundamental. There is a kind of didacticism to my work (intended to increase environmental awareness) but the messages are often pluralistic, open to an amount of individual meaning. The installations and photographs are experienced, so the readings are open-ended. Even in the field and lab studies ideas from the participating public are explored and we experience the process of enquiry as a group. This is the praxis of my method, which diverges from standard pedagogical practices. […]

Chamberlain Do you see your work as part of a re-knowing about nature by urbanized populations?

Ballengée I see my work as a reaction to what I find in nature. These results are shared with wide audiences, often living in cities. Urbanites have always been fascinated with nature. In the mid nineteenth century the artist and ornithologist John Gould received over 75,000 visitors to his display of taxidermized hummingbirds in London's Hyde Park. In North America the naturalist John Muir commented on the large numbers of city dwellers who benefited from visiting forests. So many that he was concerned they might destroy the natural habitats they had come to visit.

Instead of urban exodus into nature, or the Victorian gaze, I see this as a continued rise in ecological consciousness, post-*Silent Spring* [by Rachel Carson, published in 1962]. Though this is not exclusive to urbanites, as environmental historian William Cronon and others have alluded to, there is a growing awareness that we as human beings have altered the planet and there is an impetus for us to change. These changes are often more visible in cities. Symptomatic of this rise in consciousness is the shifting effort towards valorizing local urban eco-systems. These resistant environments have historically been seen as unnatural. Urban parks, feral areas and brownfield sites don't easily fit inside our occidental 'wilderness' construct.

Several of my past projects have focused on these seemingly 'austere' landscapes. For example, the 2000–2004 work *Losing Ground* dealt with the rapidly-changing ecology of New York City's Jamaica Bay. This vast wetland contains thousands of marsh islands that filter water and create habitats for numerous species. Due to both natural and anthropogenic factors these islands are sinking at an incredible rate of between 40 to 60 acres per year. The project involved collaborating with scientists, educators, bird-watchers, students and members of the public to study the bay and create an ecological art installation at a local community centre. During the four years' work on the project, we saw first-hand the disappearance of many of these islands – it was remarkable and horrifying. The field data we collected were submitted to both environmental and scientific groups to help campaign for governmental support of remediation. Currently restoration efforts are ongoing in Jamaica Bay.

Chamberlain Does this have implications for a substantial environmental paradigm shift?

Ballengée As more than half the world's population has shifted to occupy cities, we have become an urban species. The remaining islands of 'wilderness' are becoming our new suburbia. As the palaeontologist and environmentalist Tim Flannery describes it, we have all become 'Weather Makers'. We are all trying to come to terms with what this means. Most of us are much more conscious of our impact now and want changes.

A shift is already happening. When former US president G.W. Bush spoke in China about hybrid automobiles it was symptomatic of this shift. It is coming from furthered natural resource depletion and economic necessity as well as being increased by growing public concern and pressure on governments to implement change. Reflective of this cultural shift is the increasing number of artists currently addressing environmental issues globally. It is a kind of positive feedback loop; artists are generating ecological projects in a global culture more sensitive to environmental issues. Barbara Matilsky, in her book *Fragile Ecologies,* discussed how artists can implement real world change by increasing popular awareness. Artists can bring environmental issues to the social foreground, making the public aware. This is followed by increased popular concern, which can then push for changes in government policies. Art is increasingly helping to drive an environmental paradigm shift.

Chamberlain Do your discoveries of 'deformed nature' act as metaphor or litmus paper for a rising sense of disharmony and psychological unease felt in westernized urban society?

Ballengée My work is the product of environmental disharmony as a social construct and as a biological reality. Growing up in post-*Silent Spring* America I was aware of an eco-psychological unease prevalent in many popular books and films. *Soylent Green* (1973), *Logan's Run* (1976), *Prophecy* (1979), *The Food of the Gods* (1976) and others presented dystopian visions of a near future. For better or worse they helped shape a cultural vision of landscape for a generation. Large-scale catastrophes [involving toxic waste], such as at Love Canal in Canada and Chernobyl in the Ukraine, embedded a sense of urgency. This has been reaffirmed through continued news of rapid extinctions and climate change. Without question, the fear of future environmental calamity is causing social concern. Currently some authors have begun to compare this environmental unease to post-traumatic stress syndrome on a massive scale. […]

Chamberlain Are there other ways of working – I'm thinking of Joseph Beuys and his swim in a peat bog?

Ballengée This performative work by Beuys was an early inspiration for me. He directed public attention towards the loss of bog habitats. My *Eco-Actions* attempt to focus participants on specific ecosystems through experiential methods and basic scientific wetland-surveying techniques. These are conducted with community members at local sites. By looking, getting their hands dirty and asking their own questions, the public use their senses to achieve an enriched understanding of a site. As a group we can gather important environmental data, shared with the scientific community. Past students/public participants have remarked that our *Eco-Actions* changed their prior perception of the study sites. My approach is attuned with the philosopher John Dewey, who thought that experience in nature was an important and essential part of education.

I believe currently there is an impetus for these kinds of experientially-based environmental programmes. As the ecological psychologist Edward Reed suggested, a current difficulty we face is the lack of direct sensory experience in our everyday lives. According to Reed, Western cultures have become increasingly reliant on processed or 'second-hand' information. This is leading to an experiential gap and erosion of natural mental resources. Also, the educator Richard Louv hypothesizes that an increasing lack of experience with nature is leading to a 'Nature Deficit Disorder' in today's youth.

Chamberlain Both you and Mark Dion have worked with dead specimens collected at a fish market: how do you see your work differing in its intentions and in the outcome as read by the viewer?

Ballengée The art historian Carla Yanni has discussed the way that natural history museums became the bastion of scientific rationalism during the Victorian era. Displaying specimens became a didactic and perhaps often dogmatic tool for explaining systems of life. Much of the work I'm familiar with by Mark Dion offers a critique of these institutions, along with the cultural entropy of science. Including specimens among numerous other components seems a natural way for Dion to raise his problematic.

In my work, preserved animals are often a primary artistic medium. Such as the 2006 piece *Prelude to the Collapse of the Atlantic Food-Chain*, which consisted of a large pyramid made up of hundreds of aquatic specimens. Each was carefully placed, one on top of another, to reference a marine trophic system. Empty jars recalled species extinction. The specimens were specially lit to put some fish in shadow, representing population decline. The work had a subdued palette of colours, through natural melanin saturating the spirits. The specimens represent a sad reality, a reminder that if we don't do anything, all that will be left are vast preserved collections of a once biologically rich planet.

Dion's 1992 work, *The Report of the Department of Marine Animal Inventory of the City of New York China Town Division* created the office of an imaginary governmental agency in charge of monitoring fish in New York's Chinatown. On display was a collection of preserved fish, among other components such as a desk, maps, charts, to make up the office. Through my *The Ever-Changing Tide* (2000–1) I offered a kind of 'homage' to his earlier installation, but my work was a methodological year-long survey of New York City seafood markets and focused on marine conservation. Since 1992, several of the fish Dion displayed had suffered population declines and some had even become commercially extinct. With a team of collaborators, we systematically surveyed these markets to collect data and monitor encountered species. Through the project a sustainable seafood multilingual guide was developed, with lifesize fish photographs, installed at participating markets and the Queens Museum of Art, New York, along with the preserved specimens. The intention was to increase consumer awareness and influence behaviour.

Chamberlain Both you and Dion have been described as artists who 'blur' the boundary between art and science: how fine can such a dividing line be explored between disciplines, where it also intrinsically retains its definition, thereby allowing each to remain a skilled technician in their own field?

Ballengée My practice falls into a transdisciplinary approach. This way of working involves the utilization of both artistic and scientific techniques. The art is an expression derived from an experience with animals in natural or artificial conditions. While conducting primary research, biological scientific methods and standards are rigorously followed. The blur comes from the way these seemingly divergent techniques inform one another. Through scientific techniques I can achieve a better understanding of natural phenomena, thus further substantiating my artworks about nature; whereas my artworks can more readily carry knowledge to a wider lay audience. […]

Brandon Ballengée and Tim Chamberlain, extracts from interview, *Antennae*, no. 10 (Spring 2009) 10–14.

Jesse Ashlock
Please Don't Feed the Animals//2006

Museum gift shops are notorious price gougers, but even that couldn't explain the twenty-dollar PowerBars at the last Whitney Biennial. What made these energy bars so special? The answer lay in the nutrition information graphic on the back of the wrapper. 'Nutrition Facts for Birds', it read, and recommended a serving size of one pinch. The PowerBars were art.

Well, yes and no. As with most projects by the New York-based Australian artist Natalie Jeremijenko, this one wasn't quite so easily reducible. One of the best-known talents working in the hybrid spaces between art and technology, Jeremijenko creates what she calls 'spectacles of participation' – often with her 'corporate' arts collective, the Bureau of Inverse Technology – that draw on a dazzling array of disciplines, including engineering and design, environmental science, political economy, sociology, architecture and conceptual art.

Jeremijenko has several engineering degrees, and in 2004, when she was on Yale's engineering faculty, a profile in the *Yale Alumni Magazine* archly declared, 'It's art, all right. But is it engineering?' The question has dogged her throughout her career. In fact, her work may not be engineering or art, depending on whom you ask, but such rushes to categorize seem to miss the point. Everything is connected, as they say, and Jeremijenko actualizes this bromide in playful, unexpected, often instructive ways. She calls herself an interactive artist, although she means that in a particular way. 'The tradition of interactivity has taken people to computers, and not to collective, cumulative action', she says. 'Working in this realm of action is very interesting to me.' […]

As an artist, Jeremijenko isn't interested in working in the realm of personal expression, but her intelligence, offbeat wit and sometimes baffling freeassociativeness were all on display in her multiple – and, as is common of her work, continuously evolving – contributions to the last Biennial. Created with fellow Bureau member Phil Taylor, these included the on-site *Whitney Biennial for the Birds*, and its companion in the Hudson River, the *Whitney Biennial for the Fish*. Both projects ask us to reconsider our relationships with urban animals, or as Jeremijenko coyly refers to them, 'non-humans', by recognizing our interdependency with them. The bird project consisted primarily of translucent perches, first displayed in 2005 at MASS MoCA, on the walls of the Whitney's outdoor courtyard (with images of the artwork indoors mounted nearby – literally, a Biennial for the birds). When birds landed on them (though few did), they triggered human voices that 'translated bird concerns into human dialect'. These wry, recorded messages made a case for maintaining biodiversity by keeping bird populations healthy, so as to avoid diseases like an avian flu pandemic.

This might seem like an exercise in high-concept anthropomorphism, but that's a word Jeremijenko resists. 'It's not a pretence that animals are human', she insists. 'It's an understanding that we're solving similar problems, that we can learn from each other, that we have similar conceptual resources, that our brains are just not that radically different from other brains that exist.' The energy bars, designed to be 'delicious and nutritious' for birds and humans alike, argued the same point. So why make them prohibitively expensive? The symbolic price point – $20.06, actually, to match the year of the Biennial – was a way of using the gift shop as a frame, Jeremijenko explains. 'It marks it as precious.' But while bars may have been more conceptual than practical, Jeremijenko is serious about scripting mutually beneficial interactions in which humans actually do feed animals. 'It's a very visceral way of demonstrating that we share the same natural resources, we eat the same stuff – they're not inhabiting a different world, but, in fact, the same one. The interaction of sharing food is very much how we define who we're related to, who are your friends.'

This is the main aim of the still-unrealized *Biennial for the Fish* installation, planned for a site on the Hudson River at the end of West 15th Street. Following on past theoretical work with experimental aquatic architecture, Jeremijenko designed a 'fish interface' of motion-sensitive buoys at water level; the buoys light up when schools of sturgeon and bass swim past, indicating their presence to humans above. Humans can then feed them seaweed-based fish bars containing PCB-chelating agents that transform the heavy metals in their systems into harmless salts, helping clean up the river, one of the world's largest Superfund sites. What's good for the fish is also good for us.

Jeremijenko groups both projects under the rubric 'Hudson River School 2.0', a reference to the group of nineteenth-century Romantic landscape painters whose pastoral depictions of the Hudson River Valley offered an aestheticized view of nature as a world apart from human beings. It's a perspective she believes informs the conservationist ethos of traditional environmentalism, which she finds problematic. 'The idea that we don't interact with natural systems is bogus, a consensual hallucination, that nature is out there and we're in here', she argues. 'The way to understand the environment is not as nature out there, but through our political and economic systems.' It isn't news that human actions have negative consequences on the environment, but we still often think of those consequences as abstract and remote – in terms of rising sea levels or the vanishing snows of Kilimanjaro. For Jeremijenko, closing the perceptual gap between nature and the city, by recognizing gritty urban wilderness and grubby, un-aesthetic urban wildlife as participants in a dynamic and reciprocal natural system with human beings, is a strategy for fostering environmental awareness.

Throughout her career, Jeremijenko has consistently sought to make complex, unseen social phenomena intelligible by rendering them experientially. Early tangible media projects like *Trigger* and *Bull Ride*, mechanical bulls which allowed participants to 'ride' the Lorna Prieta Earthquake and the 1987 stock market crash, respectively, highlighted this approach. With subsequent public experiments like *One Trees*, in which she planted a thousand genetically identical saplings around San Francisco to see how varied urban conditions affected their development, and her ongoing releases of feral robotic dogs, in which she sets loose toxin-sniffing electronic canines at sites of environmental contamination, Jeremijenko has sought to generate social discourse by confronting scientific claims in mediagenic ways. She knows how to leverage a metaphor for maximum effect.

But it wasn't until 1999, when she moved to New York and experienced life with rodents for the first time, that she became interested in the relationship between humans and urban wildlife as an area of inquiry. As she observed feral mice, it struck her as incongruous to use endlessly bred lab mice as our animal proxies in scientific testing. 'I wanted Manhattan mice, living a Manhattan lifestyle!' she exclaims. As an experiment, later exhibited at Yale (as *Milgram's Mice*, in honour of the famed social psychologist who once occupied her lab there), she built a dollhouse model of her own habitat at mouse scale and placed human substances inside – including jellybeans, muscle relaxants, antihistamines, antidepressants, vodka and gin – curious what the mice would do. She reports that they self-administered the muscle relaxants and antidepressants, and preferred vodka.

As a worker extricates the last sticks of furniture from Jeremijenko's nearly empty studio one afternoon, she ruefully explains that these mice experiments, and subsequent efforts to lure birds which could provide competitive population pressure and keep the mice in check, touched off a years-long battle with her building's co-op board that is finally culminating with her moving out. This conflict by no means deterred her investigations into urban species interdependence, however. In 2003, this interest took her to the Dutch landscape art centre De Verbeelding, where she was taken by the way the local goose population had adapted to human technologies by nestling beneath the eaves of De Verbeelding's pavilion. Seeking to learn more about geese, she designed her first fully realized human/animal interface, a robotic, remote-controlled goose that offered users a goose-eye-view of the animals' social life, and came preloaded with speech samples to facilitate interaction with other geese, and a video camera to record these interactions. The geese turned out not to respond as well to the robotic interloper as ducks did, so Jeremijenko designed a robotic duck she later released in Dublin (she spends a lot of time explaining herself to airport security). She grouped these and other animal interfaces as *Ooz*, choosing the backwards spelling of 'zoo' to connote an inversion of the usual relationship between humans and animals. In this 'zoo without bars', animals come to us in their own habitats, forming mutually beneficial and theoretically educational interactions.

In honour of the Biennial, Jeremijenko is incorporating *Ooz* this year, an effort to extend the legal personhood enjoyed by corporations to animals. She's selling fish buoys as shares. There was also another, secret component to her Biennial project, a wild garden she has been cultivating on the overhang above the Whitney's entrance, comprised of plants that have adapted to Manhattan's unique ecosystem. She intends it as an additional stage for the city's bird population, and as another way of asserting that humans' built environment is part of the natural system. 'If art museums are part of nature', she jokes, 'then we're really getting somewhere!' [...]

Jeremijenko's work is informed by scientific inquiry, but she's not especially interested in getting good data, since she believes that information alone has proven insufficient to change behaviour. 'Truth is not a centralized authority', she insists, 'it's shared meaning'. She often references the Slovenian cultural critic Slavoj Zizek's idea that ideology persists more in our actions than in our beliefs. 'I think we need to interact with natural systems', she says, 'Instead of this thesis, 'do not touch, do not interact', it's like, act, and make it good. It's a shift in environmental thinking, which I think is the new environmentalism.'

Tell that to an environmentalist, you might say. In fact, Jeremijenko works with many environmental organizations, from Friends of the Urban Forest to the National Oceanic and Atmospheric Administration. And in a world where governments ignore overwhelming scientific evidence that the planet is getting warmer, and people who know better keep buying SUVs, it does seem wise to consider new approaches.

'Environmentalism has been more about hand-wringing – drive less, use less electricity, less packaging – and less about the engagement of wonder',

Jeremijenko says. 'Understanding, through the spectacle of adaptation, that animals and natural systems are dynamic, not static images to be conserved and preserved, gives us a responsibility, or opportunity, to change.'

Jesse Ashlock, extracts from 'Please Don't Feed the Animals: Natalie Jeremijenko's Hands-On Environmentalism', *RES magazine* (July/August 2006) 52–4.

Mark Sheerin
Marcus Coates//2010

Marcus Coates arrives wearing neither badger fur nor stag antlers. He drinks tea, not peyote, and does not bark, yelp or fall into a trance. In fact there is no evidence at all this man has a hotline to the animal kingdom.

His genial conversation is a far cry from the spooky rituals which have made the artist's name. In order to tackle social issues, Coates has after all consulted with plover, moorhen, sparrowhawk and deer.

The resulting performances might suggest he has a true gift and you could speculate there were years living with some remote tribe, learning their ways, but no.

Of his shamanic training, he says, 'I haven't really had any.' Although he does have a weekend course under his belt. 'I think what I possibly take is an idea called core shamanism. The idea that the fundamentals of the shamanistic technique are open to everyone.'

Instead of magic, Coates uses meditation in what he describes as a 'watered-down' version of indigenous tribal practices. The sceptics among you were right all along.

'I think firstly I should say that I am deeply sceptical myself, particularly about new age culture', he says. Disappointment soon gives way to relief.

'Usually I kind of expect people to walk out', he says of his rituals, 'and I'm quite open to people calling me a charlatan and laughing. I quite like people not to be so reverential.'

But those who stick around until Coates snaps out of his trance may be surprised at the vivid descriptions he brings back and even benefit from the advice he dispenses.

'When I went to Israel I did a series of rituals in a shopping centre and people would come and ask me questions which were very serious', he recalls. 'One woman came up to ask me about her anorexic daughter and that's when I realized I had an enormous responsibility.'

The same day Coates was besieged with long queues, despite the deeply held religious beliefs of people from that part of the world. It was enough to make him consider giving up shamanic work. 'Maybe religion isn't extreme enough', he muses.

Faced with real problems of any scale, Coates looks to his imagination for a solution. The possession-like trance is in fact a creative process.

'It's really just an elaborate and extended form of meditation where I conjure up an imaginative world where I don't control it. I don't run it. I'm just very separate to my imagination. I'm guided by it', he explains.

His art background is what he claims has given him 'some fundamental skills' to do shamanic work.

'It wasn't like one day I thought I'd be a shamen. For years I had this strategy as an artist to become animal. I suppose that was to reconcile the gap between myself and another being.'

In doing so, Coates was influenced by a 1974 enquiry by philosopher Thomas Nagel: 'What is It Like to be a Bat?' 'There are degrees to which we can know each other and know of each other', says the artist.

Which prompts the questions of what our native fauna might make of contemporary art: 'I think the fact about wildlife is its indifference to us. It reacts to us. It responds to us, but in terms of caring, that doesn't really come into it.'

Art in turn is not just cut off from the natural world, according to Coates: 'I see it as cut off from the world generally. I think lots of artists are very interested in art itself. I'm not particularly interested in art. I see art as a by-product of what I do.'

What primarily he does is explore the present day resonance of indigenous belief systems, the power of ritual, and the leaps of faith needed to create and enjoy art.

It needs pointing out that humour is another strong by-product of his endeavours. But, says Coates, 'That is totally undeliberate. The attempts are very serious, but I think the incongruities that are formed create the humour.'

But the strength of his performances lies somewhere between mischief and make believe. Indeed, he says, 'Most of the work comes from the idea of being an eight-year old.'

Mark Sheerin, 'Marcus Coates' (2010) (www.criticismism.com)

Denise Markonish
Rachel Berwick: *Zugunruhe* (2009) //2010

What a serendipitous occasion to find myself standing in Rachel Berwick's studio on 1 September 2009. For it was on that very day ninety-five years ago that Martha, the last passenger pigeon, drew her final breath. This was a sad end to an awe-inspiring and horrific story of scientific intrigue, human greed and environmental devastation. It is no wonder then that Berwick's studio is strewn with amber casts of this most famous bird, frozen in time and captured in memory.

The story of the passenger pigeon is essentially one of wonder but also of warning. First-hand accounts of passenger pigeon sightings are filled with amazement. For example, in the early 1800s Alexander Wilson stated, 'I was suddenly struck with astonishment at a loud rushing roar, succeeded by instant darkness… I took [it] for a tornado, about to overwhelm the house and everything around in destruction.'[1] Later, in 1813, John James Audubon similarly recalled: 'The noise which they made, though yet distant, reminded me of a hard gale at sea, passing through the rigging of a close-reefed vessel. As the birds arrived and passed over me, I felt a current of air that surprised me … The Pigeons, arriving by thousands, alighted everywhere, one above another, until solid masses were formed on the branches all round … It was a scene of uproar and confusion.'[2] Two of America's most respected ornithologists of the nineteenth century seemed downright dumbstruck at the sight of these birds, whose numbers were estimated in the millions per flock. These are not your usual accounts of pleasant, tweeting birds sitting in a nearby tree; they are visions not unlike descriptions of natural disasters. Given this overabundance it is even more astonishing that these birds no longer exist.

The extinction of the passenger pigeon was one of the greatest and quickest in the history of North America. Swarms of birds would move from one area to the next, seeking out old growth oak and beech forests. The sight of the birds, as noted above, was magnificent, but it was also plague-like and destructive. Due to their sheer numbers, when the birds descended they would darken the sky, tree branches would snap under their weight, and one hardly need mention or imagine the hailstorm of bird droppings they would leave in their wake: a real-life Alfred Hitchcock moment. So what happened to the passenger pigeon? Plainly stated, we, the human race, happened to them, as their numbers dwindled both as a result of deforestation and hunting. At each spectacular arrival of passenger pigeon flocks, hunters would gather and begin to take the birds down, shooting them, netting them or just using sticks to knock them out of trees.

Billions of these birds existed in the 1870s, only dozens by the 1890s, and by 1900 they were extinct in the wild (Martha, who lived at the Cincinnati Zoo, would hang on for another fourteen years).[3] This extinction is perhaps the first in history to teach us about the fragility of the environment, the first where we could see disappearance as the result of our own hands, whether it be for food, sport, fashion or pest control. For many years, people speculated about what happened to the passenger pigeon, not willing to accept culpability, and instead theorized that the birds were hiding elsewhere. However, the inevitable was made all too clear when in 1947 the Wisconsin Society for Ornithology erected a monument to the passenger pigeon in Wyalusing State Park. The dedication of this monument was written by Aldo Leopold, one of the first conservationists, and included the following elegiac statement: 'Trees still live who, in their youth, were shaken by a living wind. But a decade hence only the oldest oaks will remember, and at long last only the hills will know.'[4] Here Leopold hints at the wonder of these birds but more palpably he mourns their loss.

Aside from teaching us about our own destructive capabilities or awakening our sense of wonder, one could postulate that – due to their vast numbers and movement from one area to the next – the passenger pigeon was one of the first visible examples of species migration. At the time, the science of migration was in its infancy and would not be fully explored for another few decades. There has always been a sense of mystery around migration; early on it was believed that birds perhaps went underground or hibernated, for it seemed improbable that they would fly across the globe in search of warmer climes. Even today scientists have not yet determined how and to where some species of birds migrate. The first breakthrough in migratory science came in 1949 when German ornithologist Gustav Kramer built a series of orientation cages – cylindrical structures with glass bottoms for observation. The purpose of these cages was to test how birds move and why. Was it the orientation of the stars, the sun, magnetic forces, etc.? In some studies birds were put into cages surrounded by mirrors to shift the location of the sun, in others magnetic fields were placed around the cages, and later, in the 1960s, scientist Stephen Emlen would take these cages into planetariums to shift the location of the stars to determine how certain birds oriented themselves. The 'why' that compels the act of migration is particularly interesting to Berwick, and it is from this 'why' that she chose the title for her work: *Zugunruhe*. This term, coined by Kramer, describes the restlessness in birds; the compulsion to move or to migrate.

For Berwick there is a kind of poetry in *zugunruhe*, in the fact that it is a mysterious force that is felt but not seen. This becomes all the more palpable when viewing her work. Upon entering the gallery, viewers are confronted with a large ten-foot diameter, nine-foot high heptagonal structure made of smoky two-way glass. It appears almost like a monumental version of an orientation cage, a new device for another form of observation, as much about humans as birds. Inside is complete stillness, as a number of passenger pigeons cast in amber sit amongst the branches of an old tree. Here *zugunruhe* is arrested. There is no movement, only the memory of movement, and compulsion is therefore replaced with thwarted desire. Berwick's *Zugunruhe* is a monument to the lost migration of these now extinct birds, as much as it is a monument to science, optics and spectacle.

This convergence of science, optics and spectacle evident in Berwick's work comes from the sense of nature as entertainment or constructed experience, an evolution which can be traced from the pre-Renaissance to the Victorian age (and even continuing today in our zoos and museums). For Berwick, another inspiration for *Zugunruhe* comes from Athanasius Kircher, the seventeenth-century German Jesuit scholar known as 'the master of a hundred arts'. Indeed, Kircher was an intense polymath, studying geology, hieroglyphics and most intensely, magnetism. Kircher believed that magnetism was the defining force of all nature. To support this he created devices in which he would embed magnets in small figures and then suspend them in water-filled globes to test the forces of the external world on these magnets. These are like proto-orientation cages, for migration as a result of magnetism was a subject that Kircher also took interest in. Kircher's environments in globes or mirror boxes (small landscapes constructed of wax and placed in mirrored display cases) were scientific but they were also concerned with the theatricality of display and the construction of nature, much like the eighteenth-century curiosity cabinets that held natural history collections (of both actual and created specimens) that were popular in Renaissance homes and early museums.

Kircher merged the investigations of science and display, a practice that would continue in the nineteenth century, evolving from the curiosity cabinet and expanded in scale and scope with the Crystal Palace. The Crystal Palace; built in 1851 for the Great Exhibition or first World's Fair in London, was said to be 'a giant structure of iron and glass dedicated to a new way of looking …'[5] Inside the Crystal Palace one could find international exhibitions about industry and culture alongside fine fashions, furnishing, and natural and artificial wonders as far as the eye could see. Included in the Great Exhibition were magnificent hummingbird trees created by British ornithologist John Gould. These small glass-enclosed display cases held branches inside of them that were populated by hundreds of taxidermy hummingbirds of different species. In these cases, Gould constructed a specific kind of nature experience through theatrical display, an idea that also emerges in Berwick's constructed forest of amber passenger pigeons. Both, however, hint at the impossibility or fantasy involved in how we view nature in these 'created' situations: in Gould's case, the number and species variety of hummingbirds would never be seen together, and in Berwick's installation the impossible vision is even more palpable due to the extinction of the birds on view. What replaces nature in the hummingbird trees and in *Zugunruhe* is instead stillness and the awareness of perception.

In addition to showcasing these 'natural' wonders, the Great Exhibition demonstrated all that was amazing about and could be constructed as a result of modernity, starting with the building itself. In 1845 taxes on the importation of glass from France were lifted, enabling the Crystal Palace to exist and exposing the world to the kind of voyeuristic experience of looking that glass can offer. It is no accident that Gould's hummingbird trees have become so engaged with ideas of perception, for glass offered the opportunity to re-evaluate just how things get looked at. Berwick beautifully exploits these qualities of glass in *Zugunruhe*. Her use of smoky two-way mirrors presents viewers with a choice of observation points as they walk around the sculpture, leading to the recognition of their own reflection as well as those of fellow onlookers. The tree and birds inside Berwick's 'mirror box' are lit from within, so the reflection of the viewer sits on the surface of the glass, spectrally hinting at the culpability of mankind in these birds' disappearance but linking as well to the looking and awe evident in early passenger pigeon sightings as much as in the Crystal Palace or even the contemporary museum. Nature here has become a phenomenological experience; it is a new kind of theatre. By using two-way glass Berwick reaffirms the fact that her reality is a construction, for as viewers look through the piece the single tree and amber birds are mirrored kaleidoscopically to create a seemingly endless forest befitting of one of Kircher's mirror boxes. By merging the orientation cage with the mirror box and the hummingbird tree, Berwick creates a willing suspension of disbelief. We, as viewers, are transported by our own phenomenological experience, and in this realm, abundance has been returned to the passenger pigeon.

'And it can be said in particular of Wonder that it is useful in making us learn and retain in our memory things we have previously been ignorant of, for we wonder only at what appears rare and extraordinary to us.'[6] This story of passenger pigeons, migration, mirror boxes and crystal palaces is certainly rare and extraordinary; through Berwick's conflation of these histories she brings the wonder of it all back for our eyes to behold. Rachel Berwick's *Zugunruhe* is, as P.T. Barnum wrote in 1886, 'A stupendous mirror of departed empires'.[7]

1   [footnote 3 in source] Alexander Wilson, *American Ornithology*, Volume 2, with a continuation by Charles Lucian Bonaparte; illustr. notes by William Jardine (London: Whittaker, Treacher and Arnot, 1832) 201–4.

2   [4] John James Audubon, *Birds of America*, Volume V. For the online version of the 1840 'First Octavo Edition' visit http://www.audubon.org/bird/BoA/BOAjndex.html. For a full account of the passenger pigeon go to 'Extinct Birds'.

3   [5] Jennifer Price, *Flight Maps: Adventures with Nature in Modern America* (New York: Basic Books, 1999) 3.

4   [6] Aldo Leopold, *A Sand County Almanac* (Oxford: Oxford University Press, 1949) 116.

5   [7] Celeste Olalquiaga, *The Artificial Kingdom: On the Kitsch Experience* (Minneapolis: University of Minnesota Press, 2002) 31.

6   [8] René Descartes, article 75: 'Wherein Wonder in particular is serviceable', *The Passions of the Soul* (1649); trans. S. Voss (Indianapolis: Hackett Publishing Company, 1989) 59.

7   [1, revised] P.T. Barnum (1810–91) in 1889, promoting the ethnographic exhibits at his 'Grand Travelling Museum, Menagerie, Caravan and Hippodrome'. See Bluford Adams, *E. Pluribus Barnum: The Great Showman and the Making of US Popular Culture* (Minneapolis: University of Minnesota Press, 1997) 188.

Denise Markonish, 'A Stupendous Mirror of Departed Empires', in *Rachel Berwick: Zugunruhe* (Providence, Rhode Island: Brown University, David Winton Bell Gallery, 2010) 7–11 [retitled].

Carl Zimmer
Justine Cooper: The Awe of Natural History Collections//2009

A natural history museum is really two museums, and when you're in one of them, you can hardly imagine the other. I don't know how many times I've wandered around the halls of the American Museum of Natural History, among the armoured fish and the stegosaurs. But it wasn't until I was a 26-year-old science writer that I had the chance to pass through to the other side. I wanted to learn about pterosaurs, those stork-faced, bat-bodied reptiles that soared for 150 million years. I found out about a Brazilian man named Alexander Kellner who was getting his Ph.D. at the museum, studying new fossils of pterosaurs from the Santana Formation. Kellner invited me to the museum, to take a look at the bones and talk about his ideas about what pterosaurs had actually been like in life.

I followed his directions and came to the Grand Gallery. I waited by the Great Canoe, and eventually a gangly palaeontologist emerged from the acoustic fog of school groups on field trips. He led me through exhibit halls, and then, between two dioramas, he stopped. At first I thought he was lost in thought, and then maybe that he had forgotten something. There was no reason, after all, to stop by a dim wall between a pair of displays. But then I heard keys ringing in Kellner's hand. He slipped one into an invisible lock, and the wall swung open. We slid through and Kellner locked the door behind us. I was in the other museum.

'You've never been back here?' Kellner asked. The answer was obvious; I was staring like a gobsmacked tourist at the rows of storage cabinets, which loomed overhead like wardrobes for giants. I knew that natural history museums kept fossils and other objects in storage, but I assumed that most of their material was on display, back in the other world. As we walked down long hallways, with drawer after drawer pressing in on either side, I realized how wrong I was. We could look into rooms as we passed, most of them with cabinets and drawers of their own. Kellner reached out to a hallway drawer and opened it. A hip bone from a dinosaur sat inside, knobbed and flared like a Calder sculpture.

It was the first of many journeys I've since taken to the other side of museums. Scientists love to show off their collections by pulling drawers open at random, the way Kellner did — exposing me to an army of flies from Peru neatly pinned to slips of paper, or a flock of lyrebirds lying on their backs as if dozing in a collective nap. I've gawked at fossil whale feet and jars of tapeworms, at leeches and Mesozoic ferns. But Justine Cooper's photographs at the American Museum of Natural History take me back to that first shock. They capture the crowded stillness of those halls, the unexpected treasures. The seals in the attic.

Cooper's photographs belong to an artistic tradition that reaches back over four centuries, to the origins of natural history museum collections themselves. In the 1500s, illustrators began to publish engravings of 'cabinets of wonders' – where Renaissance monarchs housed personal collections of exotic oddities, like bizarre deep-sea fish, glittering crystals, exquisitely geometrical shells. Kings and queens would retire to these cabinets to contemplate nature, or just use them to dazzle their visitors.

Gradually, royalty's cabinets of wonders turned into libraries of flesh and rock, where scholars could research the workings of the world. Ole Worm, a seventeenth-century anatomist, became famous for his collection of narwhal skulls, stuffed lemurs, dried armadillos, and other natural specimen. *Museum Wormianum*, an illustrated catalogue of Worm's collection, was published posthumously in 1655, and what makes his illustration so mesmerizing is the strange way in which nature's fractal beauty appears so unnaturally organized. It's the same jarring effect seen in Cooper's photographs of modern natural history collections.

Museum collections may have their roots in the obsession of collectors and the public's love of oddities, but they've always served much greater ambitions. Worm used his collection to teach his students: 'Let us take off the spectacles that show us the shadows of things instead of the things themselves', he wrote. In the 1700s, a worldwide system for naming species arose, which depended on museums to preserve the original type specimens that naturalists used to name them.

By the mid 1700s, naturalists were using collections of fossils to study the history of life on this planet, discovering dynasties of diatoms and conodonts that gave way to revolutionary new assemblages of species. Charles Darwin had some of his deepest insights into evolution while spending years studying fossils of barnacles from the British museum. And Ernst Mayr, the German ornithologist, developed the central explanation for the origin of species while curating a collection of bird skins at the American Museum of Natural History. As he studied the plumage of the birds and charted them on maps, he began to develop a theory for how new species arose through geographic isolation.

Cooper's photographs show how, over the course of centuries, museum collections grow into their own cumbersome beasts that require much care and feeding. It is no simple task to conserve these collections. Their information remains embodied in tissue and stone, even in an age in which we prefer our information abstracted and digitized, coursing without mass along fibre-optic cables. Earlier this year, a team of scientists unveiled the *Encyclopedia of Life*, an online repository of knowledge that they hope will someday contain data on every species that calls this planet home. One could imagine that each species page might someday include a DNA barcode, high-resolution photos of its exterior, MRI scans of its interior, and movies of it in the wild. On the morning of its launch this past February, the *Encyclopedia of Life* attracted 11.5 million visitors — so much traffic that it crashed the servers. That's more than twice the number of people who visit the American Museum of Natural History in a year.

Yet it would be a catastrophe if museums offloaded their pickled fish and stuffed lizards every time a species made its Internet debut. We can never declare a collection of walking sticks or kangaroo rats exhausted of all its secrets. In 1856 quarry workers in Germany unearthed some mysterious fossil bones that became the type specimen of *Homo neanderthalensis* — the Neanderthals. Naturalists made drawings of the bones and carefully compared them to humans, but were unable at that time to conclude whether Neanderthals were human or belonged to another species. The bones were moved to the Rheinisches Landesmuseum in Bonn, which has cared for them ever since. A few years ago researchers managed to extract DNA from the bones — a molecule that was unknown when the fossil was discovered. After analysing the DNA, scientists concluded that Neanderthals are a separate lineage from our own, sharing a common ancestor with us that lived some 600,000 years ago.

Museum collections also uniquely capture nature's variety across space – a tray of butterflies can reveal the flow of genes across a river basin, the rise of new mutations, and the effects of genetic drift and natural selection – as well as time. The collections at the Museum of Vertebrate Zoology at the University of California, Berkeley, include a trove of mice, gophers and other small mammals collected in Yosemite National Park in the early 1900s. A century later, scientists from Berkeley went back to those exact sites and trapped for mammals once more. It was not an exercise in redundancy. The scientists discovered that mammals have moved up the slopes due to climate change. They are an ominous reminder that the collections that Cooper so lovingly portrays are not just a repository of the past, but a stake in our future.

Carl Zimmer, 'The Awe of Natural History Collections', *Seed Magazine* (12 February 2009) (seedmagazine.com).

Henrik Håkansson
Earth Sound Research Revival: Conversation with Jörg Heiser//2009

Jörg Heiser Recently I passed by the horse chestnut trees next to Berlin cathedral, where every year in autumn up to 40,000 starlings stop over temporarily. It's a fascinating spectacle – there they were again, with the polyphonic sounds of their voices and the way they lined up, like a string of pearls, on a building crane nearby. I couldn't help but think of witnessing you shooting 16 mm film at the site in 2002, capturing their extremely coordinated flights in formation. Another experience that comes to mind is when I watched you taking super-slow motion footage of flies at your house in rural Sweden in 2006.

The starling footage has been used for a video monitor installation and a projection, but it's yet to be decided whether you might finally also show it as a film, while the fly footage is waiting for the right moment and context to be realized and completed at all. Do you have a continuing need to revisit the protagonists of your work, reconsider them, like a biologist would revisit an animal population after years? Did you ever feel some kind of anxiety or even repulsion in terms of re-confronting a species or specimen? Or is the work done when it's finally done and you move on?

Henrik Håkansson Anxiety and the decision to move on come together at all times, as nothing is ever ended. In the cases you mention, or in general, I see the work as a process that naturally relates to the process it relates to. A form of infinity, a kind of circular movement that always goes back to where it started, but without a beginning or end. A problematic aspect, as in many ways I very often look back to works that seem finished with some kind of repulsion, as they could have come out differently, but I would never use the word, or feel repulsion towards the subject or topic of any project. In the end, to answer this question I would say that I do have an urge to revisit, or to find a way to follow up on things, or to stay with or within. I do probably consider the works I produce as being parts of one continuous project.

Heiser There are two quite distinct strands in this continuous project: on the one hand there is the observational work, often involving surveillance equipment such as remote cameras placed in the regular habitat of the protagonists, as in the series of works realized in the southern Lacandon rainforest of Mexico, for your exhibition at Museo Rufino Tamayo, Mexico City, in 2008, which included cameo appearances of tapirs or jaguars. On the other hand, there is work that involves the live performance of living beings in art spaces, whether it's the crickets on stage for *Monsters of Rock* (1997), competing against their own sounds transmitted over the speaker system, or the orchids and plants of *Broken Forest* (2006), suspended in mid-air like the fragment of a biotope catapulted into outer space. Would you agree there are these two strands? And don't they translate the typical forms of the digital age – the Big Brother/Facebook-type mutual observation and performance of the self – into the context of nature, as if to see what happens in that collision?

Håkansson The works are certainly reflective of things happening around me in a more general sense, but otherwise there has so far not been a reason to concentrate on a special technique or specific media or methods to create a series, or one defined style. The concerns are different each time, so instead I divide my work into groups that are simply media, such as 35mm or 16mm film, video, photography, text, sound, performance, installation, painting etc. Sometimes I refer to them as film stills, soundscapes, documents, observations, environments, fragments, to name but a few. More recently, there has been a more defined interest in the time, date and space aspect as well. I would say that works such as *Monsters of Rock*, or actually most works done before 2006, are now archival. My focus is now more on observation- and documentation-based works, as well as purely visual aspects including the methods of painting. The collision or the big bang, or Big Brother, is perhaps just a reference, but it is present.

Heiser Music always, in a way, is a crucial frame of reference, no? As a kind of atmosphere, timbre or sound? And also, maybe, the Romantic tradition, both in regard to methodological ideas like 'the fragmentary', but also in terms of the song, the singer, as Romantic tropes? The single bird performing a song, or even only the fragment of a song, has kept recurring in your work …

Håkansson The nature of romance is perhaps the concept of beauty, as every single note in a bird's call might be the romance of nature. This as such might be the evolution of music and so stands as a great inspiration for the kind of communication I'm trying to achieve. So in terms of method, as you put it, even fragments of music are a generating force. Behind my work desk, there are a number of guitars and amplifiers just within arm's reach, and the possibility of great amplification is a current driving force in my work. So yes, there are musical references to create the atmosphere of the work in general, and maybe this is where the worlds collide. In the distant call of a buzzard outside of my window and the distorted feedback of a Fender Jaguar [guitar] over what is currently my favourite guitar amplifier, the Earth Sound Research Revival … Even those names already generate some kind of undefined energy …

Heiser In your work electricity is not just a technical requirement, but an embodiment of psychic and bodily energies. Dr Frankenstein's monster, the other way round: not a single body composed of dead elements, but living beings fragmented into sounds, images, machineries, sometimes ghost-like presences. What do you make of the kind of cyber-animalisms, hybridities between animals and humans and technology, that theorist Donna Haraway develops, for example? She has written extensively about the National Geographic television show *Crittercams*, where turtles or whales are fitted with remote cameras etc. Do you look to this stuff? Do you, for example, see bats with their sonic navigational powers as being in some way 'technological'?

Håkansson Bats would be a great example of technology. The echolocation calls are inspiring. The whole idea of the signals transmitted to be reflected and captured, the technology of hunting, radar. Most technologies or electric phenomena have a biological source; powers that are natural but not always understood. I'm personally not too involved in human cyborg relations, but seeing the cyborg developments at the brink of animal technology is not difficult. Something like *Crittercams* might allow us to explore different angles, but still these angles just reflect the way we see things – they are not a translator of the bats' or insects' vision. Though I'm seeking ways out of the electrically powered techniques in my work, I still find an attraction in the possibilities of those cameras and the possibilities of being there but not present. To quote musician and recording artist Will Oldham: 'The unique power of recording equipment is that it actually can capture something as it's happening, something that has never happened before.'

Heiser You make music yourself with fellow artist Johan Zetterquist?

Håkansson Yes, and artist Bo Melin.

Heiser Do you see this as directly feeding into your work? Or do you see it as separate? Correct me if I'm wrong but so far you have never used music made by yourself in any of your pieces, have you?

Håkansson I do not separate the music project for myself, but I do currently see this project as separate from the works that are presented within the exhibition context. I haven't yet included my own produced sounds in works, but I wouldn't say that it would never happen.

Heiser Your fondness for 'heavy' sounds, whether avant-garde or 'plain' Motörhead type, seems juxtaposed with the fragility and beauty of a small bird peeping (or not even peeping) in front of a large, anxious auditorium, as in the Frieze Art Fair project of 2005. So how does the heavy relate to the delicate?

Håkansson Music is essential; musical improvisation, for example, expands the system, and I use it for myself to relax my mind. Imaging then a total improvisation among the birds, frogs or insects – and then using very controlled and frequency- pitched sounds. And in that regard I find it of great interest to work around the form of single delicate notes or movements; around a directed, yet uncontrolled situation, presented with the performative method that music or theatre can achieve.

Heiser I remember you once told me how as a kid you found a beetle frozen in ice. You took it home, presuming it was dead; the ice melted, and the next morning when you looked for it the beetle was gone. This surprising event, this epiphany of the wonder of nature that expresses itself in a glimpse or fleeting event, is that still something you look for when you make a new work? For example, your latest project?

Håkansson Of course a surprise is a nice element to any work you are trying to achieve, just as the beetle in this story turned up crawling on my bookshelf the next day. However the surprise itself might not be the main driving force behind my works. What I'm searching for, or think is interesting in my work, is something that deals with the organized randomness that we are surrounded by. [...]

Henrik Håkansson and Jörg Heiser, extract from 'Earth Sound Research Revival', *Mousse Magazine*, no. 21 (November 2009) (www.moussemagazine.it).

Nikolas Rose
The Politics of Life Itself//2007

The space of contemporary biopolitics has not been formed by any single event. The reshaping of medical and political perception and practice has come about through interconnections among changes along a number of dimensions. Without claiming exhaustivity I delineate five pathways where I think significant mutations are occurring.

First, *molecularization*: The 'style of thought' of contemporary biomedicine envisages life at the molecular level, as a set of intelligible viral mechanisms among molecular entities that can be identified, isolated, manipulated, mobilized, recombined, in new practices of intervention, which are not constrained by the apparent normativity of a natural vital order.

Second, *optimization*. Contemporary technologies of life are no longer constrained, if they ever were, by the poles of health and illness. These poles remain, but in addition, many interventions seek to act in the present in order to ensure the best possible future for those who are their subjects. Hence, of course, these technologies embody disputed visions of what, in individual and or collective human life, may indeed be an optimal state.

Third, *subjectification*. We are seeing the emergence of new ideas of what human beings are, what they should do, and what they can hope for. Novel conceptions of 'biological citizenship' have taken shape that recode the duties, rights and expectations of human beings in relation to their sickness, and also to their life itself, reorganize the relations between individuals and their biomedical authorities, and reshape the ways in which human beings relate to themselves as 'somatic individuals'. This is linked to the rise of what I term a 'somatic ethics' – ethics not in the sense of moral principles, but rather as the values for the conduct of a life – that accords a central place to corporeal, bodily existence.

Fourth, *somatic expertise*. These developments are giving rise to new ways of governing human conduct, and the rise of multiple subprofessions that claim expertise and exercise their diverse powers in the management of particular aspects of our somatic existence – geneticists specializing in particular classes of disorder working in alliance with group of patients and families, specialists in reproductive medicine with their public or private clinics and devoted clientele, stem cell therapists whose work becomes known across the world via the Internet and who become the focus of pilgrimages of hope for cures for everything from spinal cord injuries to Alzheimer's disease. Around these experts of the soma cluster a whole variety of new pastoral experts – genetic counsellors are perhaps the best exemplars – whose role is to advise and guide, to care and support individuals and families as they negotiate their way through the personal, medical and ethical dilemmas that they face. And, perhaps most remarkable has been the rise of a novel expertise of 'bioethics' claiming the capacity to evaluate and adjudicate on these activities, which has been enrolled in the government and legitimation of biomedical practices from bench to clinic and marketplace.

Fifth, economies of *vitality*. Energized by the search for biovalue, novel links have formed between truth and capitalization, the demands for shareholder value and the human value invested in the hope for cure and optimality. A new economic space has been delineated: *bioeconomy*; and a new form of capital: *biocapital*. Old actors such as pharmaceutical corporations have been transformed in their relation with science on one hand, stock market on the other. New actors such as biotech start-ups and spin-outs have taken shape, often seeking to stress their corporate social responsibility and combining in various ways with the forms of citizenship and expertise. Life itself has been made amenable to these new economic relations, as vitality is decomposed into a series of distinct objects – which can be isolated, delimited, stored, accumulated, mobilized and exchanged, accorded a discrete value, traded across time, space, species, contexts, enterprises – in the service of many distinct objectives. In the process, a novel geopolitical field has taken shape and biopolitics has become inextricably intertwined with bioeconomics.

I am wary of epochal claims, and it is necessary to recognize that none of these mutations marks a fundamental break with the past: each exhibits continuity alongside change. Yet, I suggest, from the point of view of the present, a threshold has been crossed. Something is emerging in the configuration formed by the intertwining of these five lines of mutation, and this 'something' is of importance for those, like myself, who try to write the history of possible futures. This is why I suggest that we are inhabiting an emergent form of life. [...]

Nikolas Rose, extract from *The Politics of Life Itself* (Princeton: Princeton University Press, 2007) 5–7.

Critical Art Ensemble
Contestational Biology//2002

> Once again, what appears to us in the mystical guise of pure science and objective knowledge about nature turns out, underneath, to be political, economic and social ideology.
> – R.C. Lewontin

Over the past five years Critical Art Ensemble (CAE) has travelled extensively doing participatory performances that critique the representations, products and policies related to emerging biotechnologies. When we do projects concerning transgenics, one of the most common questions participants ask is whether CAE is for or against genetically modified organisms (GMOs). The reply from group members is always the same: We have no general position. Each product or process has to be taken on a case-by-case basis. Some appear disastrous (primarily to the environment), while others seem soundly engineered and useful.

The real question of GMOs is how to create models of risk assessment that are accessible to those not trained in biology so people can tell the difference between a product that amounts to little more than pollutants for profit and those which have a practical and desirable function, while at the same time have no environmental impact. Making such decisions is further complicated by a general lack of understanding of safety testing procedures. For those without scientific training, the question of what constitutes scientific rigour seems to be a mystery, and reading a study on the safety of transgenic products appears to be a mountain that is too high to climb. The concerned public can be further bamboozled by specialized vocabularies. The result is that individuals are left with the implied obligation that they should just have faith in scientific, government and corporate authorities that allegedly always act with only the public interest in mind.

The perception that science is too difficult for anyone other than a specialist to understand is socially ingrained in those separated from the discipline on an everyday life basis. The walls of the division of technical labour seem unbreachable. The common English expression 'it's not rocket science', usually made as a sarcastic remark when someone has inordinate trouble with an easy task, is but one example of a manifestation of public reverence for the intellectual intensity of science and its separation from common daily activities.

However, while such perceptions have a serious degree of truth to them, they are also over-exaggerated. Within a very brief period, anyone who is modestly literate can learn the fundamentals of scientific study and ethics. To give an example of how scientific matters are often easily understood, consider the following. Studies should be replicated numerous times not just by a single lab, but in conjunction with other labs to see if the same or very similar results are consistently obtained. If each lab shows the same findings, then the hypothesis or theory guiding the tests is said to be reliable. Reliability is a key indicator of test validity. Until reliability studies are done, a given result is suspect. Obviously, one does not need to be a scientist to understand that if a study has not been repeated by independent sources, the data are questionable. If the only replications were done by the lab (usually the lab is corporate, but academic labs are suspect too) that will financially benefit, one does not need a Ph.D. in ethics to know that this violates scientific codes of conduct due to a conflict of interest that could radically skew data interpretation (if not the data itself). Currently, biotech corporations are the primary if not sole suppliers of data to the Environmental Protection Agency and the United States Department of Agriculture for commercial licensing permits for genetically modified organisms. Amateur discourse clearly has a place in the transgenic debates since some levels of study can be reviewed by non-experts. The stakes are too high for product safety testing to be left solely in the domain of corporate and scientific experts.

Representations of the transgenic face a deep contradiction, albeit one that emerges from imperial and/or corporate culture. The spectacle of transgenics, as usual, tends consistently to support profit initiatives and promote the idea that the 'free' market always works in the public interest, by saving us from environmental, health and population problems. Unfortunately for corporate culture the historical representation of the rules of social purity and pollution clashes with the utopian representation of transgenic products. While the former insists on maintaining natural purities and claims that it is unwise, if not catastrophic, to intervene in the engines of creation, the latter presents a world of molecular exchange that will benefit everyone. This second position is not doing very well at convincing the consuming public that genetic engineering is a good idea. After all, dislodging ideological imperatives that have settled deeply into every classist and racist separation for the past three millennia is not an enviable task. This ideological contradiction is all the more difficult to reconcile because capital does not want to disrupt effects beneficial to colonial and endocolonial initiatives that the current ideology of separation provides, thus the construction of a doublethink is required in which mixing the categories of nature is sometimes good and sometimes not. While the manner in which such imperatives are structured and selected actually depends on what is most profitable, it cannot be represented that way. Somehow this contradiction must be mythically represented and thereby normalized through the filtering code of the natural. Biotech companies have failed to solve this problem, and while they still try a variety of public relations campaigns, the fundamental strategy has been just to produce and deploy whatever transgenic products are predicted to be profitable, and not emphasize the quandary, hoping that as the consuming public builds habitual associations with the products, the problem of public 'hysteria' will solve itself.

As a cultural resource for artistic material, transgenics is becoming a trendy exploitable topic for savvy, career-minded cultural producers. Not that this trend is atypical: Whenever new vision technologies appear, and less endowed areas of specialization (like art production) finally gain access to them, there are those who will immediately seize the opportunity to exploit new aesthetic possibilities. It seems reasonable to assume that at this very moment, some artists are exchanging their web cams for electron microscopes. And already, the 'art world' has begun to see work derived from molecular biology drifting out of the laboratories and into various cultural spaces. With two decades of the vision-tech explosion behind us, what is ahead is relatively predictable – monumental molecular landscapes emphasizing the paradox of scale and the colourful beauty of the micro-world, and the next step in living sculpture, consisting of expressions of frankensteinian desire in the form of manufactured or intentionalized life forms (glow-in-the-dark rats and proteins performing textual patterns).

To be sure, these projects of technological and/or formal novelty will be more depressing this time around, because so much of the highly visible is and will be as apolitical (or hiding its politics) as possible and designed to further feed the cultural commodity's market for novelty. In terms of political economy in general, such work does help educate the public, but also functions on behalf of corporate culture to calm public scepticism by ripping bio-imaging out of the realm of political debate and fortifying it within the spectacularized and specialized bunker of aestheticization. Corporate and state culture could not ask for better public relations work, and hence the willingness of corporations to fund high-profile cultural manifestations such as Ars Electronica in Europe, or the museum extravaganzas at the Whitney Museum of American Art and San Francisco Museum of Modern Art in the US.

Finally, the problem of policy comes ready-made. Developments in transgenics will follow the path of all goods and services under capital – that is, they will rarely be in the public interest. Pancapitalist policy only fuels, strengthens and expands the profit machine. Molecular invasion and control is rapidly being transformed into new types of colonial and endocolonial control. The focus seems to be on consolidating the food chain from molecular structure to product packaging. With the ability better to control species expression, corporations have a better chance than ever to intensify developing nations' dependency on western corporate economy. Food must either be purchased from corporate food suppliers, or the necessary organic and chemical materials must be purchased. Either way, resource management is controlled by western capital. Farmers can be leveraged either to grow cash crops like cotton or any combination that is most advantageous to the colonizer. This plan has existed since the inception of industrial farming, so food resource hegemonies have simply been given another powerful tool that fits perfectly into the current structure of domination.

In addition, any form of molecular capital can now be appropriated – it is an open frontier. As with all named and controlled objects, now, genomes, enzymes, biochemical processes, etc., will all be privatized. What was once communal and controlled by traditional authority and common understanding is now usurped by separating its molecular or chemical value from its holistic phenotypic value. For example, a plant used in traditional medicine that had general (economic, political, spiritual) value can be transformed into something of solely economic value as a chemical compound. This compound can be patented, and while the plant could still be used, the active ingredient cannot, thus functionally removing the plant from the common resources. In a moment of eco-piracy disguised as Lockean property rights, the labour of separating the various micro-properties of the plant overrides any holistic function and collective ownership.

The standard argument for eliminating any trace of the commons is to say that common property is an inefficient way to manage resources. If efficiency is increased, more goods are available, so everyone gets more for less. However, we know after two centuries of capital that the only people who get more are the owners, while the poor and disenfranchised completely lose the little resources they once had access to. The assumption that efficiency is a totalizing good is nothing more than a disgraceful example of the particular values of the powerful being represented and internalized as universal.

Efficiency stings in other territories as well. Environmental neglect, pollution and exploitation in regard to transgenics are all occurring in the name of efficiency. Capital in the US is obsessed with speed in general, but in this case its interests are in closing the gap between the time when a product is developed and its arrival on the market. Efficiency, in this case, means profitability. Once a product is shown to function, it is ready for distribution. Transgenic products are being made available as soon as possible in order to establish a firm market niche. At present, no one knows how transgenic products will affect the environment. While the prognosis is generally optimistic for the short term, the long term is another matter. No long-term studies have been done on new types of crops and creatures, and could not be, because the technology is too new. One would hope that the producers of such products would want to err on the side of caution and wait a few decades before releasing genetically modified organisms so that proper long-term testing could be done, but for the most part it is too late now. The engine of progress (i.e., profit) moved forward, leaving the general public unaware that it had left the station. Should there be any future difficulties, those who released the GMOs will not even be held responsible for cleaning up the mess. Secondary hazards are just part of the risk of doing business.

What can be done to alter this situation? The answer is as singular as the pancapitalist machine itself – disturb the profit flows. Certainly, the use of traditional and electronic methods of contestation will be useful, but how can the new molecular/biochemical front be directly engaged as a means to disrupt profits? This is an area that is completely under-theorized, and is the subject matter of contestational biology. Two immediate hurdles that must be cleared are the connection of bioresistance to violence and the tendency of resistance to be urban-based. Given that living organisms are of concern, it is quite likely that introducing inertia into the profit system will damage genetically modified life. Industrial culture has had the environment under fire for decades (and in some areas for as long as two centuries), so CAE is only proposing returning fire. Further, the rules of engagement are pretty well established. If one assumes that bioresistance should use violent methods only as a last resort, and only to the extent necessary to be effective, a number of possibilities that will not lead to jail time present themselves. Corporate culture has long maintained that violence through secondary consequences is not the fault of an individual agent or institution. For example, if a manufacturing process causes acid rain, the manufacturers are not responsible for any ill effects on flora, fauna or other environmental elements, nor are they responsible for any type of clean-up. If the resistance can locate itself in the same fuzzy field, legal counter fire is possible that would be disturbing and effective.

The second problem is deciding how to redeploy resistant forces. Currently, the majority tends to focus its activities in urban areas. Only the green movement has developed methods for rural and wild areas. The means by which rural capital can be used for resistant purposes is only modestly theorized. Bioresistance is still waiting for the day when a demonstration of 20,000 people will be launched at a Monsanto test site in Alabama, or when farms dedicated to the development of resistant species will appear. This logistical problem and need for redeployment gives nomadic capital quite an edge in terms of maintaining its activities in territories where social and political friction is minimal. [...]

Critical Art Ensemble, extract from 'Contestational Biology', *The Molecular Invasion* (New York: Autonomedia, 2002) 3–12 [footnotes not included].

Paul Tebbs
Zhao Renhui: *The Blind*//2009

The posited origin of art within the caves of Lascaux ensures that something of the future of art (and the future of the image) appears forever inscribed within the contemporary visualization of animals. Art functions uneasily in this context (the context in which the specific work *The Blind*, and the more general artwork from which it is taken, The Institute of Critical Zoology, should be understood) as a working through and articulation of the difference between animal and human life. There is a paradox within such a function for art: it is the very possibility of art in human existence that partly constitutes humanity's separation from animal life, yet it is also within the space of art that this difference is manifested as a disturbing proximity. 'Animality' names something of the base condition from which such art is produced, to which it returns, and which it sometimes transcends. Cultural visualizations of this proximity abound, from the melancholic evictions from civil life of the Incredible Hulk to the starkly decontextualized animal sacrifices recorded in Abdel Abdessemed's video works. In one, an ethically sensitive if uncontrollable man-monster, in the other, a performance of human mastery that takes visualization within art to the limits of the ethical (animals are tethered and killed by a single sledgehammer blow).

As a multimedia fictional construct The Institute of Critical Zoology (ICZ) mobilizes artistic strategies under the methodological and liveried disguise of an authentic scientific institute. Devoted to the interdisciplinary study of zoology, it is a performance (predominantly through the website www.criticalzoologists. org) of an unlikely international collaboration between Japan and China, showcasing advances in zoological knowledge and technique, often in the wistful pursuit of ecological salvation. It purports to have a museum housing several collections – including 14,000 animal specimens bequeathed by Soon Bo, some of which can be seen online – and produces an academic journal. The tone of ICZ is dryly evangelical. Its visual performance is at once cool, if naggingly pseudo, cultish even. The execution of this artistic conceit is extremely persuasive.

The object of ICZ's critique is scientism and its languages of persuasion, both written and visual, as well as the exploitation of animals within culture generally, for example through the tragic but enduring spectacles of zoos, circuses and, seemingly, art. As an artwork, ICZ is to science what Walid Raad's Atlas Group is to the writing of recent political history: absurdist but plausible, poignant and playfully political. And it is a critique that cuts at least two ways: art lightly mocking the scientific calibration of animal and human difference, but performed knowingly within a culture of art production and art education that increasingly adopts scientific language and behaviours to determine its status as a mode of research. ICZ operates on fertile ground.

Its website provides an archive of the Institute's research and ecological initiatives. These include a process known as 'Acusis', in which an acupuncture-induced biostasis offers animals a state of limbo prior to possible extinction. A 'live' webcam allows the viewer access to their subtly pulsating bodies. Other projects include the establishment of tiger farms – a blatant adoption of commercialism to advance conservation – and a cloak, known as 'the blind', that allows the scientific operative invisibility in the field of study. This, a most desired possibility within research, is in order to eliminate observer interference within the field of study. The ICZ website explains: 'The blind works on the principle that an object vanishes from sight if light rays are not reflected as usual but forced to flow around it and carry on, as if it was not there. To make these cloaks, our scientists developed "meta-materials", meticulously patterned thin metal sheets that can bend light in precisely the right way.'

The world's leading ethologists (specialists in animal behaviour) have suggested that a critical point may now have been reached and animals are, for the first time, vengefully fighting back against the cruelty of humans. Significant increases in attacks on humans across a variety of animal species have led some to argue that we are in an unprecedented period of 'human-animal conflict' (acronym HAC). There is a certain speculative richness to this 'scientific' suggestion, that is not a fabrication from the ICZ, but was recently reported in the popular press based upon scientific research. It is a theory perhaps backed by Santino, a male chimpanzee in a Swedish zoo, who has recently been observed preparing caches of ammunition to throw at his daily parade of visitors. Santino was not reported in the context of HAC but instead presented as evidence that primates can prepare in advance and act in a premeditated way.

These two reports (HAC and Santino) testify to both the richness and poverty of the scientific account of animal life and it is into this space of indeterminacy that ICZ successfully operates. It does not take the centenary of Darwin's birth (and with it the mobilization of Creationist opposition to the theory of natural selection) to remind us that there is a still a very contemporary unease within the calibration of animal and human difference.

Paul Tebbs, 'Zhao Renhui: The Blind', *Portfolio*, no. 49 (2009).

Bruno Latour
Will Non-Humans be Saved? An Argument in Ecotheology//2009

[…] It has now almost become common sense that we were able to think we were modern only as long as the various ecological crises could be denied or delayed. As I ventured to put it, a few years back, 'To modernize or to ecologize? that is the question.'[1] The course of events has settled the matter quite firmly: modernizing will not do. What is not clear, however, is what ecologizing will mean exactly. The range of attitudes, prescriptions, warnings, restrictions, summons, sermons and threats that go with ecology seems to be strangely out of sync with the magnitude of the changes expected from all of us, the demands that appear to impinge on each and every detail of our material existence. It is as if the rather apocalyptic injunction 'your entire way of life must be modified or else you will disappear as a civilization' has overwhelmed the narrow set of passions and calculations that go under the name of 'ecological consciousness'. The camel seems to stand no chance of going through the eye of this needle. When the first tremors of the Apocalypse are heard, it would seem that preparations for the end should require something more than simply using a different kind of light bulb …

In addition to this lack of fit between the implied threats and the proposed solutions, there is something deeply troubling in many ecological demands to suddenly restrict ourselves and to try to leave no more footprints on a planet we have nevertheless already modified through and through. It appears totally implausible to ask the heirs of the emancipatory tradition to convert suddenly to an attitude of abstinence, caution and asceticism – especially when billions of other people still aspire to a minimum of decent existence and comfort. As has been so valiantly argued by Nordhaus and Shellenberger in their post-environmentalist manifesto, *Breakthrough*, it might not be the time to sound the retreat and to betray the progressivist ethos of modernism by suddenly becoming ascetics.[2] If modernism was Promethean, the massive acceleration of a green economy and clean technologies they argue is needed would be Prometheus squared. As I wrote in a review of their book, they have redefined environmentalism by 'breaking through the limitations of the notion of limits'.[3] And yet, it, is still unquestionable that there is something deeply flawed in the hubristic tone of so much hype about technological solutions to ecological crises. Is there a way to explore a positive, energetic, innovative set of passions to repair and pursue the modernist experience at a more fundamental level? Can we imagine a Doctor Frankenstein who would not flee in horror at the creature he bungled at first – a

Frankenstein who goes *back* to his laboratory? Can Prometheus be reconciled with the seemingly antithetical notions of care and caution?

If it is true according to the French proverb that it is 'always safer to direct one's request to the Good Lord than to His saints', it is probably also true that when people use 'apocalyptic terms' it is safer to go straight to religion instead of using them metaphorically. You will forgive me, I hope, if I concentrate on the religion I know best. There is no question: religion, in the various traditions, elaborated around Christianity, is all about a radical change in the make up of daily existence. 'Let the Holy Spirit renew the face of the Earth' the monks chant eight times a day and, if I have not been misled by my informant, so do the devout of the [British] Left at their meetings: 'Bring me my chariot of fire' [William Blake, *Jerusalem*].

Not only does religion demand a level of radical transformation compared to which the ecological gospel looks like a timid appeal to buy new garbage cans, but it also has – and this will be even more important for the future – a very assured confidence in the *artificial* remaking of earthly goods. As the Metropolitan John of Pergamon points out (as a rule, Eastern orthodox theology is very much at the forefront on these questions), the Eucharist is not a presentation of grains and grapes but of the actively, artificially, technically (and I would add scientifically) transformed grains in bread and grapes in wine.[4] Before the transubstantiation of bread and wine into flesh and blood, there is another indisputable transubstantiation of grain into bread and of grapes into wine that is no less mysterious than the other (and being a Catholic from a Burgundy family who has in addition spent many years studying Louis Pasteur, you may take my word for it …). So, because of these two features (radical transformation and full confidence in artificial transformations in this world, or in other words, Incarnation), religion, in its Christian instantiation at least, presents itself as a rather plausible alternative to an ecological consciousness whose ethical and emotional drives don't seem to have enough petrol (or soybeans) to carry us through the tasks it has burdened upon us. In this respect, nothing is less conservative, and nothing is more down to earth than religion. The sad histories of the Christian churches should not mislead us here. Even if they were unable to digest the shock of Science in the seventeenth century, we should not forget that the appeal to renewing everything, here and now, and in this world, is first of all a religious passion – and a Passion it is … Whereas ecological consciousness has been unable to move us, the religious drive to renew the face of the Earth just might.

Naturally, this connection between ecology and theology, or ecological consciousness and Christian spirituality is not my invention. Ever since Hans Jonas brought his immense knowledge of the Apocalyptic and Gnostic tradition to bear upon the ecological threat, a thriving field of eco-theology has been developing in many quarters of the various Churches. That it is still a marginal movement is due to the modernist history of the Church (in its Western Protestant and Catholic versions) which has never stopped restricting religion to an ever more shrinking domain.[5] Everything happens as if, the farther forward you move in time, the more the Churches have resigned themselves to save only humans, and in humans, only their disembodied souls. But what about non-humans? What about Creation itself? Moralistic, spiritualist, psychological and I would argue scientistic definitions of religion have led theology, rituals and prayers to turn away from the world, the cosmos, and to see nothing objectionable in the quote: 'What good would it be to possess the world, if you forfeit your soul?' without realizing that because of the urgency of the ecological crisis, the opposite is now far truer: 'What use is it to save your soul, if you forfeit the world?' Do you by any chance have another Earth to go to? Are you going to upload yourself to another planet?

Catholics and Protestants killed each other for a century over the rather limited question of how many of them would be saved and whether this should be by grace alone or also by deeds, without noticing that, while they were busy trying to expand or restrict the numbers of the blessed, they were abandoning the huge masses of non-humans, that is, 'the whole Creation' which, as Paul so powerfully bore witness to, still 'groans and labours with birth pangs' even now. We always forget that what modernism did to religion is even worse than what it did to science. It deprived it of its energy, restricting it, as Whitehead said, to mere furniture of the soul.'[6] It is painfully clear that this ever shrinking religious ethos will do nothing for ecologizing our world, and if we take what is preached in most sermons around the planet for religion, it would be better to prepare for the Apocalypse which is fast upon us by changing a few light bulbs and buying a Terra Pass to pay for our pollution. Yet perhaps we can postpone this seemingly inevitable Apocalypse: religion could become a powerful alternative to modernizing and a powerful help for ecologizing, provided that a connection can be established (or rather re-established) between religion *and Creation* instead of religion and nature.

I say 're-established' because the pre-modern Christian theology, especially that of the Fathers, was well aware that it was the whole of Creation that was in the throes of salvation, not only the poor floating souls of spiritually disembodied humans. Non-humans had a central place in theology, in spirituality, in rituals and of course in art which they now have almost totally lost.[7] But this was before modernism and before its politicization of science: thus it remains immensely difficult for us (and for me at any rate because of my ignorance of the Greek Fathers) to retrieve these resources which have been covered by so many layers of modernism that they seem as lost as the bones of our pre-human ancestors.

Can they be resurrected? Can those dry bones in the Valley of the Dead be assembled again? [...]

The key question is to decide whether or not nature is the *only thing* that Christian religion can encounter when it tries to reach back to the world it has been forced to exit too fast. The answer strikes at the cutting edge of anthropological theory. It becomes clearer and clearer, as anthropology moves on, spurred both by my own field (science studies) and by ecological crises and globalization more generally, that nature has never been the unified material medium in which modernism has unfolded. Under scrutiny, 'naturalism' reveals itself as a queer bundle of many contradictory traits which do not form enough of a homogeneous domain even to be defined in contrast to the domain of the soul or even less the realm of the supernatural. In the work of Philippe Descola (whose fundamental book *Beyond Nature and Culture*, to the great shame of British and American anthropology and their academic publishing industries is not yet translated into your language), naturalism is only *one* of four ways in which connections between humans and non-humans can be established – and it is the most anthropocentric of the four.[8] Whereas for its first century, anthropology could multiply 'cultures' while nature remained the non-coded category in contrast to which cultures could be defined, it is fair to say that, in this century, anthropology will go on multiplying the ways in which former cultures and former natures (now in the plural) become coded categories. It is a direct consequence of the fact that we have never been modern that the very notions of cultures (in the plural) and nature (in the singular) have been slowly dissolving (actually nature and culture could also compete for the Olympic medals of modernist obfuscation ...). 'Anthropology of nature' (the name of Descola's chair at the College de France) has very quickly passed from an oxymoron to a pleonasm.

This is now so well known and is carried forth by anthropologists and anthropologically minded historians who are so much better endowed with ethnographic knowledge than myself, that I don't want to belabour the point any further. What I want instead is to draw from this a slightly more radical conclusion made directly possible by the work done in science studies (or at least by its more philosophical version). This will allow me, following Whitehead, to extract from the ill-formed notion of nature, the third contrast I need for my acrobatic demonstration.

Remember that the key question is how to allow religion to encounter something other than 'nature'. That this is possible (if not easy) becomes clearer when one begins to realize that what is called 'nature'– or, what has been taken for the same thing, 'the material world', the world of 'matter', is made of at least two entirely different layers of meaning: one consists of the ways in which reference chains need to be arrayed so as to work, by giving us knowledge of far away entities and processes of all kinds; but the other is provided by a completely different type of mode, and that is the ways in which the entities themselves manage to remain in existence.[9] Having called the first *Reference*, I will call this second *Reproduction* (for a reason that will become clear in a minute). These two contrasts, or, to call them by a more ontological term, these two *modes of existence*, have been constantly confused by modernism, but this confusion does not need to continue with ecology. To reach something far away through long arrays of instruments, you need to make sure that necessities and constants are transported with as little transformation as possible (this is why I call them *immutable mobiles*). But that such a path is necessary to reach those entities which could not be grasped otherwise, does not mean that those entities use the same subterfuges to remain in existence, to persist and endure. Geometry, mathematical entities and inscriptions of all sorts, are powerful ways to carry heavy-duty immutable mobiles through long reference chains, but it would be extraordinary (and quite improbable) if entities such as atoms, photons or particles needed mathematics and geometry to subsist. As Whitehead so forcefully showed, the concept of matter confuses the ways entities persist with the ways we try to know them. Though *res extensa* is an extraordinary powerful way to establish knowledge, no entity has ever resided 'in' *res extensa* – except on paper when you have to show, that is, to know it. At the very least, the concept of matter has thus mixed together in the same bag two entirely different sets of practices: Reproduction is not Reference (no more than Reference is Religion).

This is why it is always so difficult to be a real materialist: matter, mistaken for the transportation of undisputable necessities through chains of cause and effect, is not the obvious, given background of the world but instead a highly elaborated, historically dated and anthropologically situated hybrid which combines the reference chains necessary to access the far away with the surprising inventions entities themselves have to go through in order to subsist. I hope you understand that I am not indulging here in the nineteenth-century game of pretending to *add* to matter some spiritual dimension (and even less am I flirting with the bogus Mind/Body conundrum). I have, on the contrary, simply (and I'd say politely!) *withdrawn* from the confusing bag of matter, *one* of its confusing elements, the most spiritual (or intellectual) one by the way: namely, the processes and the chains of inscription necessary to travel back and forth safely (that is, by maintaining necessities and constants all along the chain in both directions) from the knower to what is to be known. What is left in the bag? Entities which endures by running the risk of reproduction and repetition. Such is the third trait, the third mode of existence I wished to introduce.

I said earlier that when nature comes on the scene, religion has to exit. Well, now the scene has shifted quite a lot: first it was nature which had to exit; then,

Reference has been clearly contrasted with Reproduction. And now, you might ask, what will happen if religion is called back on stage, not to encounter nature (it is gone for good) but a world consisting of entities undertaking the risky business of sustaining and perpetuating themselves? Suspense, suspense. Or no suspense at all because I have most probably lost you … Well, I will wake you up, with one two syllable word: Darwin!

It is not by coincidence that the protagonists of the Science and Religion debate always converge on Saint Darwin, this Father of the Church – and here I am well aware that I am treading on dangerous territory, especially in England.

The confusion between Reproduction and Reference was less noticeable when we were dealing with so called 'inert' entities which, in addition, were always considered in bulk and never individually. With falling bodies, planets, billiard balls and games of chance, the ways we access them and the ways they are supposed to reproduce themselves are so similar that the collage or hybrid character of the notion of matter was hardly noticeable. There seemed to be nothing wrong in considering matter as a transportation of necessities through chains of causes and effects: The crude stitches of this category mistake could not be detected. The ways we know the world and the ways in which the world behaves seemed to be simply the same thing twice to the eyes of the physicist (though this was already less the case to the eyes of the chemist and not at all to the eyes of the engineer, even if these discrepancies could somehow be papered over with tortured distinctions like that between pure and applied sciences or science and engineering).[10] However, the hybrid character of the notion of matter was unavoidably obvious to the eyes of evolutionary biologists. Here, billions of entities undergo the risks of repetition across gaps and discontinuities in time and descent that no transportation of undisputable necessities could cover up. They face lots of causes and lots of effects to be sure but at every point there are masses of invention that intervene, so that causes and consequences don't match one another so well.[11] Creativity, seeping in at every juncture, jumped out at the naturalists. What could still be plausible for physics and engineering, namely that *res extensa* was a description of the ways entities endure and persist in the world as well as the ways we grasp them from far away, could no longer be entertained once naturalists began to reckon with biological evolution. To be sure, they could draw up tables, trees and build reference chains to attempt to grasp these processes, but this knowledge could no longer be confused with the ways in which the organisms themselves behaved. No snail, no earthworm, no virus, no acorn ever lived in the *res extensa* which is so necessary nonetheless for us to access their peculiar mode of existence.

With Darwin, living entities were at last allowed to subsist and thrive but only provided they were no longer cultivated, so to speak, in the highly artificial medium of the *res extensa* – and it is not by coincidence either that one of the most daring naturalists, Von Uexküll, invented the word *Umwelt* to describe the alternative medium in which biological organisms were allowed to reproduce, this *Umwelt* which now envelops the world under the name of 'environment' and environmental crisis.[12] To modernize or to ecologize has also always been a question for biologists. No one can deny the complete sea change that has occurred in the last thirty years: yet the major effect of ecology is not, as I have shown at length, that nature has made a comeback, but that we are finally 'out of nature'.[13] So where are we? It is not clear, but once we are out of Nature we have to realize that we all reside in some *Umwelt*. (The only thinker who has absorbed this new situation is of course the German philosopher Peter Sloterdijk, with his theory of Spheres – a radically original alternative to nature and to society).[14] And where is the *res extensa*? It has not disappeared, on the contrary, but it is safely located inside the reference chains and is no longer allowed to float dreamily in some nowhere land. (This, by the way, seems to me to have been the major contribution of science studies to anthropology).

No doubt, some of you will object that by bringing in evolution and by waving the red flag of Darwin's name, I am falling straight into the same obscure Science and Religion debate I had earlier promised to avoid. … True, unless we put to good use the three modes I have outlined. It is safe to say that one hundred and fifty years after his discoveries, the full originality of Darwin's thought has still not been absorbed by public consciousness. I am not alluding here to the masses of results and models obtained by evolutionary biologists, but to the metaphysical consequences of evolutionary theory. The problem is that the full originality of Darwin's understanding of the world is obfuscated not only by so called creationists but in part also by neo-Darwinians.

To their credit, creationists sensed that there was something deeply wrong in the way in which evolution was sold to the public: it was transformed into an ideology of nature, understood as the bearer of indisputable necessities – that is, as exactly what we have seen a minute ago to be a mixed bag of category mistakes.[15] Unfortunately, creationists, after having recognized that there was something fishy in the nature of nature, were unable to diagnose the reason for their malaise. No wonder: they had abandoned religion even more than they had misinterpreted science. They began to look at the Bible as if it were a geology book! No deeper misunderstanding of religion was ever committed than when the call to convert and renew the face of the Earth, that is, to put oneself in the living presence of the *ego, hic et nunc*, was kidnapped in order to divine within the venerable sacred texts some trace of a lost knowledge giving access to the far away, like the distant origin of the Grand Canyon. Creationism depends on a mistaken etymology for the word *geo*-logy: the science of the salvation of the

Earth is not the same thing as the science of the conservation of fossils ... As if the prophets were a bunch of failed Ph.Ds in molecular biology who, instead of Jerusalem, had their eyes set on 'evo-devo'. To call such a reading of Scripture a 'literalist' interpretation is to commit quite a blasphemy against the meaning of the Letter – not to mention the Spirit ... Creationism is neither literal nor even especially religious: it is most of all a thorn in the side of the neo-Darwinians. But I am mischievous enough to think that it is a well placed and, on the whole, a useful thorn ... [...]

Of all the scholars who have tried to highlight the emergence of the contrast that I have called Religion, it is certainly Jan Assmann, in our day, who has done the most. Before he identified and explained what he has called the 'Mosaic division', there was a great confusion between the appeal to multiple divinities and the radical departure we associate with the mythical name of Moses (and also Akhenaton, but this will lead us too far astray). The main point of his, by now, well known and admirably defended argument in *The Price of Monotheism*, is that monotheistic religion (which he, confusingly for us, calls 'counter-religion') introduced into the relations between people and gods a radically new question: that of their truth and falsity.[16] Divinities had never been asked before whether or not they were the 'true' ones. They could be added to one another, translated into one another, piled on top of one another for additional safety. The Mosaic division cut through this sort of relaxed attitude toward truth, by contesting the claims to existence of all divinities but one. From then on there would be a connection between the question of worship and a question, irrelevant until then, of an absolute (not a relative) difference between true and false. Starting from there, Assmann has developed a complex historical anthropology of the origin of both a new form of intolerance and fanaticism and also a new appeal to rationality, the narrative he calls, after Freud, 'progress in spiritual life'.

The reason I am bringing up his work here is not because of his marvellous analysis of religion's (or counter-religion's in his language) constant misunderstanding of earlier religious practices. The misdirected critique of fetishism is an old story that starts with the Mosaic division and continues to this day, even in most of the ethnographic literature. As we have collectively shown in the exhibit and the book *Iconoclash* [edited by Latour and Peter Weibel, 2002], it is another category mistake which has helped to paralyse the key notion of mediation and the very idea of what it is to make something: the fetishist's declaration, 'yes, divinities are made, and that's why they are real'; to which the others, the iconoclasts, mistakenly retort: 'If they are made, then they can't be real' – an image war that explains a large part of the complex history of the West, in science, in religion and in art.[17]

No, the reason I am introducing Assmann is that he credits monotheism with one incredible feat: it has allowed humans escape from a too close adhesion to the natural world! Without the imposition of the radical Mosaic division, we would be left, according to Assmann, with a 'religion of nature', with what he calls 'cosmotheism'. Thanks to Moses and his many descendants we have extracted ourselves from the world, stopped confusing our gods with objects: the price is high but it was necessary for 'progress in spiritual life'. What I find fascinating is that a mind as astute as Assmann's, a scholar so attuned to the historical vagaries of the most cherished modernist notions, still takes, without a hint that it could be as disputable and historically contingent, the idea that without the transcendence of monotheism we would be left with the mere *immanence* of the natural world. Without the spirit, we would be in the world of mere objects. As if the world were really made of the stuff of *res extensa*, against which, fortunately, religious spirituality struck its sword violently enough that another world could at last be seen through the gaping holes – a sword which, in passing, was also used to cut a few throats …

That this sword has not 'slept in the hands' of those who wanted 'to build Jerusalem' and not only in 'England's green and pleasant lands' is clear, but where do we get this prejudice that religion is defined by a transcendence that can save us from a world of nature which otherwise would stifle us into immanence? (or, according to its mirror image, the alternative secular narrative that the stark immanence of the natural world will save us from an escapist adherence to the transcendent world of beyond?). This is where the root of all the spite against non-humans and by consequence the complete implausibility of any form of ecological spirituality resides. If all 'progress in spiritual life' has been accomplished by removing ourselves from 'the world' (or alternatively in converting back from a spiritual dream to a 'strictly naturalistic' vision of life on Earth), we will always have to abandon non-humans in order to reach the spirit (or what we have to take as a merely material *res extensa* to protect us from the irrationality of religion).

I hope you can now get a sense of why the anthropology of the modern is so difficult to pursue. The moderns don't know where they live. They have no world to reside in. They are homeless. Whereas there is no question that this opposition between the natural and the supernatural, immanence and transcendence, mere objects and meaning, matter and spirit, fact and value, defines a large part of the official ideologies of the West, yet, it is just as true to say that this gigantomachy pays no justice at all to the very contrasts that the modems have extracted, highlighted and cherished in the course of their long history. It is this duplicity between what they say they are and what they are, that I summarize by the saying borrowed from old Westerns, that 'White men speak with a forked tongue'. But we Westerners become immensely interesting and could become, I think, frank and reliable, once we move from the ideology to the recognition of the many different contrasts we have lived by without granting them enough room. I ask for just a bit more of your patience, so that we can sketch out how to do this, in the case of the three contrasted domains we have called 'Reproduction, Reference and Religion' [in detailed preceding argument in the original text].

First, one commits an immense injustice by confusing the 'material world' with nature. There is nothing especially 'natural' in the ways entities reproduce and nothing especially material – nothing spiritual either, and, of course, nothing especially immanent. Stop imposing on one contrast (the acts and processes of entities to sustain themselves), the categories necessary to highlight another, in this case, the beauty of science. The hiatus of Reproduction, the risk taken by each individual organism in its own *Umwelt* to last a little longer, has to be defined on its own terms, with its own felicity conditions, without imposing upon it a narrative borrowed from somewhere else. There exists no material world to which some spiritual power – Blind or Intelligent – adds a superfluous meaning. Non-humans have not been emerging for aeons just to serve as so many props to show the mastery, intelligence and design capacities of humans or their divine creations. They have their own intelligence, their own cunning, their own design, and plenty of transcendence to go on, that is, to reproduce. I hope you understand that what I am doing here, by asking for Reproduction to stand alone as a mature mode of existence, is not a plea to 'overcome the limits of a mechanistic or reductionist view of the material world', but on the contrary to *stop* adding to it dimensions that have always been superfluous to its pursuit of its own peculiar goals. It was the ideas of nature and matter that were laced with a spurious spirituality. Let us at last secularize the world of reproduction. Saint Darwin pray for us to succeed.

Second, abandoning the awkwardly makeshift concepts of matter and nature does not mean that you abandon science and objectivity. Quite the contrary. The worst injustice that you can do to science is to confuse its knowledge with the common-sense grasp of 'medium sized dry goods'. There is nothing especially 'immanent' in the reference chains that allow one to access the invisible, the hidden, the improbable, the surprising, the counter-intuitive. Even the most modest study of the humblest scientific practice is enough to show the bewildering steps necessary to obtain reliable information through a cascade of transformations. Quite a steeple chase! Many other gaps have to be overcome, many 'hiatuses' (if you will), many transcendences. If moderns are guilty of a sin, it is that of portraying one of their main achievements, namely the discovery that nothing was out of reach of reference chains, by morphing it into the lazy contemplation of a 'natural world' made visible to rational minds without work, without instruments, without history. They failed to do justice to their own inventive genius and thus have kidnapped science, for political reasons I have outlined elsewhere, into a rather drab and entirely mythical drama of Light overcoming Darkness. Reference deserves greater respect than the hypocritical (I take the word etymologically) adherence to a 'scientific world view'. Through its complex, cascading reference chains, science can produce an objective grasp of everything but no 'scientific world view' of anything – and especially not by covering up evolution.

Third, can we respect Religion, at last, once we respect the proper transcendences of Reproduction and Reference? (And is respect not the ultimate value of the anthropological project?) At the beginning, I defined the religious tradition by its ability to operate two transformations: a radical transformation of the far away into the close and the proximate (what was dead is now alive) and a positive view of all artificial transformations (against any tendency to conserve what it is). And I suggested that this could be exactly what was needed to extend the range of concerns, passions and energy that the overly narrow 'ecological consciousness' could not possess because of its unfortunate adhesion to the 'conservation of nature' and its ilk. When religion encounters nature, one of them has to go. If religion flees from any involvement with non-humans and with science, it becomes irrelevant and will be damned for having forfeited the world to save only the souls of humans in a spiritual nowhere-land. Incarnation would have been in vain. But what happens if religion is allowed to weave its highly specific form of transcendence into the fabric of the other two modes of existence, Reproduction and Reference?

I am well aware that such an encounter has never taken place, either because in modernism religion had to deal with the hybrid form of nature it never knew how to handle, or because in premodern theology there was neither science nor an ecological crisis to raise the question urgently enough (no matter how splendid seems the Fathers' insistence that it is the whole world that is to be saved). Strangely enough, as I have argued (and not without many reservations), creationism seems to be at the right place but with the wrongest tools. It wants religion to be relevant to what is said about the world (which is sound) but it takes the world to be nature (or common-sense matter) and wishes to compete, hopelessly, against the power of scientific chains of reference (which is utter nonsense). Can we do better? Can we help prepare the occasion for an encounter that has never taken place? To put it even more brutally: can the Earth be Saved? (And here the word 'save' is not the one we use on our computer to 'save files', nor is it what we mean when we 'save' the whales: what is at stake is Salvation).

It is good that my space is up because, having reached this point, I feel a bit like Saint Christopher standing in the middle of the river: the weight of the argument is crushing me …

Just a suggestion to conclude – and maybe to escape. The word 'creation' does not need to remain forever the exclusive property of the unfortunate creationists. 'Creation' does not have to be the alternative to the 'natural world', as if the only question were to choose between the Blind Watch Maker and the Intelligent Designer. 'Creation' could instead be the word to designate what we get when Reproduction and Reference are seized by the religious urge radically to transform that which is given into that which has to be fully renewed. The dream of going to another world is just that: a dream, and probably also a deep sin. But to seize, or seize again, this world, this same, one and only world, to grasp it otherwise, that's not a dream, that's a necessity. The term 'Creativity' also designates Reproduction quite well – and it is also a fitting way to capture the immense productivity of science. Is it so absurd to think that all the alliances among values that 'nature' made impossible might be renewed within 'Creation'? Is it so far-fetched to imagine that if nature was never a place to live for long, the modernists might find a much safer and sweeter 'land of milk and honey' in 'Creation'? As the psalmist taught us to sing: 'O Jerusalem, how much I long for the safety of your walls.' I am sure I have neither bow, arrow, spear nor 'chariot of fire', but I hope I have convinced the reader that neither you nor I should 'Cease from [that] Mental Fight'.

1   [footnote 6 in source] B. Latour, 'To Modernize or to Ecologize, That Is the Question', in N. Castree and B. Willems-Braun, eds, *Remaking Reality: Nature at the Millenium* (London and New York: Routledge, 1998) 221–42.

2   [7] T. Nordhaus and M. Shellenberger, *Break Through: From the Death of Environmentalism to the Politics of Possibility* (New York: Houghton Mifflin Company, 2007).

3   [8] B. Latour, 'It's the Development, Stupid!, or. How Can We Modernize Modernization?', unpublished manuscript) commenting on T. Nordhaus and M. Shellenberger, *Break Through. From the Death of Environmentalism to the Politics of Possibility* (New York: Houghton Mifflin Company, 2007) (text can be viewed at www.bruno-latour.fr).

4   [9] M. Zizioulas, *Proprietors or Priests of Creation*, keynote address to the fifth Symposium of Religion, Science and the Environment (2003).

5   [10] D.T. Hessel and R.R. Ruether, eds, *Christianity and Ecology* (Cambridge, Massachusetts: Harvard University Press, 2000).

6   [11] A. N. Whitehead, *Religion in the Making* (New York: Fordham University Press, 1926).

7   [12] H. and J. Bastaire, *Pour une écologie chrétienne* (Paris: Le Cerf, 2004).

8   [14] P. Descola, *Par delà nature et culture* (Paris: Gallimard, 2005).

9   [15] A.N. Whitehead, *Concept of Nature* (Cambridge: Cambridge University Press, 1920) and its commentary in I. Stengers, *Penser avec Whitehead: Une libre et sauvage création de concepts* (Paris: Gallimard, 2002).

10   [16] I. Stengers, *Cosmopolitiques – Tome 3: Thermodynamique: la réalité physique en crise* (Paris: La Découverte, 1996).

11 [17] Witness the mass of examples in F. Scott Gilbert and Epel David, *Ecological Developmental Biology. Integrating Epigenetics, Medicine and Evolution* (Sunderland, Massachusetts: Sinauer Associates, Inc., 2009).

12 [18] J. Von Uexküll, *Mondes animaux et monde humain. Théorie de la signification* (Paris: Gonthier, 1965).

13 [19] B. Latour, *Politics of Nature: How to Bring the Sciences into Democracy*, trans. C. Porter (Cambridge, Massachusetts: Harvard University Press, 2004).

14 [20] P. Sloterdijk, *Sphären III – Schäume* (Frankfurt am Main: Suhrkamp, 2004).

15 [21] P. Kitcher, *Abusing Science: The Case against Creationism* (Cambridge, Massachusetts: The MIT Press, 1983).

16 [25] J. Assmann, *Of God and Gods: Egypt, Israel and the Rise of Monotheism* (Madison: University of Wisconsin Press, 2008).

17 [26] B. Latour and P. Weibel, *Iconoclash: Beyond the Image Wars in Science, Religion and Art* (Cambridge, Massachusetts: The MIT Press, 2002).

Bruno Latour, extracts from 'Will Non-Humans be Saved? An Argument from Ecotheology', paper prepared for the Royal Institute of Anthropology's annual Henry Myers Lecture, British Museum, London (25 September 2008); *Journal of the Royal Anthropological Institute (JRAI)*, vol. 15 (2009), 462–4; 465–9; 470–75.(www.bruno-latour.fr).

Giorgio Agamben is Professor of Aesthetics at the University of Verona.

Jesse Ashlock is an editor, critic and curator, and former editor in chief of *I.D.* magazine.

Michael Auping is Chief Curator at the Modern Art Museum of Fort Worth, Texas.

Aziz + Cucher Anthony Aziz and Sammy Cucher are New York-based artists who have worked collaboratively since 1991.

Gaston Bachelard (1884–1962) was a French philosopher of science and theorist of poetics.

Brandon Ballengée is a New York-based artist, activist and ecological researcher.

Gregory Bateson (1904–80) was a British anthropologist, ecologist and theorist of cybernetics.

Jane Bennett is Professor of Political Theory at Johns Hopkins University, Baltimore.

Henri Bergson (1859–1941) was a French philosopher influential in the early twentieth century.

Joseph Beuys (1921–86) was a German artist and theorist of education and society.

Claire Bishop is Associate Professor of Art History at the Graduate Center, City University of New York.

Suzaan Boettger is Associate Professor of Art at Bergen Community College, New Jersey.

Roger Caillois (1913–78) was a French sociologist and writer on art, science and anthropology.

Oron Catts & Ionat Zurr are Australian-based artists, researchers and curators. In 2000 they co-founded the artistic research laboratory SymbioticA at the University of Western Australia.

Mel Chin is an American artist based in New York.

Emma Cocker is Senior Lecturer in Fine Art at Nottingham Trent University.

Steven Connor is Academic Director of the London Consortium and Professor of Modern Literature and Theory at Birkbeck, University of London.

Lynne Cooke is chief curator at the Museo Centro de Arte Reina Sofía, Madrid, and curator at large for the Dia Art Foundation, New York.

Critical Art Ensemble is an American collective formed in 1987 by five tactical media practitioners who explore the intersections between art, theory, technology and activism.

Walter De Maria is an American artist and composer based in New York.

Jacques Derrida (1930–2004) was a French philosopher and critical theorist.

herman de vries is a Dutch-born artist based in Eschenau, Germany.

Mark Dion is an American artist based in New York and Pennsylvania.

Vilém Flusser (1920–91) was a Czech-born philosopher and theorist of science, media and design.

George Gessert is an American artist whose work explores the intersection of art and genetics.

Oliver Grau is Professor of Image Science at Danube University, Krems, Austria.

Tim Griffin is editor at large of *Artforum*, where he was editor in chief from 2003 to 2010.

Félix Guattari (1930–92) was a French psychoanalytic theorist, philosopher and political activist.

Hans Haacke is a German-born artist based in New York.

Henrik Håkansson is a Swedish artist based in southern Sweden and Berlin.

Peter Halley is an American artist, critic and co-founder of *Index* magazine (1996–2006).

Donna Haraway is Distinguished Professor Emerita in the History of Consciousness Department, University of California at Santa Cruz.

Helen (Mayer Harrison) and Newton Harrison are American artists who have collaborated since 1971. They are Professors Emeriti at the University of California at San Diego.

David Harvey is Distinguished Professor of Anthropology at the Graduate Center of the City University of New York.

Pierre Huyghe is a French artist based in Paris and New York.

Eduardo Kac is a Brazilian-born artist based in Chicago.

Bruno Latour is a French theorist of science, ethnography, sociology and ethics.

Pamela M. Lee is Professor in the department of Art and Art History at Stanford University.

Jean-François Lyotard (1924–98) was a French philosopher and literary theorist.

Tom McDonough is Associate Professor of Modern Architecture and Urbanism in the Art History department at Binghamton University, Vestal, New York.

Denise Markonish is curator at Massachusetts Museum of Contemporary Art (MASS MoCA).

Mary Mattingly is an American artist based in New York.

Ana Mendieta (1948–85) was a Cuban-born artist who worked in the US, Italy, Cuba and Mexico.

Jacques Monod (1910–76) was a French pioneer of molecular biology and genetics.

Robert Morris is an American artist based in New York.

Arne Naess (1912–2009) was a Norwegian philosopher and founder of the Deep Ecology movement.

Thomas Nagel is Professor of Philosophy and Law at New York University.

Trevor Paglen is an American artist and writer based in New York.

Jane Prophet is a British artist and Professor of Interdiciplinary Art and Computing at Goldsmiths, University of London.

Ingeborg Reichle is an art historian and research fellow at the Berlin-Brandenburg Academy of Sciences and Humanities, Berlin.

Alexis Rockman is an American artist based in New York.

Nikolas Rose is James Martin White Professor of Sociology at the London School of Economics.

Andrew Ross is a writer and critic, and professor in the Department of Social and Cultural Analysis at New York University.

Tomás Saraceno is an Argentinian-born artist based in Frankfurt am Main.

Mark Sheerin is a critic and writer based in Brighton, England.

Bonnie Sherk is an American artist based in San Francisco.

Robert Smithson (1938–73) was an American artist and writer on art and contemporary culture.

Christa Sommerer & Laurent Mignonneau are an Austrian and a French artist who have collaborated since the beginning of the 1990s. They are professors at the InterfaceCulture Lab of the University of Art and Design at Linz.

Alan Sonfist is an American artist based in New York.

Stelarc (Stelios Arcadiou) is an Australian artist and Professor in the School of Arts at Brunel University, Uxbridge, England.

Paul Tebbs is Senior Lecturer in Photographic Theory at London College of Communication, University of the Arts, London.

Rirkrit Tiravanija is an Argentinian-born artist based in New York.

Mierle Laderman Ukeles is an American artist based in New York.

Vladimir Vernadsky (1863–1945) was a Ukrainian-born Soviet mineralogist and geochemist.

Victoria Vesna is a media artist and Professor at the UCLA Department of Design/Media Arts.

Carl Zimmer is a writer, journalist and broadcaster on contemporary science.

Andrea Zittel is an American artist based in California.

Bibliography

Adams, Frank Dawson, *The Birth and Development of the Geological Sciences* (Baltimore: The Williams & Wilkins Company, 1938)

Agamben, Giorgio, *L'Aperto: l'uomo e l'animale* (Turin: Bollati Boringhieri, 2002); trans. Kevin Atell, *The Open: Man and Animal* (Stanford: Stanford University Press, 2004)

Ashlock, Jesse, 'Please Don't Feed the Animals: Natalie Jeremijenko's Hands-On Environmentalism', *RES* magazine (July/August 2006)

Auping, Michael, 'A Nomad Among Builders', *Places*, vol. 3, no. 4 (Fall 1987)

Aziz + Cucher and Thyrza Nichols Goodeve, 'These Are the Forms We Live With: A Conversation with Thyrza Nichols Goodeve' (1999) (www.azizcucher.net)

Gaston Bachelard, *L'eau et les rêves* (Paris: José Corti, 1942); trans. Edith Farrell, *Water and Dreams: An Essay on the Imagination of Matter* (Dallas: Dallas Institute of Humanities and Culture, 1983)

— 'The Dialectic of Imaginary Energies: The Resistant World', in *Earth and Reveries of Will: An Essay on the Imagination of Matter* (1946) (Dallas: Dallas Institute of Humanities and Culture, 2002)

Bacon, Francis, *A Description of the Intellectual Globe* (c. 1612), trans. Robert Leslie Ellis, in *The Philosophical Works of Francis Bacon* (London: George Routledge and Sons, 1905)

Ballengée, Brandon, and Tim Chamberlain, interview, *Antennae*, no. 10 (Spring 2009)

Bann, Stephen, 'The Map as Index of the Real: Land Art and the Authentication of Travel', *Imago Mundi*, vol. 46 (1994)

Bateson, Gregory, *Steps to an Ecology of Mind* (Chicago: University of Chicago Press, 1972)

Bennett, Jane, *Vibrant Matter: A Political Ecology of Things* (Durham, North Carolina: Duke University Press, 2010)

Bergson, Henri, *L'Évolution créatrice* (Paris: Alcan, 1907); trans. Arthur Mitchell, *Creative Evolution* (New York: Henry Holt & Co., 1911)

Beuys, Joseph, 'Interview with Richard Demarco', *Energy Plan for the Western Man* (New York: Four Walls Eight Windows, 1990)

The Body: A Reader, ed. Mariam Fraser, Monica Greco (London and New York: Routledge, 2005)

Boettger, Suzaan, 'Looking at, and Overlooking, Women Working in Land Art in the 1970s' (2008), *WEAD Magazine*, no. 1 (2009), Women Environmental Artists Directory (http:weadartists.org)

Caillois, Roger, *The Writing of Stones*, trans. Barbara Bray (Charlottesville: The University of Virginia Press, 1985)

Caillois, Roger: *The Edge of Surrealism: A Roger Caillois Reader*, ed. Claudine Frank (Durham, North Carolina: Duke University Press, 2003)

Carlson, Allen, *Aesthetics and the Environment* (London and New York: Routledge, 2000)

Catts, Oron, and Ionat Zurr, 'Towards a New Class of Being: The Extended Body', *Intelligent Agent*, vol. 6, no. 2 (2006) (www.intelligentagent.com)

Chin, Mel, Fareed Armaly and Ute Meta Bauer, interview, *Georgia Magazine* (Athens, Georgia, USA: University of Georgia, June 1997)

Cocker, Emma, 'Heather and Ivan Morison: Earthwalker', *Artists' Newsletter* (December 2006)

Connor, Steven, 'Topologies: Michel Serres and the Shapes of Thought', paper for 'Literature and Science' conference, Ascoli, Piceno, Italy (May 2002); *Anglistik*, no. 15 (2004)

Coolidge, Matthew, and Jeffrey Kastner, 'Jeffrey Kastner talks with Matthew Coolidge about the Center for Land Use Interpretation', *Artforum* (Summer 2005)

Critical Art Ensemble, *The Molecular Invasion* (New York: Autonomedia, 2002)

Cultures of Natural History, ed. Nicholas Jardine, James A. Secord and Emma Spary (Cambridge: Cambridge University Press, 1996)

The Cybercultures Reader, ed. David Bell and Barbara M. Kennedy (London and New York: Routledge, 2000)

Daston, Lorraine, 'Nature by Design', in *Picturing Science, Producing Art*, ed. Caroline A. Jones and Peter Galison (New York and London: Routledge, 1998)

— and Katherine Park, *Wonders and the Order of Nature, 1150–1750* (New York: Zone Books, 1998)

Deleuze, Gilles, *Desert Islands and Other Texts, 1953–1974*, trans. Christopher Bush (New York: Semiotext(e), 2004)

— *Bergsonism*, trans. Hugh Tomlinson and Barbara Habberjam (New York: Zone Books, 1991)

De Maria, Walter, 'On the Importance of Natural Disasters' (May 1960), in *An Anthology of Chance Operations*, ed. Jackson Mac Low and La Monte Young (Bronx, New York: self-published by the editors, 1963; reprinted, New York: Heiner Friedrich, 1970)

Derrida, Jacques, *L'Animal que donc je suis* (manuscript 1997); trans. David Wills, *The Animal That Therefore I Am* (New York: Fordham University Press, 2008)

de vries, herman, *to be* (Stuttgart: Edition Cantz, 1995)

Dion, Mark, and Dieter Buchhart, 'Meine Werke sind nicht über Natur, sondern über die Idee von Natur', interview, *Kunstforum*, no. 157 (2001)

— and Alexis Rockman, in conversation, *Journal of Contemporary Art* (Spring/Summer, 1991); reprinted in *Concrete Jungle* (Middletown, Connecticut: Ezra and Cecile Zikha Gallery, Wesleyan University, 1993) and *Concrete Jungle: A Pop Media Investigation of Death and Survival in Urban Ecosystems* (New York: Juno Books, 1996)

Endo, Toshikatsu, 'On Fire', in Toshikatsu Endo (Tokyo: Tokyo Museum of Contemporary Art, 1991)

Flusser, Vilém, 'Curie's Children', series of three texts, *Artforum*, vol. XXVI, no. 7 (March 1988); vol. XXVI, no. 10 (Summer 1988); vol. XXVI, no. 2 (October 1988)

Findlen, Paula, *Possessing Nature: Museums, Collecting and Scientific Culture in Early Modern Italy* (Berkeley and Los Angeles: University of California Press, 1994)

Foucault, Michel, '11 January 1978 Lecture at the College de France', in *Security, Territory, Population: Lectures at the College de France 1977–1978* (London and New York: Picador, 2007)

Fragments for a History of the Human Body, edited by Michel Feher with Ramona Naddaff and Nadia Tazi (New York: Zone Books, 1989)

Fulton, Hamish, 'Into a Walk into Nature', *Thirty-One Horizons* (Munich: Städtische Galerie im Lenbachhaus, 1995)

FutureNatural: Nature, Science, Culture, ed. Jon Bird, Barry Curtis, Melinda Mash, Tim Putnam, George Robertson, Lisa Tickner (London and New York: Routledge, 1996)

Gessert, George, 'A Brief History of Art Involving DNA', *Art Papers* (September/October 1996); reprinted in *Ars Electronica 99: Life Science* (Vienna and New York: Springer Verlag, 1999)

Goldberg, Ken, *The Robot in the Garden: Telerobotics and Telepistemology in the Age of the Internet* (Cambridge, Massachusetts: The MIT Press, 2000)

Grau, Oliver, 'The History of Telepresence: Automata, Illusion and Rejecting the Body', in Goldberg, Ken, ed., *The Robot in the Garden*, op. cit.

Griffin, Tim (chair), Claire Bishop, Lynne Cooke, Pierre Huyghe, Pamela M. Lee, Rirkrit Tiravanija, Andrea Zittel, 'Remote Possibilities: A Roundtable Discussion on Land Art's Changing Terrain', *Artforum* (Summer 2005)

Guattari, Félix, *Les trois écologies* (Paris: Éditions Galilée, 1989); trans. Ian Pindar, *The Three Ecologies* (New York and London: Continuum, 2005)

Haacke, Hans, and Jeanne Siegel, interview in *Arts Magazine*, vol. 45, no. 7 (May 1971); reprinted in Jeanne Siegel, ed., *Artwords: Discourse on the 60s and 70s* (Ann Arbor: UMI Research Press, 1985)

Håkansson, Henrik, and Jörg Heiser, 'Earth Sound Research Revival', interview, *Mousse Magazine*, no. 21 (November 2009) (www.moussemagazine.it).

Halley, Peter, 'Nature and Culture', *Arts Magazine* (September 1983); reprinted in Peter Halley, *Collected Essays 1981–87* (Zürich: Bruno Bischofsberger, 1988)

Haraway, Donna J., *Simians, Cyborgs and Women: The Reinvention of Nature* (London and New York: Routledge, 1991)

— *When Species Meet* (Minneapolis: University of Minnesota Press, 2008)

Harvey, David, extract from 'Between Space and Time: Reflections on the Geographical Imagination', *Annals of the Association of American Geographers*, vol. 80, no. 3 (September 1990)

Harrison, Helen Meyer and Newton, and Thomas Sokolowski, 'Nobody Told Us when to Stop Thinking', interview, *The Quarterly Bulletin of the Grey Art Gallery & Study Center* (New York University, Spring 1987)

Harrison, Helen Meyer and Newton, 'On Ecocivility' (2009) (theharrisonstudio.net)

Heizer, Michael, and Julia Brown, 'Interview: Julia Brown and Michael Heizer', in *Sculpture in Reverse* (Los Angeles: The Museum of Contemporary Art, Los Angeles, 1984)

Huyghe, Pierre, and Philippe Parreno, 'Interview', in *No Ghost Just a Shell* (Cologne: Verlag der Buchhandlung Walter König, 2003)

Irwin, Robert, *Being and Circumstance: Notes Toward a Confidential Art* (Larkspur Landing, California: Lapis Press, 1985)

Jeremijenko, Natalie, and Mihir Desai, 'Cross-Species Dining: An Interview with Natalie Jeremijenko and Mihir Desai' (www.ediblegeography.com)

Jones, Caroline A., *Sensorium: Embodied Experience, Technology and Contemporary Art* (Cambridge, Massachusetts: The MIT Press, 2006)

Kac, Eduardo, 'Transgenic Art', *Leonardo Electronic Almanac*, vol. 6, no. 11, December 1998; reprinted in *Ars Electronica '99: Life Science*, ed. Gerfried Stocker and Christine Schopf (Vienna and New York: Springer, 1999)

— *Signs of Life: Bio Art and Beyond* (Cambridge, Massachusetts: The MIT Press, 2007)

Kastner, Jeffrey, ed., *Land and Environmental Art*, including survey essay by Brian Wallis and anthology of writings (London and New York: Phaidon Press, 1998)

Katchadourian, Nina, and Ian Berry, 'Paying Attention: A Dialogue with Nina Katchadourian by Ian Berry', in *All Forms of Attraction* (Saratoga Springs, New York: Skidmore College, 2006)

Kemp, Martin, *Seen/Unseen: Art, Science and Intuition from Leonardo to the Hubble Telescope* (Oxford: Oxford University Press, 2006)

Kojève, Alexandre, *An Introduction to the Reading of Hegel* (Ithaca, New York: Cornell University Press, 1980)

Kusahara, Machiko, 'Presence, Absence and Knowledge in Telerobotic Art', in *The Robot in the Garden*, ed. Ken Goldberg, op. cit.

Latour, Bruno, 'Will Non-Humans be Saved? An Argument from Ecotheology', paper for the Royal Institute of Anthropology's annual Henry Myers Lecture, British Museum, London (25 September 2008); *Journal of the Royal Anthropological Institute (JRAI)*, vol. 15 (2009) (www.bruno-latour.fr)

Lyotard, Jean-François, *L'Inhumain: Causeries sur le temps* (Paris: Éditions Galilée, 1988); trans. David Macey, 'The Inhuman: Reflections on Time', in The Lyotard Reader' (Oxford: Blackwell, 1989)

McDonough, Tom, 'No Ghost', *October*, no. 110 (Fall 2004); reprinted in Tom McDonough, *The Beautiful Language of My Century: Reinventing the Language of Contestation in Postwar France, 1945–1968* (Cambridge, Massachusetts: The MIT Press, 2007)

Markonish, Denise, 'A Stupendous Mirror of Departed Empires', in *Rachel Berwick: Zugunruhe* (Providence, Rhode Island: Brown University, David Winton Bell Gallery, 2010)

Mattingly, Mary, and Shane Danaher, interview, *Rough Copy* (2010) (http://roughcopymag.wordpress.com)

Mendieta, Ana, and Linda Montano, interview, *Sulfur*, no. 22 (Spring 1988)

Monod, Jacques Monod, *Le hasard et la nécessité. Essai sur la philosophie naturelle de la biologie moderne* (Paris: Éditions du Seuil, 1970); trans. Austryn Wainhouse, *Chance and Necessity* (New York: Alfred A. Knopf, 1971)

Morris, Robert, 'Notes on Art as/and Land Reclamation', revised version of paper for the symposium 'Earthworks/Land Reclamation as Sculpture' (31 July 1979), *October*, vol. 12 (Spring 1980); reprinted in *Continuous Project Altered Daily: The Writings of Robert Morris* (Cambridge, Massachusetts: The MIT Press, 1993)

Morton, Timothy, *Ecology without Nature* (Cambridge, Massachusetts: Harvard University Press, 2007)

Museum Origins: Readings in Early Museum History & Philosophy, ed. Hugh H. Genoways and Mary Anne Andrei (Walnut Creek, California: Left Coast Press, 2008)

Naess, Arne: *The Ecology of Wisdom: Writings of Arne Naess*, ed. Bill Devall and Alan Drengson (Berkeley: Counterpoint, 2008)

Nagel, Thomas, 'What is it Like to Be a Bat?', *Philosophical Review*, LXXXIII (October 1974)

Nechvatal, Joseph, and Catherine Perret, 'Our Digital Noology: Catherine Perret in conversation with Joseph Nechvatal', *Scan: Journal of Media Arts Culture* (Sydney: Macquarie University, 2007)

Nelkin, Dorothy, 'The Gene as a Cultural Icon – Visual Images of DNA', *Art Journal*, vol. 55, no. 1 (1996)

Isamu Noguchi, *A Sculptor's World* (New York: Harper and Row, 1968)

Oppenheim, Dennis, and Alanna Heiss, 'Another Point of Entry: An Interview with Dennis Oppenheim', in *Dennis Oppenheim: Selected Works 1967–1990* (New York: PS1, 1992)

Orlan, 'I do not want to look like', in *The Body: A Reader*, op. cit.

Ovalle, Inigo Manglano, 'Interview with Inigo Manglano Ovalle', in *Human/Nature: Artists Respond to a Changing Planet* at <www.artistsrespond.org/artists/ovalle/>

Paglen, Trevor, 'Experimental Geography: From Cultural Production to the Production of Space', in *Experimental Geography: Radical Approaches to Landscape, Cartography and Urbanism*, ed. Nato Thompson (Brooklyn: Melville House, 2008)

Pauline, Mark, Manuel De Landa and Mark Dery, 'Out of Control: A Trialogue on Machine Consciousness', *Wired*, vol.1, no.4 (1993)

Prophet, Jane, Sublime Ecologies and Artistic Endeavours: Artificial Life and Interactivity in the Online Project TechnoSphere', *Leonardo*, vol. 29, no. 5 (1996)

Reichle, Ingeborg, *Art in the Age of Technoscience: Genetic Engineering, Robotics and Artificial Life in Contemporary Art* (Berlin and New York: Springer, 2009)

Rose, Nikolas Rose, *The Politics of Life Itself* (Princeton: Princeton University Press, 2007)

Saraceno, Tomás, Stefano Boeri and Hans Ulrich Obrist, interview, *Domus*, no. 883 (July/August 2005)

Secord, James, 'The Crisis of Nature', in *Cultures of Natural History*, ed. Nicholas Jardine, James Secord and Emma Spary (Cambridge: Cambridge University Press, 1996)

Shanken, Edward, 'From Drips to Zoobs: The Cosmology of Artist/Inventor Michael Joaquin Grey', Artbyte, August/September 1998

Sheerin, Mark, 'Marcus Coates' (2010) (www.criticismism.com)

Sherk, Bonnie, 'Crossroads Community (The Farm)', Center for Critical Inquiry Position Paper, 1st International Symposium, San Francisco Art Institute (November 1977)

Silverman, Kaja, *Flesh of My Flesh* (Stanford: Stanford University Press, 2009)

Smithson, Robert: *Robert Smithson: The Collected Writings*, ed. Jack Flam (Berkeley and Los Angeles: University of California Press, 1996)

Solnit, Rebecca, *Storming the Gates of Paradise: Landscapes for Politics* (Berkeley and Los Angeles: University of California Press, 2007)

Sommerer, Christa, and Laurent Mignonneau, 'Art as a Living System: Interactive Computer Artworks', *Leonardo*, vol. 32, no. 3 (June 1999)

Sonfist, Alan, and Robert Rosenblum, 'Interview with the Artist', *Alan Sonfist* (Brookfield, New York: Hillwood Art Museum, 1990); reprinted in Alan Sonfist, *Nature: The End of Art* (Florence: Gli Ori, 2004)

Soper, Kate, 'Nature/'nature',' in *FutureNatural*, op. cit.

Stelarc, 'From Psycho-Body to Cybersystems: Images as Post-Human Entities' (1998), in *The Cybercultures Reader*, op. cit.

Stelarc: The Monograph, ed. Marquard Smith (Cambridge, Massachusetts: The MIT Press, 2005)

Tebbs, Paul, 'Zhao Renhui: The Blind', *Portfolio*, no. 49 (2009)

Tiravanija, Rirkrit, 'About the Land' (www.thelandfoundation.org/?About_the_land)

Turrell, James, *Mapping Spaces: A Topological Survey of the Work* (New York: Peter Blum Edition, 1987)

Ukeles, Mierle Laderman, 'Mierle Laderman Ukeles', artist's statement in Baile Oakes, ed., *Sculpting with the Environment* (New York: Van Nostrand Reinhold, 1995)

Vernadsky, Vladimir Ivanovich, *Biosfera* (Leningrad, 1926); trans. D.B. Langmuir, *The Biosphere* (New York: Copernicus/Springer Verlag, 1998)

Vesna, Victoria, 'Mind and Body Shifting: From Networks to Nanosystems', paper for Artmedia VIII: 'L'Ésthétique de la Communication' (Paris, 30 November 2002)

Yes Men, Yes Men FAQ at <theyesmen.org/faq>

Zimmer, Carl, 'The Awe of Natural History Collections', *Seed Magazine* (12 February 2009) (seedmagazine.com)

ACKNOWLEDGEMENTS

Editor's acknowledgements

Many thanks to the team at Whitechapel – Iwona Blazwick, Hannah Holloway, Sarah Auld and especially Ian Farr – for their counsel and assistance during the preparation of this volume. Thanks also to the Creative Capital/Warhol Foundation Arts Writers Grant Program, a generous award which supported the early research for this book, and to the many individuals who offered valuable advice, encouragement and inspiration along the way: Edgar Arceneaux, Sara Arrhenius, D. Graham Burnett, Jeff Dolven, Audrey Kastner, Sam Kastner, Nina Katchadourian, Michelle Kuo, Klaus Loenhart, David Levine, Mona Marquardt, Mary Mattingly, Alexander Nagel, Sina Najafi, Dominic Pettman, Mary Sabbatino, Tomás Saraceno, Sue Spaidl, Margaret Sundell and Christopher Turner.

Publisher's acknowledgements

Whitechapel Gallery is grateful to all those who gave their generous permission to reproduce the listed material. Every effort has been made to secure all permissions and we apologize for any inadvertent errors or ommissions. If notified, we will endeavour to correct these at the earliest opportunity.

We would like to express our thanks to all who contributed to the making of this volume, especially: Giorgio Agamben, Fareed Armaly, Jesse Ashlock, Michael Auping, Anthony Aziz, Brandon Ballengée, Ute Meta Bauer, Jane Bennett, Estate of Joseph Beuys, Claire Bishop, Suzaan Boettger, Oron Catts, Mel Chin, Emma Cocker, Steven Connor, Lynne Cooke, Critical Art Ensemble, Sammy Cucher, Shane Danaher, Richard Demarco, Walter De Maria, herman de vries, Mark Dion, George Gessert, Thyrza Nichols Goodeve, Oliver Grau, Tim Griffin, Hans Haacke, Henrik Håkansson, Peter Halley, Donna Haraway, Newton Harrison, Helen Mayer Harrison, David Harvey, Jörg Heiser, Pierre Huyghe, Eduardo Kac, Bruno Latour, Pamela M. Lee, Mary Mattingly, Tom McDonough, Denise Markonish, Laurent Mignonneau, Linda Montano, Robert Morris, Thomas Nagel, Josephine New, Hans Ulrich Obrist, Trevor Paglen, Jane Prophet, Ingeborg Reichle, Alexis Rockman, Nikolas Rose, Andrew Ross, Tomás Saraceno, Mark Sheerin, Bonnie Sherk, Christa Sommerer, Alan Sonfist, Stelarc, Paul Tebbs, Rirkrit Tiravanija, Mierle Laderman Ukeles, Victoria Vesna, Carl Zimmer, Andrea Zittel, Ionat Zurr. We also gratefully acknowledge the cooperation of: ARS, New York; Artforum; Blackwell Publishing Ltd; University of Chicago Press; Paula Cooper Gallery; Continuum Books; Éditions José Corti; Counterpoint; DACS, London; Duke University Press; Ronald

Feldman Fine Arts, New York; Vilém Flusser Archive; Berlin University of Arts; Fordham University Press; Gagosian Gallery; Éditions Gallimard; Alfred A. Knopf, a division of Random House, Inc; Galerie Lelong; Estate of Ana Mendieta; The MIT Press; The Modern Institute; Mousse Magazine; Princeton University Press; Springer Verlag; Stanford University Press; VAGA.

Whitechapel Gallery

whitechapelgallery.org

Whitechapel Gallery is supported by

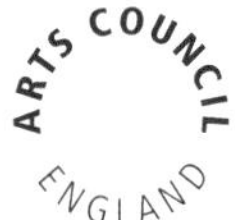